APOSTLES
INTO
TERRORISTS

APOSTLES INTO TERRORISTS

Women and the Revolutionary Movement
in the Russia of Alexander II

by VERA BROIDO

THE VIKING PRESS   NEW YORK

First published in 1977 by The Viking Press
625 Madison Avenue, New York, N.Y. 10022
Published simultaneously in Canada by
Penguin Books Canada Limited

LIBRARY OF CONGRESS CATALOGING IN PUBLICATION DATA
Broido, Vera.
    Apostles into terrorists.
    Bibliography: p.
    Includes index.
    1. Russia—Politics and government—1855–1881.
    2. Women revolutionists—Russia—Biography. I. Title.
DK221.B76   322.4'2'0947   77-4227
ISBN 0-670-12961-5

Printed in the United States of America
Set in videocomp Times Roman

FOREWORD
A Personal Note

I wrote this book because of my memories—
memories of a childhood spent among Russian revolutionaries. My
parents were Social-Democrats, Mensheviks, who passed much of
their lives in prison and exile. I knew many of my parents' friends
and contemporaries and some veterans of earlier periods. My
dearest childhood recollections are of Yuly Martov and his sister
Lydia, and of Pavel Axelrod, one of the founders of Russian Marxism. In his youth Axelrod had been a populist in Kiev and one of
his closest friends there was Katerina Breshkovskaya, later to become known as the grandmother of the Russian Revolution. She
was the first woman revolutionary to be sent to hard labour in

Siberia by a tsarist court. I knew her in her old age in Siberian exile in Minusinsk, where my mother was also exiled. A few years later, during the revolutionary years 1917–18, my mother took me to visit Vera Zasulich and Vera Figner—two famous names in Russian revolutionary history. It was difficult for me to see in these mild old ladies the terrorists of former years, but their human warmth only added to my romantic picture of them. My childhood was a storehouse of revolutionary history, and through my mother I felt a particular bond with many of its heroines. Nothing seemed more natural, therefore—when life offered me enough leisure—than to write about Russian revolutionary women.

This is not, however, a feminist book. To assign to revolutionary women the narrow partisan role of feminists is to distort their position in the revolutionary movement and to diminish their contribution to Russian history.

There is no agreed date for the beginning of the Russian revolutionary movement. The Decembrist rising of 1825, which is sometimes described as the first Russian revolution, represents rather a transition from the palace revolutions of the eighteenth century to more modern types of political opposition. It was followed by sporadic appearances of small radical groups and individuals, among whom Alexander Herzen was outstanding. But only from 1861 to 1862 does Russian radicalism truly gather momentum and only from 1868 to 1869 does a numerically significant revolutionary movement come into existence.

If 1861–62 is taken as a starting point, then it can be shown that women participated in the revolutionary movement from the very beginning, and from 1868 to 1869 they did so in ever increasing numbers. In fact, there were more women in the revolutionary movement in Russia—and at an earlier date—than in any other country in Europe.

That this should have happened in backward, rigidly patriarchal Russia, where women had been almost totally confined to the home, can only be understood in a larger historical perspective. And this I have tried to give. The position of women in educated society had not changed overnight; it had been changing gradually under the influence of the liberal, radical, and feminist ideas that pervaded mid-nineteenth-century Russia. During the reign of Alexander II, which spanned the years 1855 to 1881, the intelligentsia expected to be granted political freedoms, including the emancipation of women. The failure of the tsar to meet these expectations led to a sharp radicalization of the educated class and to the formation of the revolutionary movement. Women had shared both the expectations and the subsequent disappointment of the intelligentsia, and many of them were as ready as the men to join the revolutionary movement.

The first, populist phase of the movement ended with the assassination of Alexander II, and I have not attempted to continue my story beyond that. The role played by women did not, in fact, change much in later years. The socialist parties formed around the turn of the century all had their contingent of active and often outstanding women. The only exception was the Bolshevik party, in which the status of women declined very markedly. It is a sad thought that almost a hundred years after its beginning the Russian revolutionary movement should have produced no woman worthier of its proud traditions than the late Mme. Ekaterina Furtseva, Minister of culture from 1960 to 1974.

Born and bred in Russia, I naturally brought to my work a much wider range of reading than my bibliography reflects. It represents, in fact, only a selection of sources for the use of those interested in pursuing specific problems.

I should like to thank the library staffs of the London Library, the British Library, the London School of Economics, the London School of Slavonic and East-European Studies, and the Internationaal Instituut voor Sociale Geschiedenis, Amsterdam. While resident at Wassenaar, I also received much assistance from the library staff of the Netherland Institute for Advanced Study in the Humanities and Social Sciences; to them, too, I am most grateful.

But above all I should like to thank Ellen de Kadt, my husband, and my son for reading and criticizing the manuscript.

London, 1976   V.B.

Contents

Illustrations on pages 4, 42, 55, 103, 159, 170, 182, and 200.

APOSTLES
INTO
TERRORISTS

INTRODUCTION
Who Can Live Happily in Russia?

"Who can live happily in Russia?" [1] asked the nineteenth-century Russian poet Nikolay Nekrasov, and the answer was—nobody. His seven peasants who set out to walk through the country in search of a happy being met and questioned peasants, landowners, civil servants, priests, merchants, but found no contentment among them.

The most obvious reason for Russia's unhappy state was her backwardness: almost two and a half centuries of subjugation under the Tartars (1237–1480) had prevented her from sharing in the general development of Europe. Moreover, her religion, which came

1

from Byzantium, intensified her isolation, since the Orthodox Church was very hostile to the West. But above all her monarchy kept Russia back. While the countries of western Europe, having had their fair share of despots, were moving towards constitutional or even republican forms of government, Russian monarchy remained uncompromisingly absolutist. This meant that while in western Europe large sections of the populations were drawn into participation in the government, in Russia they were kept rigidly out of it. Not until the twentieth century were constitutional experiments begun in tsarist Russia, and even then they remained very tentative.

Russian tsars saw themselves as benevolent patriarchs, but in reality they were paternalistic and tyrannical—aiming at owning their subjects body and soul. They tolerated no independence of deed or thought. They deprived the Church of its power, reducing it to abject subservience, and appropriated to themselves the spiritual as well as temporal leadership of the people. They gave and took away lands and honours, rights and privileges in the most arbitrary manner, with the result that no class or group could develop into a stable social body. And they governed the country with the help of a vast bureaucracy, corrupt and inefficient—a kind of huge quicksand that engulfed all good intentions, including those of the more enlightened tsars themselves. The most damaging aspect of Russian monarchy was its arbitrariness. Since the tsars did not abide by any set of laws, the law itself fell into disrepute. The concepts of "civic rights," "civic duties," "equality before the law," even "citizenship" in the modern sense of the word had no chance to develop. And as everybody, from provincial governors to village policemen, aped the tsar and was an arbitrary autocrat in his sphere, there was no redress from injustice or oppression.

By far the worst evil in nineteenth-century Russia was serfdom. Over three-quarters of the population consisted of peasant serfs, owned either by the nobles or by the crown or by the Church. These peasants were no better than slaves, were often mercilessly exploited and sold or given away like cattle. But Russian peasants had never accepted serfdom as a permanent institution. They knew that it had originated in an agreement entered upon by their ancestors in times long past, by which peasants served the crown in exchange for protection from invaders and marauders, or else served the nobles when the nobles had to serve the tsar. But time had passed, and with it the danger from invaders and marauders, while nobles were released from state service in the second half of the eighteenth century. Serfdom should have come to an end then— but it lingered on for almost a century.

During this time the relationship between the serfs and their masters deteriorated in a manner damaging to both. Many landowners no longer cared for their lands or their serfs and squeezed all they could from both, sometimes ruining themselves in the process. And the serfs accordingly lost their respect for the gentry and cheated their masters whenever they could. At the same time they felt insecure, and this often expressed itself in drunkenness and senseless violence. Yet the peasants never lost hope that one day they would regain their original status of freemen and repossess themselves of the land that had originally been theirs. This lent them a peculiar dignity, which even the most abject *muzhik* never lost.

In spite of the demoralizing effect of serfdom, the peasants were the steadiest class in Russia. They derived their moral strength from the traditional Russian culture, a culture that combined Byzantine influences with a particularly rich native folklore. They were also sustained by the bonds of traditional village community. Each community constituted a *mir*, or *obshchina*, which in principle decided all problems jointly and which elected its own elder, that is, a spokesman to represent it before the landlord and the rural officials; all taxes and dues were paid by the *mir* on the basis of joint responsibility. Only vestiges of this semicommunal, semi-self-governing way of life survived during serfdom, but after the abolition of serfdom the government revived it to serve its own purposes. In an idealized form it supplied the radicals with a basis for belief in a "natural socialism" practised by Russian peasants.

The peasants were steadfast in their loyalty to tsardom and to religion. They never blamed the tsars, only the nobles for their

Russian peasants (The Mansell Collection)

misery. Moreover, in the countryside the prestige of the Church was still unimpaired. Though many village priests were demoralized by poverty and fear of the temporal authorities, there were also many parish priests and monks of great spiritual strength. Russian Orthodoxy had always produced men of exceptional charisma and to them the people turned with deep affection and reverence.

But the Church was backward-looking, viewing new ideas with deep distrust and hostility. And so were the peasants. Their ambition was simply to revert to the state of affairs before serfdom and, like peasants everywhere in the world, they were not interested in foreign countries or developments.

On the other hand Russian intellectual tradition largely derived from foreign countries, and Russian intellectuals were intensely interested in ideas and all the newest trends of west European thought. This kind of contrast exists everywhere between educated and uneducated, but it was particularly stark in Russia. Only in moments of great national danger, such as the Napoleonic invasion, did all Russians exist in the same historical moment; at other times they were centuries apart.

Russian tsars stood somewhere between the backward peasantry and the precocious educated class. Some of them were very ignorant and others quite well educated, but all were medieval in their attitude to their own role and truly Asiatic in their love for ostentation. Yet, since their coffers were often empty and their prestige in Europe precarious, they knew that they had to modernize Russia. The problem was how to do this without weakening their autocratic position—a dilemma that in the end proved insoluble. However often the tsars expressed their intention to initiate reforms, they invariably drew back the moment their absolute power seemed threatened by the forces these reforms were bound to release. With the exception of Peter the Great, the greatest autocrat of them all, none of the Romanovs had the stature or the vision to risk their power; they clung to it, as they clung to the traditional image of the all-wise, all-powerful, God-anointed father tsar. They came to believe in this image of themselves with an almost fanatical conviction. Had the tsars been less obsessed by this image and had they followed Peter the Great's lead, Russia might have developed gradually and naturally, and not fallen behind western Europe. She might even have preserved a modified patriarchal monarchy. In itself this form of government suited Russia very well—it answered to something very deep in the Russian character, and was a unifying bond in a vast country with a sparse population.

By the middle of the 1850s Russia's backwardness was dramatically revealed to the eyes of the whole world. In the Crimean War it became obvious that she had neither the industry to support her war effort nor the railways and proper roads to move her armies about and to keep them supplied. Equally obvious was the inefficiency of the Russian administration.

The economy of the country had indeed long been in a lamentable state. Centuries of serfdom and predatory methods of agriculture had devastated the countryside. Serfdom had also retarded industrial development, which needs a free flow of labour. Native Russian industry developed very sluggishly, until foreign industrialists woke up to the vast potentialities of the country and flocked there. And even then industry did not really get under way in Russia until the very end of the century.

Russian trade had always been very active and enterprising and many Russian merchants became fabulously rich and lived in grand style, often in palaces that had formerly belonged to the nobility. Some rich merchants—Pavel Tretyakov, Bakhrushin, Ivan Morozov, and the brothers Shchukin—became great patrons of the arts, supported orchestras and theatres, and amassed great collections of paintings.

Yet the merchant class never acquired a social standing or political influence and neither the merchants nor the industrialists amounted to a bourgeoisie such as had moulded the political life of modern Europe. In Russia, it was left to the educated class to champion political liberties. This class was concerned not with the needs of commerce and industry but, rather, with its own needs for free cultural development. It was a vigorous, forward-looking class, which grew out of the nobility but soon assimilated large numbers of commoners. The history of the Russian revolutionary movement is inseparable from the history of this class.

The growth of the educated class followed naturally upon the spread of higher education. By the beginning of the nineteenth century there were six universities in Russia, and ten at the end of the century, when there were also some fifty or sixty higher technical schools spread over the country. But though the actual number of students was small—only 1,700 in 1825 and 30,000 in the 1890s (when the total population was 126 million) [2]—mere numbers do not express the spiritual influence that the educated class exerted. Unfortunately the universities were administered in a manner that prevented their developing freely and made future conflicts inevitable. Professors had very little say in university affairs, all authority being vested in two persons: the inspector and the *popechitel*—an untranslatable Russian word, meaning approximately guardian or warden. But since these two officials invariably called in the police whenever there was the slightest sign of a dispute, they were completely discredited in the eyes of both students and professors.

It had been the intention of the government to make secondary and higher education available to the nobility only, but attempts to exclude other classes failed. The nobles themselves helped to frustrate the official policy by sending large numbers of their illegitimate offspring, begotten with peasant women and servant girls, to school and university, or sometimes by paying for the education of particularly bright sons of their favourite serfs. And inside the universities these less privileged students mixed happily with young noblemen in a democratic spirit that was in strong contrast to the hierarchical tradition of Russian society. The universities thus became a kind of classless oasis.

Very soon, the educated class proved to be a thorn in the side of tsardom. By virtue of its wider intellectual horizons it was able to see through the iniquities of the regime and to draw comparisons between Russia and the countries of the West. The intellectual development of young Russians could not be arrested by banning whole subjects, such as philosophy, political economy, and natural sciences.* Russians are naturally communicative and inquisitive. What they were not permitted to learn, to read, and to talk about openly, they read and discussed in private. And foreign travel, however restricted most of the time and often altogether forbidden, established an intermittent link with western Europe which the government was never able to break.

Educated Russians formed a new social force in the life of the country, and in this sense they can be called a class. It was not, of course, a homogeneous class: not all of its members were interested in ideas or politics, but those who were came together in the "intelligentsia." In 1866 the writer Boborykin defined the intelligentsia as "the highest cultural stratum of society, characterized by a democratic spirit and by a deep interest in the people, and by its defence of freedom of conscience against the absolutist state." [3] A young man writing in 1874 said that members of the intelligentsia had shed the interests of their own social class in pursuit of truth for all.[4] And the twentieth-century writer and politician Pavel Milyukov said of the poet Nekrasov, whom he described as a typical member of the intelligentsia, that he represented a synthesis of a penitent nobleman with a sick conscience and a commoner with a new kind of pride.[5] It is certainly true that the intelligentsia inherited many of the qualities of the enlightened nobility of the eighteenth century—a lofty if somewhat quixotic idealism and high notions of personal honour—and that it received an infusion of new strength and energy from "men of all ranks," the so-called *raznochintsi*.

Russian culture flourished in spite of unfavourable conditions. The reign of Nicholas I, father to Alexander II and one of the most retrograde of the nineteenth-century tsars, coincided with the Golden Age of Russian literature. Russian poets and writers— Pushkin, Lermontov, Gogol, Bylinsky, and a score of others— blended western influences with the Russian sensibility and heritage

---

* The Minister of education Shirinsky-Shikhmatov is quoted as saying in 1850: "philosophy has not been proved useful, and may well be harmful." (Nikitenko, A. (1), vol. I, p. 395.)

and established a brilliant literary tradition. Because they did not slavishly follow the doctrines of the Russian monarchy and the Orthodox Church, they encountered much official hostility, but the educated class ranged itself enthusiastically behind them. Indeed throughout subsequent history literature proved a more unifying force than any party or government—it was truly "the conscience of the nation."

The rapid growth of culture alarmed the tsars precisely because they recognized in it a rival claimant to the loyalty of their subjects. They would have liked to pose as gracious patrons of the arts and sciences in return for grateful submission, but Russian poets and writers, as well as their readers, were fast outgrowing the stage of submissiveness. Only with regard to architecture was the patronage of the tsars fruitful and it deserves much praise: Peter the Great, his daughter Elizabeth, and Catherine the Great all encouraged architects, foreign and native, and thus helped to form one of the most distinctive and brilliant architectural traditions in the world. With regard to other arts, the interference of the tsars was less fruitful and aroused nothing but antagonism. Unable to meet the challenge in more sophisticated or subtle ways, the tsars were apt to fall back on age-old methods of knout and kindness, in alternate bursts. The imprisonment of critical writers became a formula that persists down to the present day.

Both the knout and the "kindness," or "kindly persuasion," were usually administered by the tsars' most trusted servants, the secret police. There had always been some kind of secret police in Russia, at least since Ivan the Terrible. But in its modern form it was the creation of Nicholas I, in response to the rebellion that occurred at his accession in December 1825. Several groups of high-ranking officers, almost all belonging to the most illustrious families of Russia, had dared to come out publicly with demands for the abolition of serfdom and a constitutional form of government. These officers had spent some time abroad, in Paris and in Vienna, after the defeat of Napoleon, and they had returned home full of ideas for the improvement of Russia. This was the first time that the army had turned from plots of palace revolutions to concerns of public good. It was a momentous change: from that day onwards the tsars had no trouble with rival pretenders to the throne, but they were harassed by fears of civic disobedience.

The Decembrist rising was the first concerted expression of the oppositional spirit in Russia and it contained the seeds of both liberal and radical movements, for some of the plotters preferred a reformed tsardom, while others opted for a republic. Nicholas I chose to regard the rebellion of 1825 as a personal insult, hanged five of the rebels, and sent over a hundred in chains to the Siberian mines. Altogether about a thousand people were arrested, many interrogated by the emperor himself, and even those who were not punished were thoroughly intimidated. The tsar had thus dealt a double blow—at the high nobility for presuming to teach him his business and at all would-be reformers of whatever class. It was highly successful in the first instance, in that the old nobility never recovered from the blow, particularly since it was further weakened by the influx of the new "service nobility" which rose automatically from the higher ranks of the civil, military, and naval services. Henceforth, the great nobles tended to retire to their palatial mansions or country estates and eschew public office, though they kept the habit of directing "addresses" and "proposals" to the tsars. But the future reformers were not intimidated. The rebels of 1825 became the martyred heroes of the intelligentsia and inspired later generations with readiness to suffer for their ideals.

Nicholas I had a passion for military drill and would have liked to turn the whole of Russia into an army camp. He was a strong and self-reliant man, asking for no acclaim and tolerating no criticism. He once reprimanded a journalist for *praising* a government measure—he considered it an impertinent thing to do. He dismissed public concern in affairs of state as inconsistent with the dignity of his government. What he expected from his subjects was simple— silence and obedience. Having dealt with the Decembrists, he set out to prevent any future rebellion with unimaginative thoroughness. To start with, he put everybody, from veterinary surgeon to schoolboy, into uniform. Next, he created a new special police in addition to the ordinary one.[6] It was to be known as the Third (civilian) Section of His Imperial Majesty's Chancellery (to indicate the personal closeness to the tsar), and it was to work in double harness with the military Corps of Gendarmes (to give it martial stiffening). The new police was to be more efficient than any of its predecessors, but it was also to be benevolent and just. A possibly apocryphal story tells how when the first head of the police, Count Benckendorff, asked him for a directive, the tsar handed him a handkerchief with the words: "Here is all the directive you need. The more tears you wipe away with this handkerchief, the more faithfully you will serve my aims." [7] This story should rank high among the many instances of misunderstandings between the tsars and their people.

In any event, the new police incorporated all Nicholas's meanest qualities without his drive and energy. The benevolence did not last long and the efficiency left much to be desired. This was partly due to lack of funds, low salaries, and poor-quality personnel. Officers and other ranks of the Corps of Gendarmes were volunteers from the regular army, where the salaries were even lower. The civilian Third Section consisted of a small nucleus of professional detectives and a mass of poorly paid agents, spies, and informers. Since according to Russian law non-denunciation of a crime, of an intended crime, or even of a suspected crime, was punishable just as severely as the crime itself, it was easy to bully servants, waiters, caretakers (*dvorniki*), shop-assistants, and other small fry into co-operating with the police. The *dvorniki*—each town house in Russia had one and he was on duty sixteen hours a day—were required to report to the police any suspicious conversations or movements. All these elements increased the scope of police activities, but they were also unreliable.

The new special police was given very wide powers: its brief was to detect and persecute sedition in act, word, or thought. Since Nicholas I mistrusted everybody, he set his police to watch and to spy on his heir and the rest of the imperial family; on ministers of the crown and on high officials; on professors and students in universities and teachers and schoolboys in schools; on aliens sojourning or residing in Russia and on Russians travelling abroad; and, of course, on writers and poets. The new police was empowered to investigate and prosecute provincial administrators, sectarians, money-forgers, fraudulent officials, and, above all, political dissenters, real or merely suspect; and it could imprison and exile people without trial, by the notorious "administrative" method. Censorship, the scourge of Russian literary life, was also supervised by the new police and censors were appointed by it. In the case of Pushkin, Count Benckendorff and the tsar arrogated to themselves the right to censor and to criticize his writings.

The new special police was a law unto itself, answerable to nobody but the tsar. The strong personality of Nicholas I kept it in check, but in later reigns it became so powerful that it intimidated the tsars themselves. Its effect on cultural life was deadly. Nobody was safe from persecution. In 1836, Pyotr Chaadaev, a friend of Pushkin, was declared insane for publishing one of his *Philosophical Letters*, in which he described Russia as having had no history. The journal that dared to print it was banned and the editor exiled to Siberia; even the censor who had passed it lost his job. Two years earlier, in 1834, a group of three friends—Alexander Herzen, Nikolay Ogarev, and Vadim Passek—was effectively dispersed and Herzen sent into provincial exile for six years. Alexander Herzen, who was to become one of the most considerable radical figures of the century and a memoirist of genius, probably derived some benefit from this enforced contact with Russian provincial reality before becoming a voluntary expatriate for the rest of his life.

The experiences of Fyodor Dostoyevsky in 1849 were more harrowing.[8] He had joined the group around Petrashevsky, a cultured and politically rather moderate man, who kept open house on Friday evenings for anyone interested in political and social ideas. This discussion group was by no means conspiratorial and everybody was welcome—students, army officers, or civil servants. It had attracted a considerable number of interested debaters and listeners before they were rounded up by the secret police in 1849.

The extraordinarily harsh punishment meted out to Petrashevsky and his friends was undoubtedly due to the fact that the European revolutions of the year before, 1848, had alarmed Nicholas I. The *Petrashevtsi* [9] were placed in solitary confinement in the Peter and Paul Fortress. This old fortress, its handsome walls washed by the waters of the Neva, the slender gold spire of its church gleaming in the sun, is one of the best-known sights of Leningrad even today. Situated across the river from the Winter Palace, the elegant residence of the tsars, it typified the sinister underside of tsardom. Its most notorious part was the Alexey dungeon, where the Decembrists and all other "state criminals" had been kept. The damp cells and the toll of church bells every hour of the day and night combined to destroy the unfortunate inmates, in body and soul alike. The wretched Petrashevsky and his friends spent eight months in it. Incongruously they were then tried by a military court, and twenty-one of them, including Dostoyevsky, were sentenced to death. And although Nicholas I had decided in advance to commute the death sentence, he gave orders for an elaborate mock execution, with every possible theatrical effect. Military units flanked the huge execution square, drums rolled, black-robed priests stood by. Escorted by mounted gendarmes, the condemned men were driven in separate carriages through the snow-covered streets of St. Petersburg, in glittering sunshine—a drive which they believed to be their last. When they arrived in the square, the young men were lined up, their sentences were read out to them, sabres were broken over the heads of the nobles among them, and all were clothed in white linen shrouds.* The priests administered the last rites, and the first three prisoners, Petrashevsky among them, were led in front of the firing squad and the order was given to take aim. Only then was a rider seen to gallop up to the commanding officer—it was the emperor's last-minute reprieve. The effect on the nervous system of the victims of this grim practical joke can be imagined; it is said that Dostoyevsky developed epilepsy as a result of it. But the point

---

* Police archives show that many letters were exchanged between the official departments involved in an effort to decide what kind of cloth should be used for the shrouds, how and where the graves should be dug, and so forth. After the trial Petrashevsky was presented with bills for eight pairs of shackles, seven swords, linen used for shrouds and the like. (Grosman, I., p. 684.)

was taken: gatherings for the discussion of current affairs, domestic or foreign, and of political ideas, *could* be punished by death.

The new police drove thought and talent underground, but it did not succeed in killing them altogether: prose and verse circulated in handwritten copies, as in the *Samizdat* of today, and writers developed a special cryptic language to fool the censors. "Everybody," said Pyotr Kropotkin, "learned to read between the lines and knew what was meant by 'A critique of the Chinese finance system'! [10]

In such a country the educated felt themselves to be foreigners—foreigners, moreover, exposed to the full blast of xenophobia. There seemed no place for them, for all that the country had never needed them more. The alienated intellectual is a stock figure of Russian literature, yet there are still too many misconceptions about the causes of the phenomenon. It cannot be said that it arose from any disinclination on their part to do useful and practical work. Again and again intellectuals tried to fit into the practical life of Russia by working in the professions or in the administration. Indeed it was compulsory to enter one of the government offices after graduation and this meant that everybody had to go through the bureaucratic machine. But no cultured and honest man could work in the bureaucracy, run by retrograde and ignorant officials who distrusted and despised the young graduates. Even if they were neither radical nor libertarian, they were soon labelled as such, and worse still—as revolutionary.

The experiences of the lawyer and writer Bervi-Flerovsky, who graduated in law from the St. Petersburg University in 1849, illustrate the point particularly well. [11] One of the three best graduates of his year, he was spared the usual preliminary years in the provinces and immediately accepted into the ministry of justice. Starting as a junior clerk he was told to enter in a ledger all incoming and outgoing documents—and at this task he was kept for *six* whole years, while far less educated clerks were promoted to more senior positions. He ascribed his failure to advance in his career to the fact that the head of his department once saw a volume on political economy on his desk!

Clerks and minor and senior officials all took bribes, and anyone who refused to do so was victimized in various ways. Bervi-Flerovsky's friend and work-mate Beketov, an equally talented and cultured young man, was informed on his first day in the office by other clerks that all bribes went into one kitty and were later shared equally. When he replied that he did not intend to take bribes, nobody believed him; they simply assumed that he did not want to share with them and hated him for it. Cases not backed up by bribes often remained in the files for years. Corruption and sloth were still worse in the provinces. And even apart from the question of honesty, the subservience and self-abasement that were generally expected from a beginner were quite unacceptable to educated men.

It is no wonder that such men could not find a useful place for themselves and were forced to live in a kind of vacuum. They gradually lost touch with practical work and fell into a state of inertia. Russian literature has exposed these maladies perhaps too mercilessly: the "Byronic heroes" and "superfluous men"—the Onegins, Pechorins, Rudins, Oblomovs—were not found on every street-corner or in every nobleman's retreat, and in any case they were not altogether negative, for they had idealism and integrity and they kept these qualities alive and passed them on to the next generation. This next generation was much tougher. A more aggressive intellectual type was rapidly developing—particularly, though not exclusively, among young people of "lower" social origin, such as sons of priests, merchants, even peasants. These men undoubtedly brought a new and uncompromising vigour and a greater impatience, even intolerance, to intellectual life—a healthy corrective to the indolence from which many of their elders suffered.

By the middle of the century interest shifted from western philosophy to western political thought, particularly utopian socialism and the history of European revolutions. The appetite for news from abroad was enormous. Western Europe offered such a wealth of new ideas, so much was happening there. But Russian journals were not allowed to print political news or to discuss "dangerous" events, and the information that filtered through was incomplete and often misleading. No wonder that conclusions drawn from such misinformation were often nonsensical. Everybody in Russia would have benefited from an open exchange of information and views and from public lectures and discussions on controversial subjects. This being impossible, exasperation led to extremism, and the emergence of a radical movement became inevitable.

However, in the late 1840s and early 1850s Russian radicals were radical only in the abstract; there was as yet neither a movement nor even large groups that could be properly called radical. Individual writers and students might incline to radicalism, but most of these called themselves simply "democrats." Moreover, around the middle of the century, these elements temporarily transferred their attention from political and social to moral problems, leaving it to the more moderate elements to worry about freedom of press and speech and the like. This was not the last time that radicalism and liberalism changed places in Russia, now the one and now the other heading the fight for political freedom. In the Russian context they were indeed often indistinguishable. The hopeless tangle of Russian life at times made radical solutions acceptable to the most moderate of men. Even among conservative elements there were many men who entertained liberal and radical ideas.

But so long as Nicholas I was alive, no political trend could make much headway.

THE NIHILIST PROTEST

In the years before and just after the death of Nicholas I in 1855, radical elements mounted an attack on the social and moral foundations of Russian society. They took up a very extreme position, totally rejecting all institutions and conventions of the past. This wholesale rejection of Russia's way of life, which later went under the name of nihilism, was violent and often ridiculously exaggerated. Yet it was a healthy reaction against the corruption of Russian public and private life, against the injustice and inhumanity of serfdom, and against the identification of religion with tsardom and of both with the police.

It should be stressed that the terms "nihilism" and "nihilist" were not introduced by the movement itself but applied to it by others—and often by its critics in a pejorative sense. Later the terms were applied indiscriminately to all radicals and to terrorists. And this in itself shows how little either movement was understood. The original nihilists were in any case not as bad as they were painted. Though they rejected traditional morality and Christianity, they had absolute moral values of their own, and even their own religiosity.

Nihilism was the creed of the very young, of those in their late teens or early twenties. Its theoretical ammunition came from only slightly older writers—Dobrolyubov, who died at the age of twenty-five in 1861; and Pisarev, who died at twenty-seven in 1868; while the long-lived Chernyshevsky produced all his nihilist writing between the ages of twenty-seven and thirty-four from 1855 to 1862. Inevitably much of the outward manifestation of nihilism was crude and blatant. Today we would call it the "youth revolution" and recognize many of the symptoms. Indeed, the young student protesters of our own times show a most striking resemblance to their Russian precursors. The true Russian nihilist wore his baggy trousers tucked into unpolished and clumsy boots, his peasant blouse of cheap cotton was held round the waist by a leather strap; and a so-called plaid, or rug, was hung over one shoulder. The hair was worn long and the face overgrown with beard and further obscured with dark glasses. Many of the students were indeed very poor and underfed, and this contributed in some measure to their drab appearance. The female counterpart—a very new phenomenon and one that will be the subject of later chapters—also dressed with deliberate plainness: heavy boots showed under sombre black skirts topped by high-necked blouses; the hair was worn short; and there were, of course, the dark glasses and, worse still, the cigarettes. All this was in protest against the smart uniforms of official Russia, and indeed the contrast could not be greater than between the gruff manners and drab garb of the nihilist and (that emblem of tsarist Russia) the gendarme resplendent in sky-blue tunic, white gloves, and plumed helmet.

Nihilist theory was also often crude, leaning heavily on spurious and sterile scientism and such half-baked concepts as rational realism and rational egoism. But it had its positive and even its heroic side, as Turgenev, who coined the term "nihilist," was quick to perceive and which he described in *Fathers and Sons,* published in 1862.* [1] Its insistence on honesty and integrity in human relationships, its attack on the status of women in family and society greatly contributed to a healthy evolution of social mores. Older generations of educated Russians were shocked by nihilist dress and manners, but they were nevertheless profoundly influenced by nihilist moral tenets—more than they would have liked to admit. Eventually a fusion of the new notions with older cultural traditions resulted in the appearance of the typical Russian cultured home, a uniquely attractive and enlightened institution.

The two main targets of nihilist attack were religion and the family. We have it from the revolutionary Sergey Kravchinsky that religion was most easily discarded [2] because the Church had long lost the respect of the educated class. Indeed, even a believing Christian observed that "our Church is inwardly completely divorced from the people and from society; it is just another administrative department." [3] It was thus the Church rather than religion that was hated by the nihilists. As for traditional family and marriage—they held that these were entirely rotten and should be replaced by more modern forms.

Placed in their historical setting, the nihilists can be seen as fighting a double battle: their own immediate generational battle against their fathers, and a long-term battle against patriarchal despotism, in which they were simply the latest recruits to the struggle that had already involved several earlier generations. In both ways they helped the educated class to emancipate itself.

The nihilists were also whole-hearted champions of the emancipation of women and the first to proclaim full equality of the

---

* Dostoyevsky was one of the few who understood the author's intention; in a letter to Turgenev, he said of the hero of *Fathers and Sons:* "Bazarov, for all his nihilism, is restless and pining (these are the symptoms of a great heart)." (Turgenev, I., p. 336.)

sexes. And they practised what they preached: it was in nihilist circles that women first found complete recognition and acceptance as human beings and were given a chance to develop their intellectual capabilities. This was indeed a major achievement in view of the position women occupied in Russian society.

Russian women, whether peasant woman, merchant's wife, or general's daughter, had been kept in strict submission to a rigidly patriarchal family life; they were thus victims of two patriarchal orders, one superimposed on the other. Although, by a whim of Russian law, women could inherit property, they had no other rights. In villages, serf women were made to work as hard as the men, particularly during *strada* (harvest time—a word related in Russian to suffering, *stradanye*); were beaten savagely by their husbands, knocked about by their mothers-in-law, and worn out with child-bearing. If pretty, they ran the risk of pleasing the serf owner and usually paid with lifelong misery and humiliation for the brief glory of being his mistress. If both pretty and talented—and there was much native talent in Russian villages—they might be taken, together with male serfs, into the private theatre, choir, or orchestra that many a rich landowner kept for his own and his friends' delectation. In that case they might be petted and become famous, only to revert to their former status once their master's favour or finances ran out. Usually these unlucky people had meanwhile acquired civilized manners and considerable culture and their despair was often acute enough to lead to suicide.

In small provincial towns, life was hardly different from village life: the same log houses badly in need of repair, the same unbelievably muddy or dusty unpaved roads, the same stray hens and goats and cows, and the same or even greater poverty, drunkenness, and brutality. Artisans, small shopkeepers, and petty clerks in such towns were very insecure, and it was not unusual for their wives and daughters to have to beg. As in the villages, famine was always near at hand and fires periodically reduced the inhabitants to complete destitution. The spectacle of whole "burnt-out" communities (*pogoreltsi*) roaming the countryside or camping in the fields and begging at the roadside was as common as it was heart-rending.

In the centre of small towns there were a few paved roads and some municipal buildings of stone or brick and a few prosperous private homes of higher officials and richer merchants. But the level of culture in these homes was hardly higher than in the humbler ones, except that the women were brought up to an idleness which passed for genteel. Intended simply for the marriage mart they were, if possible, even more truly ignorant. The only spiritual preoccupation of women of all these classes was religion—but often it was religion of a special kind. These women were strongly attracted to the intense and intimate religiosity of the "holy" beggars, pilgrims, and other wandering "saints," hordes of whom were for ever tramping up and down the vastness of "holy mother Russia." They propounded a fantastic mixture of Christian faith with heretical beliefs, and held their listeners spellbound with horrendous tales about the Last Days and the Last Judgement, the rewards of Heaven and the frightfulness of Hell. These apocryphal stories accorded well with traditional folk tales, of which Russia has such a rich store, and they were often told with great artistry.

The heretical sects—of which there were many in Russia—presented a different case. Usually they had high standards of literacy, honesty, and abstinence. And though they were patriarchal in their family life, they treated their women better and taught them to read and write.

Few noble families were rich enough to afford culture. Most of them lived modest, secluded lives in remote corners of the country, where they enjoyed a certain local esteem. But they cut a poor figure in the cities, when they ventured there, for in both manner and dress they seemed relics of a bygone age. And it was quite against their traditions to let their daughters stray outside their own narrow universe of domestic virtues and Christian piety.

The rest of provincial society lived, in the words of Alexander Herzen, who got to know it intimately during his exile, in a "swamp," [4] where careers and riches were made by dishonesty and extortion. Social life was often on quite a lavish scale—local ladies eagerly following the latest fashions and attending local balls, while the men spent their evenings over cards at the local club of the nobility or in a brothel. Cultural life was confined to the small group of professional men, who were poor and snubbed by local society and usually succumbed to melancholia or vodka or both. It was still so in Chekhov's time, some fifty years later.

However, the few hundred noble families who either resided permanently in the larger cities or spent the fashionable season there, and who might even travel abroad, belonged to an altogether different world. For a long time culture and refinement of mind and manners were to be found only in this world, along with genuine patronage of arts and sciences. The imperial court, with all its ostentatious splendour, remained uncouth by comparison. The aristocratic "salons" of St. Petersburg and Moscow were a curious mixture of the literary and the pleasure-seeking. It was here that the brilliant generation of Pushkin and Lermontov found encouragement. And some of the fashionable hostesses were women of superior understanding and wide interests.

At a somewhat later date, with the advent of the intelligentsia, the tea-tables in the humbler drawing rooms of intellectuals came to play a similar role to the salon. Only in the home was it safe—away from police curiosity—to exchange ideas and opinions freely, and the salon and the tea-table thus became the true nerve centres of cultural life. And in the domestic setting, women could develop their minds and their talents. In cultured homes, rich or poor, girls were encouraged to read and think and often received very good tuition, on a par with their brothers. In the long vacation, when many noble families retired to their country estates, their sons and their sons' friends from the universities often descended upon them, while impecunious students were usually engaged for the summer as tutors for the younger children. All these young men were full of the newest ideas and events in the world and their conversations and heated arguments worked powerfully on the imagination of the younger women of the household. This was the milieu in which the compulsive talkers of the type of Turgenev's Rudin were to be found, casting their spell upon the inexperienced but receptive female mind.

This situation has been described repeatedly by Russian novelists, and usually the young women emerge as strong and consistent characters, as opposed to the unsteady young men. In fact, the strength or, as it is often called, the wholeness (in Russian it is *tselnost*) of women was one of the major themes of Russian literature from Pushkin's Tatyana in *Eugen Onegin* onwards. And it is not difficult to see that the women owed their *tselnost* to their sheltered lives, while the men had been "broken" by their conflict with Russian reality.

The poet Nekrasov dedicated many of his poems to strong female characters, whom he found in villages as well as in the salons. His long narrative poem "Sasha" [5] was particularly popular in his lifetime and many young girls were inspired by the heroine. It is the story of a typical provincial miss, daughter of simple and modest landowners. She is brought up in the seclusion of their country estate, free to roam in the meadows and to learn domestic arts but not burdened with book-learning. Then a neighbouring nobleman, who had been abroad for many years, returns to his neglected estate and becomes a frequent visitor. Happy to find in Sasha an avid listener, he talks at length of foreign lands, laments over human misery and the deeper roots thereof, and vaguely predicts a happier and better future for mankind. Even more vaguely he refers to some useful work which should be done and which he would have liked to undertake, if only. . . . And then the summer is over and Agarin—that is his name—departs for the metropolis, giving no thought to the mischief he has wrought. Sasha is a lost soul—her former pursuits no longer satisfy her, all day and often night long her nose is stuck in books. And soon this is not enough: she begins to go to the villages, among the peasants, to teach their children and nurse the sick. She is translating the ideas caught from Agarin into deeds, and she is happy doing the useful work he had hinted at. Two years pass before Agarin returns, his hair somewhat thinner and his face more worn. She, at nineteen, has blossomed into a little beauty, full of health and energy. She pours out to him at once all she had read and done in his absence, but his response is luke-warm. He is now telling her that mankind is worthless and all attempts to help it equally so. When he surprises Sasha one morning working among the peasants, he mocks her: "A child amuses itself with a new toy!" [6] But her work is deadly serious to Sasha; while he has lost all purpose in life, she has found one. She loves him, has probably loved him from the start, yet she rejects him when he asks her to marry him—she could not marry a weakling. "Sasha" was devoured by countless young women all over Russia, all eager to learn and to study and to lead useful lives.

Such, in broad outline, was the situation of women in Russia when the nihilists entered the lists on their behalf. The nihilist motto was: *skazano-sdelano,* that is, no sooner said than done, and accordingly they interested themselves primarily in problems that could be immediately tackled. The family was felt to be the foundation of society and therefore should be attacked first of all. And since the liberation of women, who next to peasants were considered to be the most underprivileged part of society, was felt to be a precondition for the transformation of family, it was naturally included in the attack.

The "new" family advocated by the nihilists was to ensure freedom for all its members. The "new" relationship between parents and children was to be based on tolerance and mutual respect. In practice this proved easier said than done and often deteriorated into mutual abuse and misunderstanding. Neither the old nor the young could change quickly and painlessly. Turgenev, in *Fathers and Sons*, gave an inimitable portrayal of the dilemma. But he was concerned with the tensions between fathers and sons and neither he nor any other writer explored the relationship between fathers and daughters—in fact this dilemma seems to be deliberately avoided. It is amazing how many of Turgenev's and Goncharov's heroines are fatherless and brought up by mothers or grandmothers. But whether son or daughter—their position within the existing family structure proved difficult to change. It became clear that new forms of family would have to be found and—*skazano-sdelano—*

the nihilists began to experiment with new forms of family and of marriage.

The "new" marriage was to rest on complete equality between the sexes, on sexual freedom for both, and on perfect honesty, tolerance, and mutual respect. All social behaviour was, in fact, to rest on these principles, and on rational egoism, a concept based on the naive assumption that a) everybody was capable of rational thought, and b) individual needs would not conflict with each other but, on the contrary, harmonize with those of everybody else.[7] What was best for the individual was also best for society, and a rational and dispassionate analysis of any given situation would inevitably show it to be so. For a married man to be happy, his wife should be happy too, and therefore unselfishness in marriage constituted the highest degree of egoism.

It was more or less generally conceded that the ideal new marriage could not be achieved at once and that at first men should accept second place, to give women time to outgrow their past servitude. Nikolay Chernyshevsky was particularly insistent on that score: "Every decent man should put his wife above himself," and to start with, "the stick should be bent the other way." [8] These are indeed noble as well as rational considerations. Unfortunately Chernyshevsky pushed them to absurd lengths both in his own marriage and in his embarrassingly naive novel *What Is To Be Done?* In it Chernyshevsky shows the "new" husband helping and encouraging his wife to educate herself and to become independent and self-supporting. Husband and wife are shown as living in separate rooms and knocking punctiliously at each other's door before entering. When the wife falls in love with another man, the husband uncomplainingly fades out of her life. Obviously this is meant to show that sex should not be taken for granted and that the partners, particularly the wife, should have freedom of choice. However, the reader is left in doubt as to whether sex entered their relationship at all. Fortunately the second husband, though equally a "new" man, is altogether a more determined character, who, having knocked at the heroine's door, enters the room, and does not emerge again until next morning.

Though Chernyshevsky's novel lacked all talent, with characters unreal and sentimentalized and situations downright silly, it was the first attempt to deal with "new" morality in fiction. And for this reason perhaps, as well as for the early portrayal of an idealized revolutionary (Rakhmetov), the novel had an enormous and lasting success.

In his own marriage Chernyshevsky failed to find a "new" woman in his wife, Olga, whom he married in 1853. On his side, he acted according to his theories and was considerate and even subservient to her—"my character is . . . such as to obey"—but she proved a shallow and pleasure-loving woman and shared neither his selfless love nor his intellectual interests.[9]

Several other famous attempts were made to live according to the new marital morality. One marriage that is well documented was that of the Shelgunovs.[10] Both husband and wife as well as the third party left memoirs and letters, so that we can form a fair opinion of them and of their relationship to each other. Nikolay Shelgunov, who was to become a very popular radical writer, married his lively cousin Ludmilla in 1850. A gifted and intelligent woman, she was very attractive to men and loved being surrounded by admirers. On one of her frequent visits to the masked balls, where she went to indulge her passion for what she called "mystification," [11] though "flirtation" would have described it equally well, one of her victims was the young poet Mikhail Mikhaylov, who fell deeply in love with her. Soon he moved in with the Shelgunovs and became as close a friend of the husband as he was a passionate lover of the wife. In fact the bond between the men proved stronger and more durable than between Ludmilla and either of them. Shelgunov had put it on record that he wanted marriage to be based on equality and comradeship and on complete honesty. He dreamt of having next to himself "a rational, thinking, feeling, and beautiful being." He was prepared to be tolerant, and to "obey his wife not out of weakness but out of magnanimity." [12] He seems indeed to have been a strong man as well as a truly magnanimous one, and to have taken upon himself more than his fair share of responsibility and of suffering. As for Mikhaylov, he was an exceptionally talented as well as an honest and charming man. Ludmilla Shelgunova undoubtedly matured with the years and fully shared the political ideas and activities of the two men. Yet she remained egocentric and self-indulgent to the end.

A better-balanced marriage was that of Pyotr Bokov to Maria Obruchova.[13] It was generally believed that the novel *What Is To Be Done?* was modelled on their real-life relationship, but Bokov, who seemed to have been a man of good sense as well as good taste, entirely repudiated it. His usual good-humoured rejoinder was, "Do I look like a hero of a novel?" [14] As none of the three people concerned left personal memoirs, we can only reconstruct their history from the numerous comments of their contemporaries. It appears, then, that Bokov was born into a peasant family and worked his way up through school and the medical faculty by sheer dogged determination, supporting himself by giving private lessons. Maria's brother Vladimir Obruchov, a fellow student who was later condemned to hard labour for writing one of the earliest radical proclamations, asked Bokov to help his sister to prepare for examinations. She was apparently determined to study medicine, but in order to matriculate she had to pass the school-leaving examinations. Bokov agreed but was soon being asked to help her in a more personal manner: she had met with parental opposition—most parents still considered it immodest for a girl to want to study—and had decided to resort to a fictitious marriage. This was a device much practised among young people and one that helped greatly to free women from parental authority. In those days, unmarried women were entirely in the power of the father: if they wanted to leave home, he could not only refuse financial support but also his permission for the necessary residence permits; he could even have her brought home by the police. A married woman, on the other hand, became dependent in all legal matters on her husband, and her dowry was paid out to him. It was considered a point of honour among young progressives not only to offer "their hand and name" to any young woman who wanted to become independent, but also to hand her dowry over to her, which enabled her to study. After this the scenario varied. Some couples separated at that point, never to meet again, while others went together to study abroad and still others genuinely fell in love with each other and their marriage ceased to be fictitious.

Bokov, a gentleman in all things, readily agreed to marry his pupil. At first this marriage was, as such marriages were, a scrupulously platonic affair, but eventually their friendship turned into love and for four happy years they were truly man and wife. He still helped Maria with her studies. In those days it was a continuous struggle for a woman to study, and Maria Bokova belonged to the first generation of women who became doctors—a brilliant pioneer generation which, however, had to fight every inch of the way. When in 1864 women were barred from lectures at the St. Petersburg Medical Academy, she had to finish her studies abroad: in Vienna, Heidelberg, Zurich, and finally London, where she became well known as a specialist in eye diseases.

But to go back to the beginnings of her story. The Bokovs were not only the happiest of married couples but also the best of friends, so that when she met the young scientist Sechenov in 1861 and they fell in love, Dr. Bokov retired, though remaining on friendly terms with both. Later in life he met and married another woman and settled with her in Moscow, where the "Bokov Sundays" [15] became popular tea-table gatherings of intellectuals. When Sechenov was appointed to the chair of physiology at Moscow University, the two couples met in the most cordial manner. Sechenov rose to be one of the foremost Russian scientists and his wife established herself both as a doctor and as a translator of scientific books. They were very busy people but never failed to welcome friends at tea-time, when, we are told, it was he who poured the tea! [16]

What emerges from all the marital experiments described here is that to be successful all the people concerned had to submit willingly to the very painful process of mutual adjustment and tolerance. This required considerable maturity from both partners. Thus the nihilist marital experimentation promoted maturation of both men and women and played an important part in the liberation of both sexes in Russia. In most other advanced countries men had gone through a difficult and lengthy process of adjustment to a postfeudal, modern society; they had had to fight for their rights and they had won. They thus consolidated their position in society before women came to claim their share in it, a task that was correspondingly more difficult since the men, even the most progressive, had by then settled into firm modes of life and repressive attitudes towards women. It was exceptionally lucky for Russian women that they entered an open and fast-changing society in which the position of men was almost as insecure as their own. Their bid for emancipation coincided with a parallel claim by men, and they were welcomed as partners and as comrades-in-arms. It will be seen later that the same whole-hearted acceptance of women in the revolutionary movement established an atmosphere of mutual help and trust, in which many outstanding Russian women were able to develop to the full their various talents.

It is to Mikhail Mikhaylov that we owe the clearest and fullest exposition of women's aspirations in Russia. In an article entitled "Women, Their Education and Importance in Family and Society," published in 1860,[17] Mikhaylov formulated the premises on which the bringing up of women should rest in future: respect for their dignity and personality and for their desire for independence and work, and active support for their efforts towards self-fullfillment. So far the role of women had been restricted to motherhood—but how could a mother living in mental stagnation bring up her children otherwise than on "old prejudices, superstitions, and fear of life?" [18] Only a liberal education and an early physical training would enable women to bring up healthy and mentally alert children. And, of course, women should be able to take part in public life if they wished; it could only benefit the society. In the traditional Russian marriage, love was not considered essential, and husbands habitually sought "romance" outside it while demanding strict fidelity from their wives. This was no better than slavery, and all slavery was corrupting. The moral depravity of Russian society,

Mikhaylov concluded, was directly due to the enslavement of women, originating to some extent in male jealousy and fear of competition.

From this survey of past wrongs Mikhaylov turned to demands for a better future. Equal educational opportunities for both sexes, co-education in day schools, admission to all professions and occupations and full civic rights—such were the basic needs of a healthy and dynamic society. As for the physical disability of women due to child-bearing, this should be provided for in the general organization of society. Nor need women be completely "eclipsed" during the child-bearing period—which was unlikely to exceed eight or ten years—if they had active sympathy and cooperation from their husbands.

Mikhaylov's article was enthusiastically supported by radical writers, such as Pisarev: "Respect for the personality, the independence and work of women, sympathy for anything that would facilitate their development . . . it is on these ideas [advanced by Mikhaylov] that the young generation should be brought up; only ideas such as these, when realized, would ensure the emergence of women harmoniously developed, capable of useful activity, morally free and consequently happy." [19]

The term "equality of sexes" was used by most liberal and radical Russians to denote simply equality of opportunity, and both sexes were expected to find their own identity. But a small minority took the meaning literally—in these circles women sported men's clothes *à la* George Sand and practised free love. Pyotr Zaychnevsky, extreme in all his pronouncements, wrote in 1862: "We demand the complete liberation of women, and that they shall be given the same political and civic rights as men; we demand the abolition of marriage because it is a highly immoral institution, irreconcilable with the equality of sexes; equally we demand the abolition of the family." [20]

But most radicals held more sensible views on the future of women. And the fact that they were also endorsed by well-known liberal men of the day gave them a validity far beyond any particular progressive clique. The famous liberal surgeon Pirogov said that "women ought to occupy in society a place more in keeping with their human dignity and their intellectual potential. . . . So far we have completely ignored the wonderful talents of our women. . . . When women get the appropriate upbringing and education, they will be as capable as men are of organizing their scientific, artistic, and civic culture." [21] And already in 1856, the influential educationalist Boehm wrote that "women's education is of the foremost importance to State and Church, since the enlightened maternal influence is not only beneficial to the family, but is also . . . essential to all national education." [22] In the same year, Pirogov's famous article "Problems of Life" [23] also advocated better education for women—the article was widely read by the public and even, it was rumoured, in the Winter Palace.

But the changing attitudes to women's education constitute a separate, though of course related, subject. It belongs properly to the reign of Alexander II, and to this we must now in any case turn.

ALEXANDER II AND 2 REFORM

Nicholas I's official doctrine of "Orthodoxy, Autocracy, Nationhood" had proudly proclaimed the spiritual unity of all Russians in their triple devotion to Church, Tsar, and Fatherland. How hollow this claim was became obvious the moment he died: Russians hailed his son as a liberator from oppression.

The new reign began in 1855 with a genuine enough breeze of freedom. Censorship was relaxed, the secret police seemed to melt into the shadows, and the first five or six years were spoken of as the "honeymoon of the emperor with society." Time was to show that this love affair was largely based on illusions. But while it **33** lasted, it offered Russians a period of near freedom of speech and the press, and they took full advantage of it. The flexing of intellectual muscles manifested itself in vigorous polemics. Jurists, educationalists, political thinkers of the right and left burst into print. New journals sprang up everywhere, including a *Women's Journal*; there was an epidemic of public lectures; and, particularly in the capitals, in Moscow and St. Petersburg, cultural life boomed. Contemporary witnesses all speak of the general enthusiasm and optimism, of everybody being swept along in one common vital upsurge,[1] as if all the energy that had been dammed up for generations was now on the point of release.

Russia was tense with the expectation of reforms. Among the educated there was hope that even the autocracy itself might be modified; all shades of political opinion agreed that a constitution with some kind of parliament or elected People's Assembly was what the country needed.

The task confronting the new tsar was formidable. Because his predecessors had procrastinated, he was faced with the need for wholesale change. Was Alexander II the man for such a task? What kind of man was he? He had been brought up by the poet Zhukovsky, who served as his tutor, a humane and cultured man but somewhat sentimental and naive in worldly affairs. A staunch monarchist who nonetheless held very liberal views, Zhukovsky instilled in his pupil idealistic notions of the duties of a "perfect ruler": love for his people and a concern for its wellbeing as well as respect for law and justice and for public opinion. He was opposed to the military upbringing usual in the Russian imperial family and tried to prevent his pupil from "seeing his people merely as a regiment and his country as a barracks,"[2] as Nicholas I had done. But in Alexander, who loved his father very much, Zhukovsky's influence created a deep conflict. Affectionate and much in need of affection, the boy became very unsure of himself and came to dread his future. His intellect was limited, his will unstable, and he grew up into a man for ever at odds with himself, easily swayed emotionally, unable to take clear-cut decisions, touchy and resentful of criticism. He was given to bouts of depression and apathy, and to occasional outbreaks of violent temper. Yet he also had many admirable qualities: he was simple and undemanding in his personal habits and courageous in the face of danger. Moreover, he possessed exceptional good looks and great charm, was infinitely better educated than his father or brothers, and had made a tour of western Europe (including England) and of Russia in the company of his tutors before he ascended the throne.

In public as in private affairs there were two sides to him. Alexander II was at first undoubtedly sincere in his liberal intentions. Zhukovsky's influence was strong in him, and he really planned to liberalize and to modernize Russia, though not, of course, to the extent envisaged by his subjects. But the idea that he *owed* reforms to the country would never have entered his head. He believed in autocracy every bit as fanatically as his father, and saw reforms as gifts to his people, and himself as a benefactor. Indeed, he was much more like his father than appeared at first. He shared Nicholas's love for public displays. The imperial court was for ever celebrating something or other with great ostentation and at immense cost—often at the same time as famines ravaged whole provinces of Russia and the country's coffers were empty.

The enthusiasm that greeted the new tsar gave him heart, and he at once set up commissions to work out the terms of his first reform—the abolition of serfdom and the distribution of land. Unfortunately the work of these commissions ran into difficulties almost at once, and these proved in the end to be insoluble. It appeared that there was enough opposition to the reform to split the country. On one side there were the long-suffering serfs who expected freedom to be granted together with the ownership of enough land to live on. Opinions varied as to how much land they should get. Naturally they all expected to get the individual land strips they had always ploughed and had come to consider their own. But since these strips were usually much too small to support a peasant family, it seemed only fair to expect some additional land, and also the free use of pastures, woods, rivers, and the like. There were some who argued that all arable land should be equally distributed among all Russians, poor or rich, since they were all free men now.

On the other side, among the serf owners who had for centuries lived on the fruits of unpaid labour and no longer knew how to support themselves otherwise, there was panic. In their determination to sabotage the work of the commissions, they were supported by large numbers of hangers-on and petty officials—parasites who thrive on that kind of society. More seriously they were also supported by many high dignitaries of State and Church who were afraid that Old Russia might crumble once such a prop as serfdom was removed.* All these elements were known as *krepostniki*—upholders of serfdom.

In between stood the enlightened conservative and liberal landlords who were prepared to sacrifice their interests for humanitarian reasons, and the educated public as a whole. But unfortunately they had little influence on the progress of the reform.

The tsar himself was not only determined to abolish serfdom, but also to see that the peasants had enough land to live on. Several liberal statesmen were of the same mind, and so was the Empress Maria, his wife, his brother Konstantin, and his aunt Grand Duchess Elena, the best-educated woman in his family. But there were too many *krepostniki* in his entourage—that grasping and self-seeking "cluster around the throne" [3] so scathingly denounced by the poet Lermontov.

The fact that there was widespread unrest among the peasants due to natural impatience to get their freedom played into the hands of the *krepostniki*—they were able to frighten the tsar with the spectre of peasant revolts. He was never at his best when things went wrong; and this time, too, he blundered. Early in 1861 he ordered troops to be placed in all rural parts of the country with instructions to shoot to kill, to disperse crowds with bayonets, and to raze villages to the ground "where necessary." At the request of the minister of justice the Holy Synod instructed the rural clergy to preach gratitude and obedience to the God-anointed tsar, without "giving away the fact of having received official instructions." [4]

---

* One of the most energetic opponents of the reform was the Metropolitan Bishop of Moscow, Filaret; among the bishops only one, Gregory of Kostroma, denounced serfdom as unchristian. (Kornilov, A., p. 49.)

In the capitals, army patrols were stationed everywhere, even inside the Winter Palace. Secret police spies swarmed all over the towns; all *dvorniki* were instructed to inform the police if anybody had more than three visitors. They were also told *not* to talk of the liberation of peasants and to report anybody who did. This directive prompted one unfortunate *dvornik* to confide to his cronies that freedom must indeed be coming, for which lapse the poor fool was given 230 lashes of the knout! [5]

After several postponements, the peasant reform became law on 19 February 1861. It was solemnly proclaimed in all churches on the eve of the Great Lent, but it fell singularly flat—it satisfied nobody, not even the *krepostniki*. The serfs were set free *without land*; they were to be allocated portions of land, but these were not large enough to feed a peasant family and its cattle. And for this land the peasants were expected to pay an exorbitant price. The owners of the land were to be paid a lump sum by the state at once, but the peasants were to pay by annual installments plus interest over a period of forty-nine years—only then would they receive a clear title to their holdings. It was to become apparent later that these annual payments and the high taxes and dues payable to the state pauperized the peasants and made the introduction of modern farming impossible. Many small landowners, too, were ruined, since they were left with too little land and too little money to support themselves.

The peasants received the reform with complete disbelief; they even suspected the authenticity of the Imperial Manifesto. They could not believe that the "little father tsar" had been a party to the unjust terms of the reform. Clearly, the "greedy nobles" and the corrupt officials had once again deceived the tsar—perhaps even forced his hand? Soon spokesmen for the peasants, the *khodoki* ("walkers"), trudged by the hundreds along the interminable Russian roads to see the tsar and to tell him of the injustice and hardship suffered by his people. Most of them were picked up by the police before they got anywhere near the tsar and were soon trudging in fetters on the even longer roads to Siberia. But their fate, if the news ever reached their native villages, only confirmed the belief that "truth was being withheld from the tsar."

The land reform was slow to take effect. The terms were sufficiently vague and confused to foster the belief that this was not, in fact, the "true" freedom but some preliminary rigmarole; and the peasants confidently waited for the true freedom, *with land and plenty of it*, to be announced soon. But the prophets of a violent and bloody revolt were proved entirely wrong—there was now less unrest than before the liberation. The countryside was becalmed in a dispirited, stunned kind of silence. When, gradually, the passive resistance to the reform began to express itself in refusals to go through with the formalities, these sporadic and unarmed protests were suppressed with the whole force of the imperial army, which did indeed "shoot to kill," and thousands of peasants were nearly flogged to death or sent to Siberia.

Liberal-minded landowners saw clearly the injustice of the reform and many of them voluntarily gave their former serfs sufficient land free of charge with, sometimes, money to purchase cattle and tools. Several corporate bodies of landed nobility urged better terms for the peasants and at least one, that of Tver, refused to accept payment for the land allotted to former serfs. The Tver nobility did not endear itself to the tsar by its quixotic generosity—its leaders were arrested.[6] The writer and lawyer Bervi-Flerovsky, outraged by such disregard of legality, wrote a letter of protest to the tsar—*he* was put into a lunatic asylum for six months.[7]

Of all missed opportunities, the land reform was surely the greatest in Russian history. "Poor, poor tsar and poor, poor people—so to misunderstand each other!" said a contemporary observer.[8] But it was, of course, more than just a misunderstanding, it was a grave political blunder and was to have dire results in the future. Indeed the peasants' unappeased hunger for land was to become one of the strongest causes of the Revolution of 1917.

The reforms that followed were better formulated. The legal reform of 1864, designed by outstanding Russian jurists, put the judicial system on a par with, or even above, the best European models. It introduced trial by jury, equality of all citizens before the law, and the irremovability of judges; simplified and expedited legal procedure; and established a Russian bar. The local government reform of the same year also represented a great step forward by creating elected *zemstvos* (councils), which included representatives of merchants and peasants as well as nobles, for the administration of certain limited local affairs, such as education and medical care. Unfortunately both reforms suffered from subsequent governmental interference, since in practice the tsar would not tolerate initiative or independence in either judge, juror, or member of a *zemstvo,* and was quite capable of altering or annulling their decisions.

The excellent army reform of 1874 fared somewhat better—a complete reorganization of the armed services was indeed needed and the tsar did not interfere with it.

One side of Russian life remained quite unchanged, though it was the one that most needed to be changed—this was the character of the central government and the autocracy itself. The government machine was cumbersome and inefficient, and there was no collective cabinet responsibility and no prime minister. The tsars presided personally over the Council of Ministers and had the final word in all its decisions, as in the decisions of the individual ministers. The tsars neither trusted nor respected their ministers, appointing and dismissing them with extraordinary ease. This state of affairs meant that with very few exceptions, only time-servers and nonentities were willing to serve. "We have bureaucrats, even notables, we have courtiers, but no statesmen,[9] noted the diarist Alexander Nikitenko. In short, all power in the land was vested solely in the person of the tsar. By a stroke of his pen he was still able to reverse or annul any law.

The educated public was naturally disappointed. Its initial enthusiasm for Alexander II had been exaggerated, and so was its disenchantment; the honeymoon with the emperor was over. But it left a deep discord in Russian society. Liberal elements were inclined to make the best of the situation, arguing that half a loaf was better than no bread and that something useful could still be achieved within the framework of the reforms.

The radical attitude to the peasant reform was entirely negative.

Even the joy over the abolition of serfdom was eclipsed by anxiety over the economic plight of the peasants. The radicals foresaw a time of terrible hardship for the people, who in their view had been precipitated from one slavery into another, this time an economic one. Their first reaction was to rouse the educated public and the people itself to protest, and there was a spate of illegally printed leaflets and proclamations. The first to appear were three leaflets addressed to "Great Russians" and written by Vladimir Obruchov, brother of Dr. Bokova-Sechenova. He appealed to the educated class to "take over the conduct of affairs from the incompetent government," to "replace arbitrary rule . . . by legality," and to demand the convention of elected delegates for the free formulation of a constitution—a demand that foreshadowed the call for a Constituent Assembly. The leaflets proposed that a direct appeal be made to the tsar to assemble such a convention, couched in most moderate terms "so that all liberal-minded people could sign it." [10] But it was also hinted that if the government disregarded all appeals, it would bring popular wrath upon itself. Similar veiled threats were contained in the manifesto addressed "To the peasants" [11] composed probably by Chernyshevsky, in which the peasants were urged to get ready to fight for real freedom, such as existed in France, Switzerland, England, and America. Another proclamation composed by Mikhail Mikhaylov, probably in cooperation with Nikolay Shelgunov, addressed itself to "The Young Generation," which it encouraged to work for the people and for an "elected and constitutional government." [12] Much more extreme and violent language was used by Pyotr Zaychnevsky in his proclamation "Young Russia," [13] in which he damned the whole existing order and called for a bloody revolt, with unsparing use of the axe, and for the physical destruction of the entire Romanov dynasty. The manifestos reflected, in fact, the whole range of radical feeling, from the moderate to the extreme.

These were the first stirrings of the revolutionary movement in Russia. The first secret revolutionary "party" was indeed formed in 1862; it called itself Zemlya i Volya (Land and Freedom), and although it was almost at once suppressed by the secret police, its name and appearance at that moment were symptomatic.

The tsar reacted to the hostile reception of the peasant reform with great bitterness. He had expected gratitude and not criticism; he felt misunderstood and unloved. If he had studied Tocqueville, he would have known that "the most dangerous moment for a bad regime is usually when it begins to reform. . . . The abuses that are removed seem to reveal those that remain, and to make them more galling; the evil has lessened, it is true, but the people feel it more keenly." [14]

The liberalism of Alexander II did not stand the test of time. The very word "progress" was so hateful to him that he forbade its use in official documents.[15] The censorship was tightened again and the secret police set to hunt radicals, real or suspected. An ever growing mass of citizens was classed as *nenadezhnye*, that is, politically untrustworthy, and faced a constant threat of arrest or exile without charge or trial. Scores of plays, including some by Turgenev and Ostrovsky, were banned, the publication of many journals was stopped, secular Sunday schools for the children of workers and peasants were closed, and so was the liberal Chess Club in St. Petersburg!

Attempts by students in 1861 to form corporate bodies such as existed in foreign universities, and generally to establish the independence of universities, were frustrated by the police and led to mass arrests and the closing of St. Petersburg University. From the very beginning of the conflict, which started very quietly, the police and the governor general of St. Petersburg moved in. Even the university *popechitel* could not find out what was going on, except indirectly through the Third Section, which had its spies on the spot.[16]

Between 1861 and 1866 every more or less prominent radical writer was arrested, kept in the Peter and Paul Fortress for a few months or years, and then exiled: Mikhail Mikhaylov, Nikolay Chernyshevsky, Nikolay Shelgunov, Pyotr Lavrov, Bervi-

Arrest of a revolutionary student (The Mansell Collection)

Flerovsky, Dmitry Pisarev, and many others. The tsar intended these punishments to be a warning to the general public; accordingly, while the trials were held in secret, the so-called "civic executions," staged with a clumsy showmanship worthy of Nicholas I, were held in public. The sentenced men were made to mount a platform erected in one of the big squares in St. Petersburg and to stand, chained to a pole, with placards on their chests saying "State Criminal," while the sentence was read out; in the case of noblemen swords were broken over their heads to signify loss of privilege and civic rights. Then they were taken back to prison and sent into exile, often in chains. The capital was soon emptied of "dangerous" men. All active elements and possible trouble-makers were continuously weeded out and shut away, while the general public was held under severe police supervision.

Yet neither the radical writers nor the short-lived Land and Freedom party had been a real threat to the regime and most of the arrests and sentences were based on trumped-up charges. The persecution engendered much anger among the radicals, and, in the young, anger overflowed into desperation. It was certainly an act of despair that made the young student Karakozov shoot at Alexander II in April 1866. Karakozov had been one of those idealistic landowners who had given away all their money to their former serfs. Disenchanted by the peasant reform, he had joined a secret group in Moscow which called itself Hell and resolved to eliminate the tsar as the main obstacle to a better future for Russia. But though he fired at close range, the young assassin missed.* He was executed. His was a foolhardy attempt to rid Russia of autocracy or, at least, to shock society and rouse it to action. It did indeed shock society but not in the sense he intended—society as a whole rallied to the throne, and many wavering liberals moved hurriedly over to the right. It certainly further embittered the tsar. Instead of a revolution, Karakozov's shot unleashed an orgy of police terror. A deadly hush seemed to settle over the country—the ghost of Nicholas I was abroad.

---

* A soldier on sentry duty in the Summer Gardens where the attempt took place, one Dyadin, cried out: "That is not the way to shoot!" and paid with twenty years' hard labour for his unguarded tongue. (Burstev, V., part 2, p. 69.)

FEMINISM AND WOMEN'S EDUCATION

Almost the only cause that was not abandoned during the dead years that followed Karakozov's shot was that of feminism. It was a well-established movement by then, having been born in the mid-1850s, carried along on the wave of liberal, radical, and nihilist ideas, and expressing the widespread desire of women for self-determination in the social and intellectual life of Russia. One of the few women who had already won an independent position for herself—Maria Vernadskaya, an accomplished economist and co-editor, with her husband, of an economic journal—wrote in an article in 1858 that women should be allowed **45** to work for their living and yet "be respected and received every-where in society" and not "be laughed at and despised" [1] for it. And even the proverbial "young girl of good family," previously expected to be no more than a well-dressed doll, now spurned conventional restraints. As one of them wrote: "We were determined to fight old prejudices, we walked in the street without a footman, rode in hired hansom cabs, and even before I was married, I began going to social functions unchaperoned." [2] But most women had, of course, more serious ambitions.

The first feminist group which was to become the core of the movement had been founded by Maria Trubnikova,[3] who was the daughter of a Decembrist and was born in Siberia. She married in 1855 and moved with her husband to St. Petersburg, where she soon came in contact with educated and cultured men. We are told that she felt the gaps in her own education very acutely and was determined to become more knowledgeable. She read widely, mostly on social subjects, foreign authors as well as Russian—Vico, Michelet, Heine, Proudhon, Lassalle, Saint-Simon, Louis Blanc, and, of course, Herzen. Around her tea-table could be found radical, even nihilist, intellectuals as well as socialites. This mixture of the intellectual and the fashionable was indeed typical of contemporary cultural life in the capitals.

When Maria Trubnikova decided to form a feminist group, she found invaluable allies in Nadezhda Stasova [4] and Anna Filosofova.[5] Stasova never married and dedicated her entire life to their common cause. Anna Filosofova—gay, beautiful, and married to a high dignitary, who was a particular protégé of the tsar—was not afraid to use her high connections in the interest of feminism. She made herself such a nuisance to the authorities that in 1875 she was asked to leave Russia and to reside abroad, and it was made clear to her that but for the friendship that the tsar bore her husband, she would have found herself dealt with much more severely.

The feminist group found followers among women in all walks of life, from Grand Duchess Elena Pavlovna and the wife and daughter of Minister for war Dmitry Milyutin, to the young "nihilist" women in spectacles who were burning to storm the citadels of learning. But above all it was enthusiastically received and supported by the male intelligentsia. Perhaps because of this male backing feminism never became as aggressive in Russia as it did in other countries, where women met with opposition from men of their own class. Russian feminists were also spared the need to fight for the legal and political rights of women, since the educated class was already fighting for those rights—for both sexes, and for all classes.

Russian feminists could thus concentrate their efforts on obtaining better educational and professional opportunities for women. Of course they were aware that these could not be won without drastic changes in social conventions and even in the social structure—and to that extent they were politically involved from the start. In fact in many ways their views coincided with those of the radicals and even the nihilists, and they did not shrink from alliance with them. And loyalty to these erstwhile allies survived into a later period when many of them turned into proscribed revolutionaries. We know that Anna Filosofova defended young radicals in letters to Turgenev. And Maria Trubnikova's own children and their friends, all of them involved in revolutionary activities, were never denied her sympathy and help.

The first concern of the feminists was to create training facilities for women who had to earn, or were already earning, their living, so that they should qualify for better-paid and interesting jobs. The projected Society for the Propagation of Women's Work, for which Pyotr Lavrov wrote the statutes, failed to materialize; but smaller ventures were successful. Thus an *artel*—a traditional Russian form of cooperative team—of women translators and publishers became well established, the illustrations and bindings for their books being provided by a sister *artel*. However, such limited experiments were obviously not going to satisfy large numbers of women or to solve the economic and social problems created for women by the reforms of Alexander II.

As we know, the peasant reform ruined not only many of the liberated serfs but also numerous small landowners. And not only men, but many women, single or widowed, found themselves destitute. They joined the already existing "female proletariat" consisting of widows and unmarried daughters of poorly paid petty clerks, bankrupt merchants, and the like. These unfortunate women had no skills to earn their living with—except perhaps embroidery—and there was already a glut of untrained governesses. Thus the need for professional and semiprofessional training for women was dictated by life itself. But apart from these economic pressures, young women all over Russia had begun to ask for and to expect better education. And it was apparent that women aimed as high as they could go—the feminist group was hopefully planning a University for Women! [6]

These high hopes were, of course, too sudden and too extravagant to be fulfilled under Russian conditions. It was more realistic to work for elementary and secondary schools for girls. And in this the feminists were supported even more enthusiastically by educationalists and academics. The educationalists would have liked to see the whole school system reformed, but this had become very difficult after 1866, when Count Dmitry Tolstoy, the Procurator of the Holy Synod (secular head of the Orthodox Church), became minister of education, for he imposed a rigid classical education on boys' schools, to the neglect of history and natural sciences favoured by progressives.

Significantly, the famous formula that inspired all policies of Nicholas I—"Orthodoxy, Autocracy, and Nationhood"—had been the brain-child of Count Uvarov, his minister of education. And it certainly had been most uncompromisingly imposed on the educational system. It was held that it was better for pupils to be ignorant than to stray from the narrow path of piety and patriotism. Every school had attached to it a priest who closely supervised the morals and the trends of thought among pupils and teachers. Every school district was similarly watched over by a government inspector. Both boys and teachers wore uniforms and spent a great deal of their time learning military drill and discipline. A familiar sight on Russian streets was that of pink-cheeked infants in long, heavy greatcoats and gold-braided caps, skipping along to school and suddenly stopping in mid-skip and jerking up elbow and hand to salute a passing pedagogue. Nothing could be more ludicrous than these miniature soldiers.

A reform of boys' schools thus presented formidable obstacles. Girls' schools, on the other hand, were a new field for action and a unique opportunity for introducing new teaching techniques and a more enlightened educational spirit. This consideration certainly played a part in the energetic support given to feminists by educationalists—girls' schools were to be the thin end of the wedge.

In fact, girls' schools were practically nonexistent in mid-nineteenth-century Russia. The daughters of the nobility were usually educated at home or in closed boarding schools, called *pensionat* or *institut*—the Smolny Institut in St. Petersburg, which supplied ladies-in-waiting for the imperial court, being rather a superior example. The level of teaching in these establishments was extremely low, the young girls being instructed in religion and deportment, dancing and good manners, but very little else. The best education available for girls was probably in the orphanages, which were designed to supply the *instituts* with cheap instructresses and private families with governesses. Little was done for teaching girls of lower social strata. Parish schools were open to sons and daughters of the poor, but the children were taught very little there.

The official attitude towards women's education was clear. Higher education was quite out of the question—it was much too advanced an idea, offending against all the conventions. The government was prepared only to allow special training courses in midwifery, nursing, elementary teaching, and so forth, all of which met immediate needs. It also encouraged the opening of elementary and secondary schools for girls of all social strata, in the towns as well as the larger villages. Unfortunately it had no money to finance such schools, the coffers being empty after the Crimean War, so it recommended that local nobles and merchants foot the bills. The response was lukewarm—the purses of private donors were equally empty. And provincial Russia was in any case not very interested, as the schools were considered too daring an innovation.

Typical of the prevailing feeling was the petition of the Recruitment Committee of the town of Vologda (a war-time body), dated

22 December 1855,[7] for permission to endow an *institut* for fifty daughters of the nobility so that "the enemies of Christ and Church should know that Russians are not and never will be afraid of hostile hordes, and that while brandishing a sword to smite the evil-doers with one hand, with the other they are scattering the seeds of faith, love, and hope. In full consciousness of which, acknowledging that the source of all faith, love, and hope is in the mothers of families and in the sisters,'' the committee throws itself on its knees before the monarch and begs for permission "to adorn the [future] *institut* with the adored name of the ruling empress" and also to join to it the already existing orphanage "for the supply of servant girls for the *institut* and for the better education of the particularly gifted among the little orphans"—no doubt to supply equally cheap teachers for the *institut*.

Where provincial society decided to follow the recommendations of the government, the results were often no less comical. Thus in the town of Kostroma,[8] the local inspector of schools addressed the townspeople as follows: ". . . It stands to reason that an educated wife is better able to smooth the wrinkled brow of the husband . . . and as He desires every one of us to have a happy family life, the Tsar Emperor, Alexander Nikolaevich . . . pronounced His Imperial command that schools for young girls should be instituted in His beloved Russia . . . the funds . . . to be supplied by the estates that would benefit by such schools, since every State kopek had already been allocated. . . . If to you, as to every Russian, every word and wish of the Emperor is sacred . . . if you . . . believe that God Himself is making His Will manifest through the mouth of His Anointed—then how could you fail to carry out God's will and the Emperor's?" Accordingly it was proposed that voluntary taxes should be levied on every christening, wedding, and the like. In Kazan, the inspector of schools suggested a voluntary tax of ten kopeks on each new pack of cards used in the local club of the nobility—this gave the considerable sum of 400 roubles in the first year.

In 1858–59, to set a good example, four day schools for girls, named in honour of the ruling Empress Maria, were opened in St.

Petersburg.[9] These schools were attended by daughters of noblemen, merchants, and artisans; and by Russian Orthodox, Roman Catholics, and even Jews; and the teaching was in accordance with the most up-to-date educational theories. Some of the larger provincial towns opened similar schools on more conventional lines, and several excellent private schools appeared at the same time. But none of these schools conferred on the pupils any rights to further education, whether they completed the four, seven, or even the eight years' course; and in many of them the teaching was poor. Some ten years later, the Minister for education, Count Dmitry Tolstoy, was unable to give the tsar a very rosy picture: "unfortunately, women's education, on the whole . . . is in extreme decay . . . girls' schools can hardly survive on the meagre funds." [10]

Where economic necessity overruled tradition, some women had already penetrated into certain occupations even without schooling. Moreover, women proved to be very good at a variety of jobs, given a minimum of training. They certainly excelled as nurses and midwives, but also as teachers. As the Moscow *zemstvo* was to concede later, they were "preferable to men, even when not sufficiently qualified, because they were at least free from the universal male vice of insobriety." [11]

Women also moved into academic life wherever they saw the least opening. Thus they applied for and received the permission of several professors, first in St. Petersburg and later in Kharkov, Kiev, Kazan, and Odessa, to attend lectures as unmatriculated students. Some professors went so far as to help them in their studies and to allow them to sit for examinations, despite the opposition of the authorities. The first to appear at university lectures in St. Petersburg, in 1859, were the two sisters Korsini, and they were soon followed by others. It caused a mild sensation, but these first women students did nothing to encourage that—they dressed and behaved modestly and they were often chaperoned by aunts or brothers. The St. Petersburg Public Library extended reading rights to women. Some professors even allowed them to work in their laboratories, while others invited them to take part in geological and botanical field work.

But all this was chicken-feed. Women petitioned the special commission convened in 1861 to review university statutes to admit women as matriculated students. Most university councils approved of the scheme. The St. Petersburg council, for instance, unanimously recommended that women be admitted on absolutely equal terms with men, as was "only just and sensible." [12] The two dissenting universities were Moscow,[13] which objected on moral grounds and because it believed that the presence of women would interfere with the work of men students, and Derpt,[14] where the Chancellor did not believe "that women possessed a brain capable of understanding logical sciences."

Unfortunately, when the political climate changed again after the announcement of the peasant reform, and tension was expressed in student unrest in 1861 and in the Polish rising in 1863, there was no further question of more concessions to women. That citadel of profeminist feeling, the Medical Academy in St. Petersburg, was forbidden in 1864 to admit women to lectures. The few courageous professors who still allowed some women to work, unofficially, in their laboratories, risked and sometimes suffered dismissal. When the plan for a Women's College,[15] prepared for the feminist group by a voluntary committee of forty-three university professors, was submitted to Count Dmitry Tolstoy, he refused to sanction it. He allowed only a course of public evening lectures open to both men and women.

This was a terrible disappointment but the sponsors made the best of the opportunity offered. The lectures were begun in January 1870, and at once 900 people (767 of them women) registered. The fees were low, the range of subjects wide, and the lecturers often quite brilliant. The highest academic standards were maintained, and it was considered that nowhere in the world were women privileged to receive such excellent teaching. Congratulations arrived from abroad, from John Stuart Mill and Harriet Mill in England, and from feminist leaders in America. Unfortunately the lectures had to be discontinued after five years for lack of funds and because no permanent home could be found for them. Throughout that time the feminist group—which did all the work and collected all the money—was made to feel the antagonism of the police. The head of the Third Section, Count Shuvalov, bombarded the tsar with hostile reports, and his successor, General Drenteln, reported that the feminist group "aimed at obtaining equality for women through higher, semiclassical education" and that some of the women students were "politically unreliable." [16] The chief of police of St. Petersburg, General Trepov, complained that the appearance of the young women students clearly showed that they belonged to the "St. Petersburg Society of Nihilists" (no such society existed), and that in the intervals between lectures young men and women strolled in the corridors in semidarkness. [17]

But not all feminist plans failed, and there were some notable successes. In 1869 the Alarchinsky Courses [18] opened in St. Petersburg, and somewhat later the Lyubansky Courses opened in Moscow. [19] These courses, designed to prepare women for academic studies, attracted many gifted young women, some of whom later entered the revolutionary movement. Then, in 1878, the famous Bestuzhev Higher Courses for Women [20] were founded, which provided from 1881–82 onwards a four-year course of studies of almost university standard. Russian woman failed in her ambition to become a *studentka*, but *kursistka* was almost as good. Finally, in 1887, a Women's Medical School was constituted.

But to obtain full university degrees, women still had to go abroad. It needed determination to do so, since most Russian parents were appalled at the idea of their gently bred and sheltered daughters going to live alone among foreign students, reputed to be rowdy and licentious. But the enthusiasm of the young women overcame all objections, and they were encouraged by the sympathy of their male contemporaries. The revolutionary Chudnovsky, who was exiled to the southern town of Kherson in 1869, witnessed the departure of two young women for Switzerland, an event that assumed heroic proportions:

They were pioneers in 1870 and had to fight a long and dogged battle against their parents. . . . When the steamer was about to leave for Odessa, the entire embankment was crowded with young people . . . ; when the two young women appeared, they were received with respectful bows on all sides—from those who knew them and those who did not; and at the actual moment of departure, all young men present took off their hats and stood uncovered in solemn silence, until the steamer disappeared from view.[21]

The University of Zurich was the first to admit women students, at first to lectures only and later to regular degree studies, and most Russian women went there. Smaller numbers went to other Swiss and also to French and German universities. But they still faced great difficulties when they returned to Russia; with a few exceptions either their degrees were not recognized or they were forbidden to practise in medicine or law.

Yet many women in that first generation achieved great academic success. Sofya Kovalevskaya [22] became the first woman ever to hold an academic chair, when she became professor of pure mathematics at Stockholm in 1883. Her friend Anna Evreinova obtained a doctorate of law at Leipzig; the young woman scientist Volkova was elected a member of the St. Petersburg Society of Chemistry—presumably the first woman to be thus honoured. These pioneers were followed by many more, whose academic achievements in a number of fields are beyond dispute. Feminism did this for women—it opened the way into higher education and into the professions. And it is not to disparage the feminists to say that they succeeded mainly because they had the moral support and active help of many outstanding men of their day.

All the factors that had helped Russian women to emancipate themselves—feminism, the support of male intelligentsia, and improved education—also helped them in their first attempts to enter public life. Almost the first chance to do so was offered them by the civic movement (*obshchestvennoe dvizhenie*) which flourished in the 1850s and early 1860s. It was not so much a movement as a surge of enthusiasm among the liberals for organizing hospitals, schools, libraries, and so forth for the poor of town and country. Vladimir Stasov, the brother and biographer of the feminist Nadezhda Stasova, described the atmosphere: "there was such thirst for activity . . . Russians . . . were all as if infatuated. . . . Blood was boiling and hammering against the temples, and eyes were all aglow. . . . Nobody could bear to stay at home, all were for ever flitting about . . . just as if they were all in a fever of love.'' [23]

In 1858, the idea of opening free schools for poor children or adults, to be run entirely by volunteers, ran like wildfire through Russia. Socialites, landowners, merchants, priests, army officers, university professors and students, ordinary men and women flocked to help, with money or with offers to teach at these schools—at evening or morning classes, on weekdays or on Sundays. Sunday being the generally preferred day, since most of the pupils had to work for their living during the week, Sunday school [24] became the name for all schools of that type, though it had nothing in common with its English equivalent, being entirely secular. The voluntary helpers and teachers brought a tremendous zest to their work. The teaching was humane and enlightened, and

A Sunday Reading (after the painting by Bogdanov Belsky)

the pupils were treated kindly and politely, to raise their self-esteem.

At first the government and the imperial family were sympathetic.[25] The emperor instructed all government departments to lend accommodation where required, and informed provincial governors that Sunday schools were deserving of support and patronage. The empress, perhaps somewhat anxious to strengthen the religious side of teaching, had 125 booklets distributed in the Sunday schools of the St. Petersburg district, with titles like "Examples of Spiritual Piety," "Moral Tales," "On Faith and Christian Life," "Parables." But soon the head of the Third Section reported to the emperor that an anti-Church and anti-State spirit was abroad in these schools, and recommended their suppression. The charge was partly justified, since there were many radicals among the teachers, but the movement as a whole was largely liberal. The emperor tried an interim measure by installing a priest as a supervisor in each school, but eventually—in 1862—he ordered them to be closed, causing much bitterness and frustration among those who had worked in them.

Two years later, after the so-called *zemstvo* reform of 1864, which gave elected councils limited powers in local affairs, public enthusiasm was once again rekindled, and all over Russia liberal landowners, doctors, and others—again involving many women— threw themselves into various civic activities, only to be repeatedly rebuffed by the government. The systematic suppression of the civic spirit antagonized the liberal gentry and contributed in a great measure to its becoming more radical. To women the civic movement had given the first opportunity to work together and on equal terms with men. They had shared their enthusiasm for the work and their disappointment when the work had to be abandoned; inevitably many of them became also more radical.

4 EARLY RADICAL GROUPS

For several years after 1866, intellectual life lay dormant. The more cautious sector of the educated class avoided political activities and discussions and pursued the safer pleasures of Italian opera and the fashionable restaurants. Those of a more active and speculative cast of mind reserved their opinions for the family circle and the company of a few intimate friends. In many ways the atmosphere resembled that of the 1830s, which Alexander Herzen had described as the decade of silence.

The students found themselves doubly isolated: the police had thrown such a cordon of suspicion around the universities that peo- **57** ple were afraid to associate with them. That had an intimidating effect on many students, who shied away from "dangerous" pursuits. Others were keener than ever to find out about forbidden topics. With all the radical writers in foreign or Siberian exile, they were left without intellectual leadership, but they soon found certain advantages in their enforced isolation. Routine university life offered opportunities to exchange ideas which no police could detect and which did not exist elsewhere. This gave the students a heightened sense of community and solidarity and encouraged them to get as much out of those precious years as possible. There was a new wave of "self-educatory" fervour and much as yet unsystematic reading and discussing, not only among university students but now also among pupils of technical, medical, military, naval, and theological schools and academies, and, for the first time, among women students of various courses and schools.

From small groups in shared lodgings and in the *zemlyachestva* (groups of students from the same province or town or of the same ethnic origin), the discussions spread in the late 1860s to larger gatherings. As the authorities did not allow meetings in official buildings, students met in private houses and even set up special committees to hire halls and other possible premises. The attendance at these gatherings, or *skhodkas*,[1] grew steadily, students of various faculties and institutes mixing to mutual advantage and often forming lasting friendships. When the popular director of the Forestry Institute near St. Petersburg, Professor Engelhard, gave permission to hold students' evenings there (he was later dismissed and exiled for ten years), hundreds came, in spite of the considerable distance from town and the ever present risk of harassment from the police.

There was renewed interest in foreign developments. Great things were happening in the world: the European working class was stirring, and Karl Marx had founded his International. Information was difficult to obtain, since the police were especially watchful over news from abroad, but enough filtered through with the help of Russian expatriates. A handful of these, scattered throughout Europe, in London, Paris, Geneva, and Zurich, were continuing the work of the "laboratory of theory," as the saying went, which had been silenced in Russia. Russians abroad were gluttons for new European social and political theories, and for socialist and communist ideas, "utopian" and "scientific." They easily succumbed to the heady cult of the "inevitable revolution" which had found so many followers in western Europe since the French Revolution. Russians hungrily picked up all these ideas, even though under Russian conditions they hardly applied.

Still, socialism and communism—untried and unproven as they then still were—seemed infinitely more attractive than the bourgeois order that Russians abroad had ample opportunity to observe. They were repelled by its injustices and its vulgarity; they rejected the despotism of money and industry as they had rejected the despotism of privilege and autocracy. In Russia herself, the early stages of the industrial revolution and the emergence of a native bourgeoisie were equally, or even more, unattractive. There was child labour and misery in the factories, and an orgy of easy profits by speculators in league with officials. It was a situation from which all decent feeling revolted. If such were the fruits of capitalism, Russia would be much happier without them. Hopefully Russian radicals looked for an alternative for their country. Even though most of them reluctantly conceded that Marx's bourgeois phase of history could not be altogether avoided, they persuaded themselves that in Russia its ill effects could be considerably reduced and its duration shortened. Russia, they argued, possessed two saving characteristics: she came late on the scene, when the operation of capitalism was better understood, and she already possessed—or so they thought—a form of primitive communism in her traditional peasant commune, the *obshchina*, which could, with encouragement from the radical intelligentsia, take over from the capitalist order. Perhaps Russia could attain socialism sooner than other countries precisely because she was backward. "We are a backward people," wrote Mikhail Mikhaylov in 1861, "in this lies our salvation." [2]

All these speculations were reflected in the writings of Russian expatriates and exercised a kind of remote control over Russian minds at home. The writings were smuggled into the country by travellers at great personal risk. The precious contraband, together with foreign books and journals, was passed from hand to hand, often copied and recopied, and carried to the remotest corners of the country. Of course, not everything was available everywhere and what arrived did not represent a balanced selection, yet the very fact that it was "illegal" and came from abroad—at such high risk too—glamorized it out of all proportion. Everything was read hungrily and swallowed only too uncritically. Political opinions were espoused passionately, even fanatically. If John Stuart Mill had occasion to rebuke the French for "being led away by phrases, and treating abstractions as if they were realities," [3] he would have found this to apply even more to the Russians. The revolutionary Sergey Kravchinsky said it was "typical of the Russian national character to react with passion and near fanaticism where a European would react with simple approval or disapproval." [4] This tendency confused rather than clarified ideas, already rendered hazy by such current clichés as "eternal truth," "cosmic purpose," "the spirit of history," and "inevitable progress."

Just then, however, the young students were not so much in search of social and political theories as of a new faith and a new way of life. Nihilism, having done a useful job of clearance, had become a barren creed. "The generation of 'rational realists,' " wrote the contemporary novelist Vladimir Korolenko, "had reached the end of the road. . . . The whole life had been examined and the whole life had been rejected." [5] But rejection alone and hatred of life had, as the poet Nekrasov put it:

> . . . failed to feed the heart,
> brought much truth but little joy . . . [6]

Young Russians longed for a reconciliation with life and the people. The extreme narcissism of early nihilism gave way to a self-sacrificial urge to serve others, that is, the poor and the oppressed. "At our gatherings," wrote Korolenko, "we talked simply . . . about . . . how to live honestly and usefully." [7]

Almost ten years earlier, at the end of 1861, that is, after the shock of the peasant reform and the closing of the St. Petersburg University, Alexander Herzen had written to the students: "Shall I tell you where you should go now? . . . to the people, to the people . . . your place is there. . . ." [8] And in the same year Mikhail Mikhaylov had urged the radicals to become the "people's party." [9] These were the seeds that were germinating now. This was the beginning of a new faith, the faith in the Russia of the people—a Russia far older yet far more vital than that of the moribund Romanovs. It was a return to the native soil in which one could strike fresh roots and from which one could draw new strength; a return, too, to what was imagined as a society wise with the wisdom of ages and innocent of the corruption of the modern world. The attraction of this to uprooted, classless intelligentsia is obvious. Here were echoes of Rousseau and the German *Sturm und Drang*.

Inevitably, the romantic myth woven around the "people" faded somewhat on nearer acquaintance. It came as a shock to many of the young idealists to find that they knew very little about the life and habits and thoughts of the people—"the people" had become to them a pale abstraction "without nationality . . . vaguely resembling German workers of 1848. . . ." [10] wrote Korolenko. In fact they knew more about the German workers, from books. The first step, therefore, was to get to know the real people, the Russian poor. A widespread mania [11] developed for collecting statistical data on various aspects of the life of the people, in town and in the villages. It was usually done in the summer vacation when students habitually dispersed to their homes in the provinces.

There was little harm in all this; the discussions and the studies of town and village life provided a useful valve for youthful idealism. This was the opinion of the Minister of justice, Count Pahlen, who reported that the activities of the various student groups of that time were "essentially harmless" and did not "overstep the boundaries of purely theoretical discussion and youthful idealism," and did not go beyond "the usual youthful enthusiasm for universal 'brotherhood, equality, and freedom.' " [12] Given greater opportunities for the free exchange of ideas, these young people might not have become radical, or would have passed through and out of the radical phase. To quote once again Korolenko, a most perceptive and objective observer: "The young are liable to feel a special, almost innate revulsion against the beaten track. . . . Whole generations go through a fever of revolt against real life which threatens to engulf them, to de-individualize them." [13] But under Russian conditions, police harassment and persecution stampeded the aimlessly discontented young into real and lasting radicalism.* The secret police raided the students' gatherings and made many arrests. In the streets, male and female students were liable to be picked up for "looking like nihilists." By order of the governor of the province of Nizhny-Novgorod, young women wearing "nihilist" clothes, short hair, and glasses were to be taken to police stations, ordered to shed their clothes and put on crinolines (the fashion for crinolines was almost over, but the news had obviously not yet reached Nizhny-Novgorod); if they refused, they were to be exiled from the province. [14] Arrests, solitary confinement, and the threat of exile and trial were ordeals, which, while they discouraged a few, fortified many in their convictions. We have many testimonies of latter-day revolutionaries that it was, in fact, their experience of arrest and prison that first turned them into radicals.

Meanwhile the ever-present danger of police raids taught the students their first lessons in conspiracy. Large gatherings were abandoned for smaller ones and the smaller groups learned to keep their activities and their places of meeting secret. From innocent and "essentially harmless" self-education and collection of money for impecunious comrades, young men turned to conscious criticism of the social and political order and to propagating their ideas among the educated as well as among the people. The infant revolutionary movement was entering on its next stage—that of enforced

---

* There is no doubt at all that radicalism was spreading throughout Europe and would have arrived in Russia in any case; but there is also little doubt that under specifically Russian conditions it acquired its most idealistic as well as most extreme characteristics.

secrecy. Far from damping the spirits of the young, the atmosphere of danger and secrecy seemed to stimulate them. "Had the government been more intelligent and . . . less jittery," reflected Korolenko, "who knows whether the youth movement would have grown so rapidly and so violently?" [15] Certainly the government had only itself to blame for the spread of revolutionary ideas through the provinces; there was hardly a provincial town to which "politically unreliable" Russians (as well as Poles, after the risings of 1830 and 1861) were not exiled. And of course, schoolboys and other youngsters sat at the feet of these early martyrs and made a very receptive audience.

The "youth movement" to which Korolenko referred was not exactly a movement yet, but rather a large reservoir of unused young energy. This energy asked for nothing better than to be channelled into some useful, practical work. There was, therefore, a very active response to the enterprise of a small St. Petersburg group, which started by collecting small libraries for local students and went on to distribute books all over the country. This "book work," as it came to be called, enlarged the boundaries of self-education and brought the students of St. Petersburg in contact with those of other university towns. The original St. Petersburg book group,[16] which before long acquired the name of the "initiative group," consisted of only six students. They were of obviously exceptional intelligence and organizational ability, and they rapidly created a far-flung network of supporting groups in the provinces. They even found it necessary to convene a secret conference, in January 1871, in order to coordinate the work of their numerous helpers.[17] In the course of this conference it emerged that while "book work" was still immensely popular with young people in general, the members of the "initiative group" and some few others had outgrown it. They had become more politically oriented and had succumbed to belief in the inevitability of a popular revolution, which was one of the beliefs imported from the West. Russian radicals accepted it before they had time to consider the applicability or, indeed, desirability of revolution and socialism in Russia. The "initiative group" was no exception. Its members were confirmed revolutionaries and socialists—though, we are told, "the decision *to be* a revolutionary was then the extent of revolutionary activity." [18] How and when this revolution was to come about and what would happen afterwards—on this opinions varied.

As a first step it seemed to them important to convert as many intellectuals as possible to their way of thinking; later to find allies among the working people—a term applied in Russia indiscriminately to peasants and workers. Eventually intellectuals and the working people would merge into one people's party. For the time being, however, the distribution of well-chosen literature still seemed the best way of spreading their ideas, using "book work" as "the innocent canvas on which one could embroider all kinds of patterns," [19] as one of their contemporaries put it. The group soon extended its activities to importing legal and illegal books from abroad and publishing certain books in Russia. The group was greatly helped at every stage by various progressive booksellers, such as Cherkassov, the brother-in-law of Maria Trubnikova, and publishers, such as Polyakov, who supplied the group with books at exceedingly low prices and on credit. The selection of books was predictable: political economy, socialist and anarchist theory, natural sciences, and the history of European revolutions. The censorship, in its usual slap-dash way, had allowed the publication between 1872 and 1874 of several highly tendentious books that were to exert a very great influence over the young: Pyotr Lavrov's *Historical Letters*; Bervi-Flerovsky's *State of the Working Class in Russia,* his *ABC of Social Sciences*, and several others.

By the time the government became aware of the mass distribution of these books, it was too late: the police, raiding the homes of students and book stores, found very few copies. The book distributors had learnt to hoodwink the authorities. Thus when the *ABC of Social Sciences* was banned after publicaton, a whole detachment of gendarmes and police sent to confiscate the book found between 140 and 160 copies of the 2,500 printed. And even these, we are told, had been placed there expressly for the police to find—"out of politeness"! [20] A veritable witch hunt was started at once; Cherkassov's bookshop was closed and all booksellers and publishers were warned not to have anything to do with "nihilists"; armies of spies were set to sniff out dangerous books, and wherever such were found, they were publicly burned in city squares.[21] The police surpassed itself in absurdity, banning, for instance, volumes 2 and 3 of Victor Hugo's *Les Miserables*. The persecution and burning of books caused much hilarity among the students but hardly deterred them from continuing and even intensifying their activities.

It was at this stage that women entered the scene. Considerable numbers of them were already studying at the various courses open to them and were beginning to take part in university life. This was by no means easy; conservative and conventional students and professors abominated and ridiculed the "learned women," the "bluestockings," and the *"esprits forts"* (the Russian version of which was *espriforka*).[22] But the progressive students, liberal or radical, received them with great enthusiasm and on terms of absolute equality. Women students soon entered into all the interests and activities of these circles, with the inevitable result that they began to figure among those arrested, tried, and sentenced, and among those exiled without trial. They participated in student protests in 1861 and again in 1869; and a young woman, Maria Mikhaelis (sister of Ludmilla Shelgunova), was arrested for throwing a bouquet of flowers at Chernyshevsky as he stood chained to his post of shame at his civic execution.

In the spring of 1871 a "book group" of women students (Sofya Perovskaya, sisters Alexandra, Lyubov, and Vera Kornilovy, Olga Shleysner, Alexandra Obodovskaya, and several others) was formed at the Alarchinsky Courses in St. Petersburg.[23] It was a crucial date and a crucial event. Having entered the youth movement at that early stage, women became full partners in the revolutionary movement that grew out of it. In this lies the specifically Russian contribution to the emancipation of women. While in all other spheres of life—in the professions, the arts, the sciences, and in the society generally—their achievements were comparable to those of women in other countries, in this one respect Russian women found an exceptionally wide field of activity, and in it they scored exceptional triumphs.

It was a measure of their success that the women's "book group" soon merged with the central "initiative group." The merger came at a critical time for Russian radicals. The peasants were restive and dissatisfied, still waiting for the "true freedom," but a revolution did not seem likely to take place just yet. Some changes for the better might come from further reforms, as the liberals still hoped, and one was content to let liberals battle for these "small mercies." But what should radicals do? There were always some extremists, like Zaychnevsky or Karakozov, who favoured desperate measures and immediate, "instant" revolutionary action, or the so-called fire-raisers (*vspychkopuskateli*), who believed that it needed only a spark to start a popular revolution, but their number was small. Only the persuasive Sergey Nechaev succeeded in attracting a considerable number of followers with his own brand of Jacobinism. He founded the Narodnaya Rasprava (Popular Vengeance) group in 1869 and tried to bind its members to him by involving them in the murder of one of their number. He then fled abroad, where he won the support of Bakunin for his wholly fictitious secret revolutionary organization. But his deviousness and deception were exposed, and his unsavoury political manoeuvres and dictatorial methods completely discredited him in revolutionary circles. His followers were tried in 1871 and found much sympathy among young radicals, particularly since many of the eighty-seven accused had been drawn into the case on the flimsiest of pretexts. Nechaev himself was captured and tried a year later and sentenced to twenty years' solitary imprisonment in the Peter and Paul Fortress in St. Petersburg, where he died in 1882. Though Dostoevsky took Nechaev for the model of a revolutionary leader in his novel *The Possessed*, he was in fact quite untypical of the mainstream of radical thought in the early 1870s. Most young radicals rejected "fire-raising" and *nechaevstchina* in favour of peaceful propaganda.

The scope and content of this propaganda was also occupying the thoughts of the "initiative group" in the spring of 1871. There were many problems that needed thinking out and it was decided to do this during the long vacation; instead of the usual dispersal to parental homes, the group would find a place where they could all stay together. So a house was found, on a street called Kushe-levka,[24] on the outskirts of St. Petersburg, and some seventeen young men and women moved into it. It was to be a commune, an institution much in vogue among the young people of the time and an obvious extension of nihilist experiments in human relations. There had been several communes already, some of male students and some mixed. Communes had a strong appeal for the young as (in their own words) "schools of practical socialism"—though domestic socialism would be nearer the mark, since they certainly provided excellent training in shared home duties and work. Life in these student communes was dominated above all by the desire to live as simply as the Russian poor. As rural Russia was chronically suffering from famine, the diet of the communes was of the scan-tiest—there was only one main meal, at midday, consisting of horse meat usually but sometimes of dog or cat, and tea with black bread morning and evening. This is how one of the earliest communes, the Vulfovka,[25] is described to us (three of the original members of the "initiative group" had lived there):

In one of the rooms stood the samovar and all who wanted, could help themselves to tea; the commune occupied the whole house—four rooms upstairs and four downstairs; . . . [in it] lived fifteen to twenty people, two to a room. There was a communal dining room, where guests were allowed to stay for the night. All gave their money to whomever was chosen to keep house, and he issued every-body with cash as it was needed. The only meat consumed was horse meat; a live horse was usually bought, slaughtered by some veterinary student in the slaughter yard of the university and the meat was piled up in the store shed, from which other communes too could collect . . . ; only the cheapest tea and tobacco were bought; and of these and of lunch all members of the commune could partake, as well as guests, and some impecunious students who had been specially invited. . . . The samovar was huge. Only two of the members were married. Women lived upstairs, men downstairs. . . . Sometimes there were meetings to which upwards

of fifty came; on Wednesdays there were lectures . . . given by
each in turn.

The Kushelevka commune was organized on similar lines and
there was much to scandalize the neighbourhood, the worst perhaps
being the sight of young women wearing men's clothes and taking
part in vigorous gymnastic exercises, which were performed daily
by the entire commune. Incidentally, the communal house stood in
the midst of public gardens and was the object of the liveliest curiosity of all and sundry. Was it, one wonders, deliberate policy, inexperience, or just youthful bravura that made the group take this
particular house?

The program of work that the group drew up for itself included
study and discussion of the two main trends of socialist thought that
were currently influential in Russia: those of Pyotr Lavrov and of
Mikhail Bakunin. The Kushelevka group, later to become known as
the Chaykovists, on the whole sided with Lavrov, though they
remained somewhat eclectic. Lavrov, whom we have previously
met as one of the champions of the emancipation of women, had
been a professor at the Artillery Academy in St. Petersburg and a
full colonel, when, rather late in life, he became involved in radical
circles. After the Karakozov affair of 1866, Lavrov was arrested
and exiled to the provinces. It is there that he wrote his *Historical
Letters*,[26] which were an instant success with the young, and from
then on he was their venerated and beloved mentor. He was helped
to escape abroad, where he settled for the rest of his life. In 1873,
in close cooperation with the Chaykovists, Lavrov began to edit the
periodical *Vpered!* (Forward!); it became a fortnightly newspaper
after 1875. Thanks to this cooperation, and also to the presence of
an ever-increasing number of young Russians studying abroad or
fleeing abroad from the police, *Vpered!* had a strong organic link
with personalities and events at home. Lavrov's ideas evoked a
tremendous response in Russia because they coincided most closely
with the post-nihilist mood of the young and fed their new-found
sense of duty towards the people. He started, in fact, where Chernyshevsky and Pisarev had left off: *his* critically thinking individ-

uals evolved directly out of *their* rational or thinking individuals, but he found them a definite place in history.

Lavrov's argument can be summarized as follows: each individual should strive to perfect himself or herself physically, intellectually, and morally to be worthy of joining the critically thinking minority (= intelligentsia), which is *the prime mover of historical progress*. Without this enlightened and idealistic minority, society would stagnate and civilization perish. The minority has an absolute duty to promote the cause of truth and justice and to help the oppressed people, to whom it owes a debt of gratitude for its privileges of class and education. But though the minority can act as a leaven, the real changes in society can be made by the people alone. And Lavrov added a characteristic warning: the Russian people must be won over to the high ideal of justice (= socialism), but this ideal must not be imposed—the reconstruction of Russian society must be achieved not *for* the people, but *by* the people. A long period of patient persuasion and reasoning should nurse a conscious, a thinking nucleus from among the more wide-awake peasants and workers, which would provide the hard core of a strong organization, able to attract and recruit the less conscious or merely sympathetic elements in town and village. Only then can the people proceed to carry out the social revolution that will change the structure of Russian society. The task of the intellectual is thus restricted to one of teacher, adviser, helper. To be better equipped for this task, the intellectual must prepare himself or herself by study and then enter the life of the people, live and work among them. And one must be prepared for a long and patient period of peaceful propaganda.

Bakunin,[27] on the other hand, had no use for patience. He believed that the people already had in themselves a genuinely revolutionary force ready to erupt at the slightest push. This force had, furthermore, always existed—witness the natural rebels who from time immemorial had fled to the Russian forests to join the bands of robbers. These natural rebels, brought into contact with each other by the intellectuals, will rise and utterly destroy the traditional forms of life in Russia; and since the passion to destroy is a creative passion, they will create, out of the ashes as it were, a new Russia based on free associations and other equally vague societal forms. Above all there will never again be a State with its deadly machine, its master class, its enslavement of the individual. In this cataclysmic historic drama, the revolutionary élite was to be a kind of invisible General Staff, while the rank and file had simply to seek out the natural rebels, bring them together and urge them to action.* For this no particular knowledge or preparation was needed, and the rank and file was urged to leave university and school and "go to the people" without delay. One can understand how this irresponsible program appealed to some of the young. But there were good practical reasons why it tempted even more mature revolutionaries. The dilemma was a real one: under Russian conditions any propaganda was sure to attract the suspicion of the officials and the police and be stopped. So it was tempting to follow a program that promised quick results. Even the arch-gradualist Lavrov could on occasion adopt an extremist stance: in the words of Turgenev, who loved and esteemed him, he was then like "a dove trying hard to pass for a hawk." [28]

Both Lavrov and Bakunin, as well as Marx, Lassalle, and other socialist theorists, were discussed at the Kushelevka seminar in an attempt to find the right revolutionary policy for Russia. It was this that linked this group to the earlier radicals and re-established the continuity in the development of Russian radicalism that had been snapped after 1866. But study and discussion of theory were subordinated to practical considerations. The group was concerned with becoming an efficient operational unit and to this end it was considered of the first importance to achieve complete harmony of moral, social, and philosophical views. Moreover, by way of improving mutual understanding, the character and behaviour of each individual group member were openly discussed and criticized at their

---

* Bakunin was at all times attracted to conspiracy as such—even after he burnt his fingers so badly with Nechaev, who had deceived him about *his* conspiratorial activities, Bakunin tried to organize from abroad an anarchist party inside Russia so conspiratorial that members of its leadership were not to know each other. (Starik [pseudonym of Kovalik, S.] p. 18.)

meetings. Though this bears some resemblance to nihilist soul-searching, it was supposed to serve the strictly utilitarian purpose of forging a strong and efficient unit for joint future work. These people had to be ready to face police persecution, arrest, solitary confinement. It was therefore necessary that they should know, respect, and trust each other completely and unreservedly, and observe absolute loyalty among themselves. There was no room for power-seeking "generals" of the type of Nechaev, none for moral weaklings. Said Chaykovsky, their nominal leader: "We must be as clear as a crystal." [29] Only men and women of proven integrity and maturity were acceptable. The group thus elaborated a code of revolutionary ethics that was to remain the ideal of most radical groups and organizations of the future.

One of the moral issues that presented itself even before the setting up of the commune was ruled out of court first by the women and later by all—a suggestion that free love was part of socialism.[30] This view was entirely contrary to the somewhat ascetic and scrupulous friendship that united the male and female members of the commune. The suggestion discredited the man who made it, and he was later declared morally untrustworthy. On the other hand closer personal relationships between the sexes were not ruled out, and marriages as well as more or less permanent bonds outside marriage were accepted; what was not tolerated was promiscuity.

THE CHAYKOVISTS

The group that emerged from the Kushelevka semi-nar at the end of the long vacation of 1871 was not the only radical group that sprang up at that time, but none of the others proved so long-lived or influential. The Kushelevka commune had succeeded in forming a nucleus of firm friends, consisting of six men and six women. Several other members of the commune, on the other hand, could not fulfill the rigorous moral demands made on them and drifted away. The hard core that remained soon became known as the Chaykovists, though the name was often retrospectively ap-plied to the earlier "book" and "initiative" groups out of which it **73** had grown. The group gradually expanded to include some carefully chosen newcomers, but at no time was it more than thirty or forty strong at its headquarters in St. Petersburg. Together with provincial branches, it probably could count about a hundred members.

Mark Natanson,[1] a medical student, was generally regarded as the founder of the group and remained its strong backbone. A born organizer, he had a quick grasp of both intellectual and practical matters, and brought immense passion and energy to all his work. He was a warm-hearted man and a loyal friend, and one of the bitterest opponents of Nechaev's leadership methods. Nikolay Chaykovsky,[2] who lent his name to the group, was neither its founder nor was he to remain a member to the end. But he emerged, during the Kushelevka summer, as a strong and dependable character, and Natanson had no hesitation in leaving the group in his hands when he himself was arrested and sent into exile. Chaykovsky, the son of a provincial civil servant, had a clear and systematic mind, but eventually he became a mystic and left the movement altogether. Another early member of the group, Serdyukov,[3] had been brought up in an orphanage notorious for the inhuman corporal punishment dealt out to the pupils. He was among the first to go into the countryside to work as a village school teacher, and so was another Chaykovist, Sergey Sinegub.[4] One of the most colourful, and also most popular, newcomers to the group was Dmitry Klements,[5] a poet and writer and a brilliant raconteur in a pithy folk style. Though he was witty and very good company, he was also a great individualist and politically a loner, who never accepted a ruling from group or party if it conflicted with his own views.

Two of those who joined the group in early 1872 were to become world famous: Prince Pyotr Kropotkin, the future anarchist, and Sergey Kravchinsky (nom de plume Stepnyak). Both were men of exceptional calibre. Kropotkin[6] was an intrepid traveller and Fellow of the Russian Geographical Society. He had been educated from the age of fifteen in the Page Corps, a very select military establishment for the training of court pages. In due course he was appointed page to the emperor and got to know him, his family, and his entourage intimately. Sergey Kravchinsky,[7] a former officer, was a man of great courage and quick decision, also a very observant and intelligent writer on contemporary themes. Later, outside Russia, he became well known for his collection of Russian revolutionary profiles, which were published in English as *Russian Underground*. A fellow officer and friend of Kravchinsky, Leonid Shishko,[8] also joined the group and was described by Kropotkin as "the most perfect incarnation of the group's moral ideal" [9] and by Sofya Perovskaya as being "not just pure but chemically pure." [10]

Among the women, Sofya Perovskaya [11] was by far the most remarkable character. She was a slight, graceful girl with a pretty, childlike face, a sunny smile, and a ready, infectious laugh, and there was nothing in her appearance—except the steady, serious look in her blue eyes—to betray her exceptional personality. In spite of her extreme youth—she was only seventeen in 1871—she immediately impressed everybody at the Kushelevka with her uncommon strength of will and great energy. Her friend Alexandra Kornilova was to say of her later: "She is small like a piece of gold, but as precious." [12] And this is how Kravchinsky described her: "A clear and analytical mind . . . incomparable in both theoretical and practical discussion . . . always seeing all sides of the problem . . . an extraordinarily sober intellect . . . demolishing with deadly logic the illusions of her more enthusiastic comrades . . . as critical of herself as of others . . . untiring energy . . . an indomitable will and an implacable sense of duty." [13] Yet she could also be gay and carefree, and generous and loyal to her friends.

Sofya Perovskaya was the granddaughter of a minister of state and daughter of a governor-general of St. Petersburg, and she had been brought up to shine in "high society." Instead, like many other girls of her circle and her age, she longed for higher education and emancipation. At fifteen, she entered the Alarchinsky Courses, designed to prepare girls for university studies. There she met several other young girls who like herself had been influenced by the nihilist-socialist writings of Chernyshevsky, Dobrolyubov, and Pisarev; together they formed the women's "book group."

Sofya Perovskaya had been unhappy at home. Her father, an ill-tempered and tyrannical man, objected to her studies and to her friends and in the end turned her out of the house. She was not sorry to go—her only regret was the necessity to abandon her beloved mother, whom she could henceforth visit only by stealth. She found happiness among her fellow students at the courses and later in the Chaykovist group. And, indeed, the group was more of a family than a political organization. Pavel Axelrod, in his youth a member of a revolutionary group in Kiev, said of the Chaykovists: "It is difficult to convey . . . the brotherly closeness, the warmth and simplicity. . . . It was such as is sometimes found in a good and harmonious family." [14]

Most of the women who joined revolutionary groups at that time came from the nobility. A few came from the merchant class. Somewhat later they were joined by daughters of clergymen and of professional families—in short, female *raznochintsi*.

The Kornilovy sisters [15] were daughters of a wealthy porcelain manufacturer of peasant origin, and they gave considerable amounts of money to the revolutionary cause. In particular they started the political Red Cross [16]—an organization that supported political prisoners and exiles both materially and spiritually, and that continued to provide inestimable service right up to Stalin's time.

All the women belonging to the Chaykovsky group were, like the men, remarkable and often outstanding personalities: Olga Shleysner, who became Mark Natanson's wife, proved to have great gifts as a leader; [17] and Anna Kuvshinskaya [18] and Larissa Chemodanova [19] excelled as teachers.

The Chaykovists dispensed with written statutes or rules, though there were some unwritten ones. These were that: all members were equal; all were bound to secrecy, even after leaving the group; all property was shared; new members could only be co-opted by general agreement; and all major decisions had to be unanimous and all minor ones taken by majority vote. There was complete agreement that no honest human being should aquiesce in an unjust and immoral social order but should renounce all privileges of birth, wealth, and education, and "go to the people" to bring it a message of justice, equality, and freedom.[20] But there was considerable tolerance towards divergent political views. "What united us," says Leonid Shishko, "was the intensity of subjective feeling, not one or another revolutionary doctrine" [21]—and this was true of the Chaykovists as it was, to some extent, true of the whole young radical intelligentsia of the day.

Money had throughout been a big problem for the group, since the acquisition and publishing of books needed considerable funds, which the generosity of the richer members of the group could not always meet. The group was also deeply concerned with the fate of young people arrested and exiled into distant parts—it was to help them that the group founded the political Red Cross, which was run mainly by the women of the group. Occasional attempts to organize escapes were costly as well as dangerous, yet during 1872 two important exiles, Pyotr Tkachev and Nikolay Sokolov, were "sprung" and smuggled out of the country. Sometimes the group also helped young women to escape from parental restraint and arranged fictitious marriages for them.[22]

All these activities could not, of course, remain unnoticed by the police. It had watched with disquiet the queer goings-on in the Kushelevka, had raided it several times, taken the particulars of all the inmates, and posted special spies to follow them about. It had also repeatedly arrested Natanson and Chaykovsky but had to release them for lack of incriminating evidence—thanks to the group's policy of keeping as few written documents as possible. Nevertheless the police did find fragments of a draft program of future activities in the villages, which filled them with foreboding. And when a copy of the same program was also found at the Moscow Agricultural Academy, they jumped to the conclusion that a nation-wide secret society was being formed. Natanson was once again arrested and this time exiled to Siberia. Even closer watch was put on the rest of the group and, as already described, a hunt was started for "illegal" books. But searches, arrests, and burnings of books failed to disrupt the excellent organization and the net of supporting groups.

The Chaykovists were impatient, however, to carry the propaganda to the peasants. Several of them made tentative descents into the countryside: Sofya Perovskaya went as a smallpox inoculator; Sinegub and Chemodanova went as village teachers; several men and women worked on the estates of the radical landowner Yartsev. Others learned some skills in specially equipped workshops, preparatory to going to the villages as itinerary cobblers, carpenters, or blacksmiths. From 1859 onwards, but more systematically from 1871, a few individuals had experimentally worked among the peasants; and at the height of the "statistical madness" hundreds of students had invaded the countryside in search of data. But the gulf between the educated youth and the largely illiterate peasantry proved almost impossible to bridge. The peasants seemed to live in a different world, with its own logic and its own tradition.

The mass of the Russian people was deeply religious in a specifically Russian way, based on a community, "togetherness," of all believers with God, which embraced the whole of life—spiritual, social, and national. Tsardom was inseparable from this world-view, because the tsar was the defender of the Church and "God-anointed." When the intellectuals shook off religion, they placed themselves outside the spiritual community of the Russian people. They now found it extremely difficult to enter it again, particularly as they were approaching it with a mass of preconceptions borrowed from the West. The peasants were likely to distrust the *barye* (gentry) in any case. To earn their trust it was not enough to put on poor-folk clothes; one had to become wholly one with the peasants, the casual labourers, the tramps. It meant taking over their ways of thinking and their view of the world; it meant learning not only to speak, act, eat, and drink as they did, but also to swear, lie, and cheat; to swig vodka and to brawl—all things abhorrent to the idealistic intellectual. One also had to learn to sleep on hard boards in doss houses among sweating bodies, bedbugs and lice; and to do it to the manner born. Such were the conclusions of the early propagandists who had ventured among the people and had learnt bitter lessons from their experiences.

The overcoming of the practical difficulties presented a formidable task for the individual propagandist; but harder still was the next step—to carry out the actual propaganda. This required extreme tact and patience. Add to this the constant danger of detection and arrest and it is no wonder that some would-be propagandists quitted after the very first attempt. But the more stout-hearted—and the Chaykovists were certainly that—persevered with improved tactics. Obviously they had to prepare themselves more thoroughly: learn to mix more easily with the people; and train as craftsmen, village teachers, rural clerks, or medical orderlies, so as to have a legitimate reason to reside in a village. And, for a start, the tone of the propaganda might be modified—religion and the tsar could be left out, and at first only the officials, the landlords, and the rich generally attacked. If, as Kravchinsky found, " 'scientific' socialism bounced off the Russian masses like peas from a wall," [23] then one should talk instead of more immediate concerns, such as the unjust distribution of land, overtaxation, and the like. Or it might prove more effective to direct the propaganda at such discontented and persecuted elements as the Old Believers and various sectarians, or even at escaped convicts and brigands who were known to hide in deep forests and in the Ural mountains; or better still at the workers and artisans, who were more literate and more used to the ways of the towns and therefore more approachable. Among such people one might find sympathizers who would carry the word among the ignorant: being of the people themselves and having their roots in the peasantry, they would be listened to more readily.

The latter was the line taken by the Chaykovists, and in 1872 several of them went to live and work among the factory workers of St. Petersburg. By mid-winter of that year almost the entire group, men and women, was involved in teaching small groups of workers. In their tentative excursions into the countryside the Chaykovists had already encounted the twin difficulty of evading the vigilance of the police and of winning the confidence of the peasants. Towards the workers they had less need to act a part, because the workers were used to seeing students about and even had a certain sympathy with them as belonging to an intermediate class of human beings—educated and well-spoken and yet usually poor and even a little downtrodden like themselves. The difficulty here was to fool the police. Most factories in St. Petersburg were situated on the outskirts of the town or near the docks—behind *zastavas,* or toll-gates, where documents were checked and taxes collected. Beyond the *zastavas*, unpaved streets, unspeakably muddy in winter and dusty in summer, were lined with small wooden houses in bad repair, just as in any Russian provincial town. It was impossible to imagine that this was as much part of the imperial capital as the parquet-paved, clean-swept, elegant Nevsky Prospect. The workers lived in extreme squalor in the ramshackle houses or in barracks (some for married men and their families and others for unmarried men and unmarried women) constructed by the richer factory owners inside factory gates. These barracks afforded little privacy and the workers had to be in before the gates were shut at night.

Apart from possessing the appropriate papers the propagandist who wanted to make contact with the workers had to look and to behave exactly like one, if he was to get past the police patrols posted at the *zastavas*, at the factory gates, and at most street corners. Some of the propagandists brought great zest to the task and became veritable masters of disguise. Women, too, learned to dress and look like laundresses, seamstresses, or factory hands—Sofya Perovskaya was particularly good at impersonating a dim-witted type of servant or peasant girl. She rented a small house near the Nevsky *zastava*, where she lived, according to her passport, as the "wife" of a worker. In her house workers met to read and talk with the visiting propagandists. Several such homes were set up by married couples, genuine or fictitious; thus Serdyukov and his wife Lyubov Kornilova, Sergey Sinegub and his wife Larissa Chemodanova, and Charushin and his wife Anna Kuvshinskaya set up houses behind various *zastavas*, where they collected considerable numbers of pupils. Other Chaykovists went now here now there between these homes, lecturing and conducting discussions. It was usual for them to change into workers' clothes before entering factory districts. Thus Kropotkin often came directly from his spell of duty at the Winter Palace and had to leave his splendid court uniform at a flat in central St. Petersburg before making his way, more drably attired, to Sofya Perovskaya's modest little house.

These teaching activities suited the Chaykovists particularly well. At heart they were what the Russians call *prosvetitili*—enlighteners, teachers; socialist propaganda entered into their teaching only indirectly. The obvious integrity and moral purity of the teachers exercised as great an influence on the pupils as the knowledge they received. Some thirty or forty workers came to be taught by Sinegub and Chemodanova—a tribute to their teaching and their warm personalities. And the Charushins were equally popular. Leonid Shishko, himself much loved by the workers, has left a vivid description of Anna Kuvshinskaya: "A pale young woman with a strikingly intelligent face . . . she brought to her evening classes her own brand of liveliness [and] established with each of her pupils a direct and natural relationship." [24] In spite of her extreme youth Sofya Perovskaya earned great respect and affection from her pupils, some of whom later formed the nucleus of the so-called workers' intelligentsia.

Around 1870 there were approximately 800,000 workers in the whole of Russia, but only about half of them were second- or third-generation, so to speak hereditary, workers, permanently settled in industrial centres and occupied in old established industries. The rest consisted of a fluid and uncertain mass of casual or seasonal labour: peasants who worked in town during winter and on the land in summer. Often they were peasants whom their allotted plots could not feed and who had to rely on additional earnings; these were joined by large numbers of people who had been "yard and house" serfs, who had not been allotted any land at all under the terms of the peasant reform and who now flooded the towns in search of work. Not all of them could be used in industry and the residue formed an unhappy *Lumpenproletariat*. The peasants who habitually came to work in towns during winter usually arrived in groups of ten to twelve men from the same village or district and hired a suitable abode in town, where they lived and worked as craftsmen. These small house-industries were called *artel*, and there were *artels* of weavers, carpenters, dyers, and many others.

When the Chaykovists first began operating among workers, they found the casual workers much more accessible to propaganda—they were badly paid, insecure, and smarting under the injustices of the peasant reform. By contrast, the old-established workers, better paid and more secure in their jobs, were less dissatisfied. Many of them were already reasonably literate and eager to learn more. The Chaykovists were quick to perceive their different needs and to minister to them: for the seasonal workers they arranged reading and writing classes and elementary talks on the state of affairs in Russia and in the world; the others were taught more advanced subjects—geography, history, physics. Kropotkin lectured on the International, Klements on people's revolts in old Russia, Alexandra Kornilova on the German working class and so on. Apart from teaching, the Chaykovists built up a workers' library and started a workers' mutual aid fund.

The successes achieved by this handful of men and women—a round dozen of them ran workers' groups in six different districts of St. Petersburg—were very considerable. And similar activities were soon undertaken by their provincial followers in various other industrial towns. They were the first radical group to win a firm foothold among workers—in itself a milestone in the history of the revolutionary movement—and to educate sufficient number of workers to start a working-class movement in Russia. Many of their pupils indeed became leaders of that movement, while others entered the ranks of the revolutionary intelligentsia, whom they soon resembled in manners and appearance.

But to the Chaykovists, their success among the élite of the workers appeared of minor importance when compared with that achieved among the "new" proletarians. In these they saw an important link with the peasants, intermediaries between themselves and the village. Though Marx was much read and admired in Russia, his theories were thought to apply mainly in western Europe and nobody could possibly see the embryonic Russian working class as the bearer of the revolution. "The people" for Russian radicals was still the peasantry, and all future activity was envisaged as taking place in the countryside.

The Chaykovists were not the only radical group that was planning to "go to the people," and in the autumn and winter of 1873–74 all these groups were preparing for another campaign in the spring. By this time it had become clear to all that a coordination of action and a pooling of resources would benefit everyone. With the ever-watchful eye of the police upon them, the experimenters were groping not only for more effective but also for safer methods and techniques of propaganda. For practical considerations it seemed advisable to work out a common plan of action, even perhaps to merge into one revolutionary organization. The majority was not quite ready for it; in particular, many feared the emergence, in a large organization, of dictatorial leaders of the Nechaev type.

However, the very real danger of perishing in prison or in the Siberian mines before achieving anything at all—many Chaykovists and others were already behind bars—made speedy agreement desirable. A joint secret conference was held in St. Petersburg and it was decided that each existing group which intended to spread propaganda in the villages should henceforth be considered a cell of the future revolutionary organization; that the means of communication between the cells should be perfected and constant contact maintained by means of coded letters or personal visits; and that funds should be collected for the use of all. It was also decided that further experimental excursions should be made into the countryside in order to gather more experience, and that in the autumn of 1874 another secret conference should meet to hear the reports and to decide on the final shape of a joint revolutionary conspiratorial organization. But all these wise plans were to be overtaken by events.

6 "GOING TO THE PEOPLE"

In the spring of 1874 a kind of fever seized Russian youth. As soon as the snow had melted and the warmer days set in, countless young men and women suddenly took off like flocks of birds to scatter all over the countryside. Singly or in twos and threes, dressed to look like poor folk and sometimes even barefoot, they went from town to town and from village to village seeking work and trying to settle among the people. Many of them were between sixteen and twenty years old; those between twenty and twenty-five were called "the old ones" by the rest.

They found the countryside in an even more unhappy state than **85** usual—devastated by famines that had been foreseen but neither checked nor relieved by the government. In August 1873, Lev Tolstoy [1] had published a letter in a Moscow newspaper (*Moskovskiye Vedomosti*) warning that a famine was inevitable in the province of Samara, which had had poor harvests three years in succession. As it turned out the famine spread over one-third of Russia, Samara being merely the hardest hit. The peasants, pauperized by payments for their land and overburdened with taxes and dues, had no reserves of grain or food for themselves or for their cattle and could not buy any. Early in 1874 another alarm was sounded by Pyotr Lavrov,[2] who published abroad an article on the famine and appealed to young Russians to "go to the people" and help.

Had the government tried to prevent the famine or launched a campaign to help the starving peasants and invited the co-operation of young people, it would certainly have found an enthusiastic response. The idealism of the young would have been usefully employed in famine relief and in medical work in the villages. The students would have got to know the people and the people would have learned to trust them. The gap between the classes would have been narrowed and the country would have benefited. Involvement in a common task would also have improved relations between the government and the intellectuals. This, too, was a gap that needed bridging. But the government, in its distrust of the intellectuals, let the opportunity slip. The imperial court was in any case too busy to give the matter much thought—the tsar's daughter Maria was married to Alfred, Duke of Edinburgh, son of Queen Victoria, in January 1874. The "wedding was celebrated with the greatest magnificence. The bride was given a truly imperial dowry." [3]

The young men and women who were now streaming into the countryside knew that they were alone in a hostile world, but they were driven by an irrepressible impulse, half self-sacrificial dedication and half desperate courage. It was a crusade, an almost religious crusade, and the crusaders did not shrink from but rather welcomed martyrdom. They knew that they risked arrest, prison, and exile, with or without trial, and they accepted the risk. They felt themselves to be the apostles of a new religion that would bring equality and prosperity to all.

The young were inspired by an overwhelming love for the people—*narodolyubstvo*,[4] a term coined retrospectively by the revolutionary Andrey Zhelyabov. It reflects the depth of the feeling behind it. The Russian language makes a distinction between *mirovozrenie*, an intellectual view of the world, and *miroostchuschenie*, an intuitive feel of the world; and it was certainly the latter that applied here. The young *felt* strongly about inequality, injustice, and oppression and *felt* that their place was among the unjustly oppressed. They wanted to share the lowly life of the people and its misery as an atonement for what they called their privileges, including that of education. They *felt* that the privileged owed a moral debt to the people, and they were resolved to pay it.

The young idealists held a great variety of often conflicting opinions, but they shared an underlying moral conviction that could be called populism. In the broadest sense of the word populism had been endemic in the Russian educated class ever since French enlightenment had spread to Russia. Since then the concern for the people and particularly for the serfs had been the leaven of all social conscience and thought in Russia. But at that stage populism was a purely emotional and as yet unformulated doctrine. Such formidable concepts as "overthrow of the existing order," "socialism," "communism," and the like were used completely at random. The diarist Nikitenko saw in the movement of 1874

a strange awakening of the spirit of the people [against] the monstrous conditions that exist in our administration. . . . It is natural in a society that is alive and wants to go on living. This is not a revolution, but simply the transition from stupidity to something more reasonable; from all this unrightfulness . . . to rightmindedness. As for communism and socialism, they are nothing but an exaggerated figure of speech, a hyperbole, inevitable in troubled times.[5]

It is interesting to have this comment from Nikitenko, who was a professor of the St. Petersburg University, for many years a censor, and a member and sometime chairman of innumerable governmental commissions. As a censor he was often roused to indignation by the persecution of learning and literature—"revolution is made not by writers but by incompetent ministers." [6] He was no radical—he described himself as "moderately progressive" [7]—but he was a very impartial observer of the contemporary scene.

The youth movement of 1874 was spontaneous in the sense that the various established groups that intended to "go to the people" neither expected nor desired to be joined by such masses of inexperienced, raw youngsters. They had envisaged another summer of cautious and tentative exploration; instead they were swamped by hundreds of ardent and impatient crusaders. It was impossible to stem the flood, but the "old ones" did all they could to control and protect it. In particular the Chaykovists, with their wide net of supporting branches in the provinces, assumed the role of the organizational centre of the whole movement. Though their central group in St. Petersburg had been disastrously decimated by arrests, those who managed to evade the police—Kravchinsky, Klements, Shishko, Lukasevich—joined the Moscow branch: Natalya Armfeld, Varvara Batyushkova, Olympiada Alexeeva and others. The house of Alexeeva, the wife of a respectable civil servant, became a kind of headquarters through which passed by day and by night an unending stream of young men and women. Here they were equipped with peasant clothes, provided with money, forged passports, and useful addresses in the provinces, and given simple propaganda texts. These texts, usually written in a folksy style, described the poverty and the injustice suffered by poor folk in Russia or explained in simple language the unfairness of the tax system. Some of them were printed abroad or, illegally, in Russia, and others carefully selected from "legal" books passed by the unwary censor. One of the key figures in Moscow was Ipolit Myshkin, who organized and ran a clandestine printing press where many of these texts were printed—it was, incidentally, almost entirely staffed by women.

Swarm after swarm left for the wide spaces of rural Russia, until they reached the central and southern provinces—altogether they penetrated into 37 *gubernii* (that is, provinces). Bervi-

Flerovsky compared the movement to a forest fire that starts "by chance . . . self-ignited . . . and soon spreads over huge areas." [8] It is impossible to estimate the number, but apparently some one or two thousand were involved. And wherever they went they roused local youths to action, and so the ripples spread. Such unhampered progress would have been unthinkable if the enthusiasm of the young had not infected the older generation—professional men, administrators, landowners not only helped them to find suitable jobs in rural districts, but received them in their homes and gave them money. Many parents, too, encouraged their sons and daughters to "go to the people" and ran considerable risks in helping to hide them and their friends from the police. Since non-denunciation of known criminals, particularly "state criminals," ranked as an offence as serious as the crime itself, one can only conclude that the elder generation of educated Russians widely shared the feelings that had inspired the movement. There was perhaps even a little shamefaced envy of the courageous young.

Several rich landowners welcomed young propagandists on their estates and joined them in their activities. Thus one Mrs. Subotina [9] harboured two young women propagandists on one of her estates, while on her other estate two other young women were active—both members of the Moscow Chaykovists—Armfeld and Batyushkova. Mrs. Subotina had long been interested in radical ideas and had been present at one of the sessions of the First International. Her three daughters were studying at the University of Zurich and were to play an active part in revolutionary activities in 1875. In the end both mother and daughters were brought to trial and sent to Siberia.

Another estate owner, a Mr. Artsibushev, [10] invited members of the Kiev revolutionary group to learn agricultural work on his estate, and planned to establish a carpentry workshop for the training of future propagandists.

Two other rich estate owners went considerably further. Alexander Yartsev [11] left his army career at the age of eighteen to go to live on the estate of his mother in a manner worthy of Lev Tolstoy—ploughing and working in the fields along with his peasants, dressing and eating frugally as they did. Eventually he bought the estate from his mother and then resold it for a nominal price to the local peasants. He also sold his big house, leaving for himself just one peasant holding with a small house. He then petitioned the authorities to be recognized as a member of the peasant community and to be issued appropriate papers, since he no longer considered himself a nobleman; this request, however, was not granted. During his occasional visits to St. Petersburg, Yartsev became friendly with the Chaykovists, wrote a propaganda text for them, and introduced them to some peasants from his village who were working in winter in the capital as an *artel* of bricklayers. Kravchinsky and Rogachev (who had also been Army officers before joining the Chaykovists) stayed with him in the country and conducted propaganda; Alexandra Obodovskaya worked for a while in the rural school which he founded. Eventually Kravchinsky and Rogachev were arrested, but escaped; and a month later Yartsev was arrested and brought to trial.

The propagandist activities of another rich landowner, Alexander Ivanchin-Pisarev,[12] also brought him into trouble with the police. He had been very active in local affairs, having built up a book store and a school for already literate peasant boys and adolescents. But before long he involved himself in "illegal" activities: encouraging the peasants to stand up for their legal rights and openly criticizing the existing order and the tsar. In fact, he had joined the Moscow group of the Chaykovists in 1871, when twenty-two years old, and several of them came to work with him. He found loyalty and support among the peasants of his estate, though later he was betrayed by one of them. Luckily he managed to escape, with his friends, before the police arrived. He became, however, a hunted man like his fellow revolutionaries—now going abroad and now returning home to lead a wandering life, working as a coachman, a railway worker, a miner. He was finally caught in 1881 and sentenced to eight years in Siberia. His lively memoirs supply many interesting details of his early life. He tells how, when the equipment for a secret printing press arrived at his country house, the carpenters of his *artel* helped him to unload the crates from the cart. He was a little suspicious of a certain Nikolay and to mislead him said, in jest, that the crates contained rifles. As soon as Nikolay absented himself, the carpenters, who were in Ivanchin-Pisarev's confidence, dug trenches in the forest and hid the crates in them. Meanwhile, the local priest, alerted by Nikolay, who swore that the crates contained rifles, warned the police. The police arrived, found the landowner and the crates unaccountably absent but the carpenters most willing to help in the search for the crates. When they were told to dig up one suspiciously high mound in the park, they dug with great zest, and seemed as disappointed as the police when the mound yielded nothing.

The most typical and interesting group of rich landowners turned revolutionaries consisted of Sergey Kovalik, Porfiry Voynaralsky, Katerina Breshkovskaya—these three were about thirty years old in 1874—and the considerably younger Dmitry Lizogub. They all owned estates in the central provinces of Russia and some knew each other almost from birth. They began with perfectly legal activities within the local *zemstvo*—liberal-minded gentry everywhere in Russia had responded with great enthusiasm to the *zemstvo* reform of 1864 and many men and women had thrown themselves whole-heartedly into the various civic projects resulting from it. The Breshkovsky family—father, daughter and son-in-law—founded schools and donated and administered hospitals and libraries. In the aftermath of the reforms, the provinces had become battlefields between the liberals and the *krepostniki*. A key post in this battle was that of the land arbitrator elected by the local nobility, whose job it was to draw up the boundaries and the deeds of peasant holdings; obviously much depended on his fairness. Another important factor was the composition of the *zemstvo* councils, to which representatives were elected by nobility, merchants, and peasants. The liberals whole-heartedly welcomed the participation of peasants in the councils, which they considered the first step toward democracy, while the *krepostniki* feared it and attempted to manipulate the elections.

At first the liberals won on all counts: the Breshkovsky father was elected land arbitrator, the peasants elected the liberal land-owner Bidakovsky as their representative on the council, and Por-firy Voynaralsky and Sergey Kovalik were elected rural magis-trates—another progressive innovation, introduced by the law reform of 1864. But the *krepostniki* triumphed in the end—with the help of local officialdom and eventually even the central govern-ment, they had Bidakovsky exiled, Kovalik dismissed by the Sen-ate, and Breshkovsky forced to resign.[13] As the liberal aspects of the reforms were increasingly curtailed, rural schools closed, and progressive members of the *zemstvos* thrown out of their jobs, there was widespread disillusionment among provincial liberals. Some turned their backs on politics altogether, others became more radi-cal. Lizogub,[14] who was a very rich man, gave his entire fortune to the revolutionary cause. Kovalik and Voynaralsky became promi-nent revolutionaries.

In the Breshkovsky family there was a split. Katerina's father and husband remained liberal while she left her home and family and joined a revolutionary group and commune in Kiev. Together with one of her sisters and a few other younger men and women she founded a commune which became a magnet for local radicals. According to a member of this commune, Pavel Axelrod, Bresh-kovskaya had "an exceptional quality, completely her own, which . . . commanded . . . veneration. It was, above all . . . her enor-mous, vital, passionate love for the people."[15] She was undoubt-edly the outstanding woman revolutionary outside St. Petersburg. She had been devoted to her village school, she had expected to find her vocation in teaching; but all these peaceful plans were in the past now. Frustrated and embittered, Katerina Breshkovskaya turned to Bakuninist dreams of bloody revolution. In fact, the entire Kiev group was attracted to Bakunin—southern revolutionaries generally called themselves "rebels." Katerina Breshkovskaya and Pavel Axelrod even went to look for Bakunin's "natural rebel" among the robbers who were reported to have been seen in the forests.[16] They failed to find them, but another fellow Bakuninist was less lucky—he met with a horse thief, an ex-convict, whom he triumphantly introduced into the commune. Alas, when the police raided it, the "natural revolutionary" betrayed them all.[17] But in spite of these Bakuninist leanings among some of the radicals in Kiev, the Chaykovist Charushin succeeded in forming a very solid local group there, which carried out peaceful propaganda among the workers. In fact the Kiev group perhaps achieved the closest relation with the workers by organizing outings, walks, and picnics outside the town in the workers' spare time. On these occasions students and workers became really friendly, swam together in the river, and sang folk songs and revolutionary songs.

In the spring of 1874, after the swarms of young people had passed through Moscow and gone into the countryside, most of the "old ones," including the surviving Chaykovists, followed them, either coordinating and directing the movement or themselves doing propaganda in the villages. Thus Voynaralsky, Kovalik, Kravchinsky, Rogachev, and others formed a kind of flying liaison corps, going back and forth between Moscow and provincial centres, arranging transports of books, maps, and false passports; corresponding in code and watching over the developments. What began as a spontaneous movement of very young and inexperienced men and women thus became a more or less organized radical campaign, which was supported by many liberal sympathizers. And it involved practically the whole of Russia.

We have sufficient material in the memoirs of the participants, and in the letters and notes found after the Revolution in the police archives, to be able to follow the amazing course of this mass migration. But it is more interesting to see it reflected—with some degree of accuracy but with certain characteristic distortions—in the official report composed by the Minister of justice, Count Pahlen, in 1875.[18]

This is how the minister summarizes the findings of the police:

. . . it was found that many young men . . . had abandoned their studies, donned peasant clothes, procured false documents and, in the guise of simple unskilled labourers, "went to the people"—to use their own phrase. . . . [It was discovered] that somewhat earlier a secret printing press had been established in Moscow by the government stenographer Myshkin . . . on which . . . books and brochures of a criminal nature were printed . . . for the purpose of spreading propaganda among the people; that this propaganda was not limited to any one single locality, but was carried out in most parts of Great Russia and the Ukraine . . . and that the propagandists were in full agreement about their final aim as well as about their methods.[19]

The minister goes on to trace the beginnings of revolutionary propaganda back to the students' "self-education" groups which he describes as "essentially harmless"[20] until they became conversant with books of "outright revolutionary character," smuggled into Russia by Russian émigrés such as "Bakunin and other ultra-democrats and socialists."[21] Direct responsibility for the distribution of such books among students is laid at the door of the "Russian Revolutionary Party":

. . . The party of the so-called Chaykovists must be considered the first of that kind; its activities started in St Petersburg but spread later. . . . From 1873 onwards the "self-education" groups lose their original, that is theoretical, character, and gradually lead to meetings of a definitely social and democratic character. . . . This development is strengthened by the influence of the journal *Vpered!* which began to be published abroad, about then by Lavrov. In the beginning of 1874, the Moscow and St Petersburg groups decide that it is time to "go to the people," time to act. Being in full agreement on their basic aim . . . —the destruction of the existing order—the . . . propagandists can nevertheless be divided into three distinct groups. . . . Those of the first group maintain that there is no need for scientific preparation, that it is enough to be literate and to possess elementary knowledge, to be able . . . to go immediately to the people, merge with it . . . spread among it revolutionary ideas and prepare it for open revolt. Those of the second group maintain on the contrary that a serious agitator . . . needs extensive scientific education and some experience, though they attach little value to degrees and diplomas, which, they say, only demoralize and turn free men into bourgeois, that is into slaves of circumstances. Finally, those of the third group—possibly the most dangerous—not only insist on extensive scientific and general education and do not oppose diplomas and all kinds of certificates, but also intend to . . . spread propaganda not only among the lowly people but in any company. . . , among workers, soldiers, artisans or teachers, midwives, doctors, or anyone employed by the state. . . . Thus . . . the revolutionary propagandists . . . pretty rapidly penetrate into universities, seminaries, secondary schools, and village schools.[22]

At that point, unfortunately, the hitherto sober tone of the report gives way to some very fanciful exaggerations, suggesting that propagandists *"seduce* the young not only by persuasive talk and by books, but also by means of *intimate relations with the young women and girls who abound in their circle"* (my italics).[23]

Gradually the colours darken; thirty-seven provinces are described as being ". . . covered with . . . a net of revolutionary cells and individual agents."[24] More correct is the following insight: ". . . many persons no longer young, fathers and mothers of families, secure in prosperous and respectable social positions, not only did not oppose [the propagandists], but often offered them substantial sympathy, help, and support."[25]

Count Pahlen and the young propagandists can both be accused of seeing more in the affair than the reality warranted: it did not *yet* amount to an organized revolutionary movement with subversive political aims, nor was there any such thing as a revolutionary or indeed any other political party in Russia at that time. The radicals liked to call themselves "revolutionary" or "democratic" or "popular," but all these terms were quite imprecise. In fact both sides used extravagant language based on very little concrete fact. It is therefore no wonder that the ill-informed government and the illiterate police between them jumped to conclusions that were to lead to the destruction of a whole generation of young Russian intellectuals.

Throughout the spring of 1874 the police seemed quite unnaturally inactive and apparently unaware of the unusual activities of the young. We now know from police archives that the police were in fact fully aware of them. The arrests of the Chaykovists in St. Petersburg in 1873 were the beginnings of a police campaign against revolutionary propaganda. But when hundreds of propagandists flooded the provinces and the police assumed that a strong central conspiratorial organization was behind it, all the lines of investigation led merely to small groups or single individuals.* In the end, unable to find that elusive central core, the police rounded up everybody, however remotely connected with propaganda. The first to be shut down was the shoe-repair shop established by Voynaralsky [26] in Saratov which served as the regional store of books and the like; from there the books were traced to Ipolit Myshkin's printing press in Moscow. This was in June; by the end of the summer all provincial centres were discovered and raided and by the end of the year the number of arrests mounted to 1,600. According to Count Pahlen [27] 770 persons (612 men and 158 women) were finally selected for trial, a further 265 were kept in detention, another 452 were released but kept under observation, and 53 suspects were never found.† Eventually, only 193 accused were tried in the Great Trial (also known as the Trial of the 193) of 1877. And among these there were many already arrested in 1873, including most of the St. Petersburg Chaykovists. But far greater numbers were exiled without trial.

Of the well-known personalities only a few managed to escape abroad or to go into hiding. Voynaralsky, who in addition to his many other activities went on a propaganda tour in the villages in company with the barefooted Nadezhda Yurgenson, was arrested but escaped, only to be recaptured a few days later. Katerina Breshkovskaya, who had twice gone to the villages disguised as a peasant woman, was arrested on her second trip. In her memoirs she tells, with a grim sense of humour, how she was detained before she had time to read to the local peasants the subversive leaflets that she had brought with her. But as it turned out, she had a larger audience after her arrest than any she could have hoped to have earlier: the rural policeman, before locking her up, read out all her texts to the assembled and curious villagers—no doubt to show

---

* A report by the Third Section to the minister of the interior, dated 7 May, 1874, complained that the work of the police was made difficult by the fact that there appeared to be no secret organization behind the mass movement and each line of enquiry led either to a very small group or even to a single person. (Itenberg, B. (2), pp. 386–387.)

† According to Burtsev about 1,000 were selected for trial and altogether 3,500 arrested during 1874. (Burtsev, V., part 2, p. 83.)

them what a wicked criminal she was. As a result the villagers became very interested both in her leaflets and in her.[28]

The "mad summer" of 1874 thus ended in disaster. The apostolic movement was smashed, but in defeat and despair the revolutionary movement was truly born. Not for another twenty-five years or more was its membership to reach thousands or even hundreds, but it was stronger in resolution and direction. For at least another five years sporadic "going to the people" continued—mainly out of defiance—but gradually new and more decisive forms of revolutionary activity were evolved.

The government had seemingly triumphed, but it was an uneasy triumph; the sheer numbers involved showed that the youth movement was growing at an alarming rate and that some method more positive than simple police persecution had to be found to stem it. A special conference,[29] attended by seven ministers of state and the chief of the gendarmes, agreed that repression alone was no longer effective and that the whole society must be roused to help to tear out the revolutionary canker. In particular, closer relationship should be encouraged between university staff and students and, in cases of student disorders, professors rather than the police should be allowed to deal with them.[30] This was sensible, but the rest of the recommendations were farcical. Peasants were to be told that the revolutionaries wanted to reintroduce serfdom and were enemies of both the tsar and his people; and that the booklets they had been distributing in the villages were pernicious (this gratuitous testimonial greatly increased interest in the booklets). Count Dmitry Tolstoy, Minister of education, sent out a circular to all school inspectors telling them to impress upon their pupils that "the unhappy political fanatics . . . who carried their impractical fantasies into the villages . . . would stoop to theft, robbery, and even murder." This circular had been approved by the tsar, who had scribbled on the margin "very good! [31] On the other hand Professor Nikitenko commented in his diary that the circular was of an "amazing tactlessness" and "excited general . . . indignation." [32] He also thought that it was "ludicrous and stupid to see nothing but nihilism in a movement that had spread to thirty-seven provinces.'' [33]

The revolutionaries had now to draw the inescapable conclusions from their defeat. Not only had they behaved carelessly and often foolishly with regard to the police, but they had also failed to establish contact with the peasants, who had repeatedly met them with suspicion and even hostility, though it was more often the local priest or the rural clerk who denounced them to the police. The Bakuninists, in particular, had completely misjudged the situation—the peasants were clearly not on the brink of revolt, nor were they receptive to socialist propaganda. It had proved a tragic waste of lives to try to incite the people to protest. That much was acknowledged, but only with regard to the present—the future was still seen through utopian spectacles. The collapse of the summer crusade of 1874 was attributed to the large number of inexperienced, unproven participants. Many of these were frightened off by the arrests and retired into obscurity, leaving the field to the pitifully few true revolutionaries still left at large. These, however, were resolved to pursue their work. And reinforcements soon presented themselves; they came mainly from abroad, and among them was a large contingent of women. Many women had participated in the mass movement of 1874, but it was in the conspiratorial organizations of later years that they were to play a really important part.

TOWARDS / REVOLUTIONARY ORGANIZATION

As the political atmosphere in Russia grew less liberal, more and more Russians went to study abroad. Once there, they were naturally curious to inquire into subjects that were banned in Russia, for instance constitutional history and political economy; and, of course, into the history of social movements and the writings of Marx and Lassalle. In addition, Switzerland was the haven of radical expatriates—both Bakunin and Lavrov, as well as many minor figures, settled there. Young men and women revolutionaries (or just suspects) who had evaded arrest in Russia, or had escaped from prison and exile, also invariably made their way to **99**

Switzerland. Cities such as Geneva and Zurich thus became real hothouses of political indoctrination.

When Russian women went to study at foreign, mainly Swiss universities,[1] they were often received with hostility by native men students and even by professors, who were as a rule conservative and ill-disposed towards the emancipation of women. But some of the most eminent professors welcomed them warmly; and eventually the good will of others was won, as the women proved to be hard-working, conscientious, and intelligent—though the size of the female brain had been one of the stock objections to their admission!

Swiss and German burghers remained hostile from first to last; they were scandalized by the looks and clothes of Russian students of both sexes and suspected them of all kinds of "nihilist" immoralities. Women students were particularly disapproved of. In reality only their clothes were sometimes "nihilist"; their morals tended to be very strict. These girls knew themselves to be critically observed; they were still not very sure of their "emancipated" role, and this uncertainty was reflected in their defiant manners and clothes. Both seemed rather ridiculous to outsiders, though to sympathizers they were touching. " . . . can there be a simplicity in dress which does not become a girl when she is young, intelligent, and full of energy?"[2] asked Pyotr Kropotkin. In addition, many of the young women were very pretty.

Upon their arrival at foreign universities, most Russian girls were faced with great difficulties: their secondary education had as a rule been utterly inadequate and they found that they had to work very hard to satisfy university requirements. So at first these girls had no time for anything but study. But gradually they were drawn into the political interests and activities of Russian men students. They were made painfully aware of their ignorance in such matters too, and of their incapacity of putting ideas into words. They were determined to overcome this incapacity—in Zurich they even formed a special debating club for women "to learn to speak logically."[3] The club did not survive for long, as the debaters proved to be too undisciplined; whether they became more logical, we are not told. Their macabre choice of subject for the first debate was "suicide." It seemed an odd subject for young girls to choose, yet five of those present were to commit suicide later, and perhaps there was a premonition that their lives were taking a turn towards danger and tragedy.[4]

All shades of revolutionary thought were represented in Zurich, and ideological battles raged with all the heat and venom so typical of émigré politics. But again, just as they had been inside Russia, the young people who listened to these polemics were attracted by general ideas rather than by any specific program; and sometimes by certain personalities in spite of their political program. The observant Vera Figner comes very near the truth when she says that they were "Bakuninist by temperament and Lavrovist by reason."[5] It was natural enough that young men and women should be "Bakuninist by temperament"; what is more surprising is that they should have had enough sense to take the teachings of Lavrov to heart.

Bakunin attracted the young by his personal magnetism and his glamorous revolutionary past; his theories were seductive because they offered instant action and universal solutions. The influence of Lavrov was less immediately obvious but more lasting. It rested on two things: he appealed, intellectually, to the prevailing belief in science, progress, and reason; and, emotionally, to the need felt by young Russians to atone for the people's suffering. In fact Lavrov was much loved by the young, and when he set up a printing press and started the journal *Vpered!* [6] (Forward!) in Zurich in 1873, the first number was entirely set by volunteers from among the Russian students, including many followers of Bakunin. Lavrov failed to get all the émigré groups to collaborate on his journal, but he kept it open for contributions and letters from revolutionaries of all shades active inside Russia. For a few years it was indeed the voice of free Russia, as Herzen's *Kolokol* (Bell) had been earlier.

Among Lavrov's helpers was a group of young women students who were to become the protagonists of the next scene in Russian revolutionary history. They were known as Frichi, so called after Frau Fritsch, with whom all but two of them lodged. They led a semicommunal life, shared money, food, books, and helped each other with their studies. Like most Russian students they lived mostly on tea and bread, a little milk, and very little meat. Their ages ranged from seventeen to twenty and most of them came from well-to-do noble provincial families. They had received the usual education of the daughters of such families and their intellectual horizons, like their experience of life, were very narrow. They were bound together by what Sergey Kravchinsky described as a "schoolgirlish",[7] that is, an exalted yet intimate friendship which sometimes threatened to become possessive and tyrannical. Collectively they did indeed give the impression of a bunch of schoolgirls, childlike in their looks and behaviour and quite unused to the ways of the world. This is how Ivan Dzhabadari, a young Georgian student who met them in Zurich, describes them:

They were so young . . . some were so shy that they would not lift their eyes. They seemed country-bred, perhaps in some remote province; in any case the majority of them could not yet have entered so-called "society"; they had neither the serene assurance of ladies of the world nor the dare-devil brusqueness of the St. Petersburg women students with their unnecessarily dirty boots and short hair. Looking at these young girls one would have taken them all to belong to one and the same family; and indeed it was a very close family, not of blood relations but of friends.[8]

The undisputed centre of the group—they would have repudiated the notion of a leader—was Sofya Bardina. Though she was no older than most of them (she came to Zurich in 1872, when she was nineteen), she struck everybody as being by far the most mature of the group, and the Frichi, who were apt to use nicknames, called her "auntie." [9] Yet there was nothing elderly or fussy in her character, and her most striking traits seem to have been humour and vivacity. According to Ivan Dzhabadari, she "had a strikingly large head, not a pretty but a very intelligent face, a high protruding forehead and a pair of rather small but bright black eyes, alight with humour . . . her voice was soft, attractive, melodious, in the contralto range." [10] And in the words of Vera Figner, who joined

Sofya Bardina

Olga Lyubatovich

Lydia Figner

Betya Kaminskaya

Maria Subotina

Members of the Moscow Organization (*Byloe*, No. 9, 1907, St. Petersburg)

the Frichi when she came to Zurich, Bardina's "narrow black eyes were like sparks and the round . . . flushed face was arresting owing to its provocative and mocking expression. The mockery was chiefly expressed by her snub nose with which her mouth strangely harmonized." [11] But this humorous exterior obviously concealed a gentle and sympathetic nature—the same Vera Figner gratefully recalled that when in her early days in Zurich she had felt bitterly ashamed of her provincialism and ignorance, "Bardina seemed to me the only person who would not laugh at me but would help me to resolve my difficulties. When talking to her I found my tongue." [12] Many years later, Kravchinsky was to write in her obituary: "Bold, energetic, witty—she overflowed with life and good spirits. . . . It was impossible to be bored in her company. When she spoke, her blend of intelligence, gentle mockery, and fine observation never failed to captivate. . . . Bardina was beloved by all." [13] She appeared much older and more serious than her years—her "sober and sarcastic mind would not suffer sentimentality" and was combined with "stern moral standards for herself and for others," which excluded hero worship.

It seems that Bardina had a very healthy influence over the group, because she was mature beyond her years, and had sound common sense. By contrast the rest were rather young for their years and liable to fall into adolescent enthusiasms and rages. They were also on occasion excessively puritanical and ascetic —another adolescent trait. Thus Vera Figner records that one day Bardina mentioned being very partial to strawberries with cream,[14] whereupon the group was outraged and called her a bourgeoise, which in their view was the worst that could be said of anybody. And yet, after they had been three years in Zurich, Ivan Dzhabadari found these girls "the most mature, the best prepared [group] . . . not only among the female, but also among the male youth. . . . In addition to general erudition, they had an excellent knowledge of western and Russian revolutionary literature, something that one rarely saw, even among the youth of St. Petersburg." [15]

Sofya Bardina, Olga Lyubatovich, and Vera Figner became the

best-known members of the Frichi. There was also Olga's sister Vera Lyubatovich, Vera Figner's sister Lydia, the sisters Evgenia, Maria [16] and Nadezhda Subotina, Betya Kaminskaya,[17] Varvara Alexandrova, Dora Aptekman, Alexandra Khorzhevskaya, Anna Toporkova and Evgenia Tumanova. But little is known about most of these young women—too little to make them come alive if it were not for the marvellous photographs that have survived. The young faces, so full of bright intelligence and charm, are irresistible. It is no wonder that the public fell in love with them when they stood in the dock at their trial.

Vera Figner, who was to emerge as one of the band of really outstanding revolutionary leaders, belonged only marginally to the Frichi. She neither lodged with them in Zurich nor returned to Russia with them; nor did she share their subsequent activities or their trial. She was to play her important and tragic part in Russian revolutionary history at a somewhat later date, and her story properly belongs elsewhere. Nevertheless it is to Vera Figner and her memoirs that we mainly owe our knowledge of the Frichi. In describing her own childhood and upbringing she illumined theirs. In a letter to an old schoolmate, Vera Figner wrote before she went to Zurich at nineteen: "the three aims of my existence [are]: economic independence, the development of my mind, and usefulness, that is, my usefulness to others." And for the future: "I hope to found a hospital, or a school, or a workshop [for peasants]. . . ." [18]

These sentiments were shared by all the Frichi. They had all devoured Nekrasov's "Sasha" and Turgenev's stories of peasant life and longed to live and work among the peasants. But during their stay abroad they became socialists and so now they were also eager to carry socialist ideas to the people. This was dangerous work and they prepared themselves for self-sacrifice and even martyrdom. But they were resolved to finish their studies first—in this respect they accepted Lavrov's warning that a well-stocked mind was a revolutionary's most important equipment.

All their good intentions were, however, suddenly and brutally frustrated by the Russian government: in June 1873 it published a decree recalling all women students from Zurich.[19] This was not the first decree of its kind: after 1848, Nicholas I had altogether forbidden Russians to study abroad, and in 1866 men students were recalled from Heidelberg; [20] but this was the first such decree addressed specifically to women. According to it Zurich had become the centre of the most extreme radicalism; the inexperienced young Russian women were having their heads turned by propaganda; some were already taking an active part in criminal activities, others had become intoxicated with the communist theory of free love and had lost all sense of morality and feminine chastity. (This became a stock accusation against radical women and was rightly resented by them, since they tended to be rather puritanical.) The Russian government, the decree said, could not but recoil in horror from the thought that these young women would return to Russia to become wives, mothers, and teachers of the young. It was due to modern ideas propagated in some journals that women came to misinterpret their true position in the family and in society; young women were falling under the pernicious influence of Russian expatriates and were being irretrievably ruined. Yet they could have satisfied their thirst for education at home, under the benevolent eye of the government—had not various courses, for instance, for the training of teachers and midwives, already been established under various ministries and under the Fourth Section of His Majesty's own Chancellery, and were not other plans for women's education under consideration? In conclusion, the decree tersely informed women students that unless they left Zurich by 1 January 1874, they would be debarred upon their return to Russia from any further studies or examinations, and, indeed, from any activity that depended on governmental permission.

Since practically everything depended on governmental permission in Russia, this was indeed drastic. The Russians in Zurich were outraged and the young women had the sympathy of even the Swiss students and professors. Vera Figner has drawn a vivid little vignette of the Frichi returning from a protest meeting, marching down the middle of the street and belting out a popular revolutionary song: "Forward without fear or doubt!" [21] But there was nothing to be done against the decree and most of the politically uncommitted women students went home forthwith; so did many of the committed ones, to swell the ranks of those "going to the people." A cartoon circulating in Zurich under the title "To the people!" showed a line of carriages from which young feminine faces peeped, smiling and nodding, and shouting: "We are ready! We are ready!"—that is, ready, in the Lavrovian sense, for going to the people.[22] The Frichi, though more prepared than most, did not consider themselves at all ready and decided to try to complete their studies at other foreign universities. They dispersed for a time, but kept in touch. Hand in hand with their studies went various socialist activities. They had already been to a session of the anarchist Jura Federation in September 1872; they went to another in the summer of 1873 at Neuchâtel; and to a session of the International at Geneva. It was at Neuchâtel that they drew up a tentative program of a revolutionary organization. No copy of this survives, but its existence at the time shows in which direction their minds were moving.

Then came the spring and the "mad" summer of 1874—news from Russia was at first electrifying and then agonizing: the mass arrests and the complete defeat of the first mass revolutionary campaign were heart-rending. Yet among radicals there remained determination to continue the fight, and impatience to enter it. The Frichi, too, decided not to delay their return to Russia. Their Lavrovist reasonableness gave way to the Bakuninist temperament. Prepared or unprepared, ready or not ready—their place was in Russia now.

It was during this time that some of the group met a few Georgian men students who were, as it turned out, exactly of their mind. These young men had been attending a conference of Caucasians. The dilemma of Russian national minorities was the same for Georgians, Ukrainians, or Jews: they had to decide whether to fight as a national group for nationalist ends or to join the oppositional Russians, radical or liberal, in their fight against the Russian government. A conference of Caucasian intellectuals held in Geneva in August 1874 [23] voted overwhelmingly to work as a national group for the establishment of a federal Caucasian republic. Only six men dissented from this decision, on the grounds that working with the Russian opposition would not only unite all national minorities within Russian borders but also harmonize with the ultimate aims of all humanity. The six dissenters, among whom was Ivan Dzhabadari, broke with their fellow Caucasians and prepared to return to Russia. But at that point the young men met some of the Frichi and were invited to meet more of them at Geneva.

From Dzhabadari's description of this momentous meeting [24] it would seem that the Frichi had not changed much since we last saw them in Zurich:

Bardina was dressed in plain black and was sitting on a divan in front of a round table. . . . No sooner had we sat down than the others, with the shyness of very young girls, crowded like children around their "auntie," one sat down next to her and clasped her hand, another, on her other side, encircled her waist with her arm, a third, leaning right across the divan, grasped her shoulders, while a fourth pushed to get near her. . . . But Bardina, seeing herself in danger of being smothered, shook them all off with a laugh and a rebuke: "What the devil—can't you let a body talk?" They all laughed but no one yielded her hard-won position. We, too, laughed, with a vivid recollection of our own childhood—seeing ourselves as children crowding around mother when strangers called, and peeping like little animals from behind her back.

But "when the constraint of the first minutes passed . . . the girls forgot their shyness . . . question upon question was thrown at us. . . ." And after a long, animated talk it emerged, to everyone's delight, that "at that moment they had formed in their minds as in their hearts exactly the same [resolution] as myself: to leave foreign lands, leave the university and go to Russia." [25] The young men and women decided to work together in a joint organization.

The new allies found that they shared a horror of *nechaevstchina*; they agreed that their organization ought not to be overcentralized or overregimented. Equally they agreed that these dangers could be avoided, provided the members of the organization respected each other's freedom. This was possible only if the members were as carefully chosen and knew each other as thoroughly as had been the case with the Chaykovists. Fortunately the Frichi were close friends, and so were the three Georgians who joined them: Ivan Dzhabadari, Mikhail Chikoidze, and Prince Alexander Tsitsianov had known each other from school. The first two had been students in St. Petersburg from 1872; they had taken part in students' *skhodkas* and in endless discussions between Bakuninists and Lavrovists—and like the Frichi stood somewhere between the two. Tsitsianov had gone straight from school to study abroad, where his two former schoolmates joined him in 1874. A classical scholar, he was a shy and taciturn man, and inclined to brood; not surprisingly he succumbed to melancholia at the end of his life in Siberian exile. Dzhabadari, a medical student, was a man of a balanced and critical mind, cautious rather than impulsive, persevering and conscientious. His experiences in St. Petersburg had made him wary of "blabberers" and "phrase-makers," [26] who enticed enthusiastic and idealistic youngsters into revolutionary activities. Chikoidze, an outstanding mathematician, was a lovable personality, though frightening at first: he had large and piercing black eyes and a dense growth of coarse black hair, which the Frichi promptly nicknamed "the mop."

Such were the three young men who threw in their lot with the Frichi. One might wonder at their readiness to embark upon a dangerous and secret enterprise, perhaps to risk their very lives, in company with a bunch of girls whom they had themselves described as barely grown-up. One might even wonder that they should choose to involve themselves with girls at all, since their own Georgian culture allowed women no voice at all in "men's affairs." That they did so without hesitation is a measure of the complete sense of equality between the sexes that characterized that generation of radical students. We know that Dzhabadari was not in fact an out-and-out nihilist. He disapproved of the intentionally coarse behaviour and ugly clothes of the nihilist "new woman" whom he had met in St. Petersburg; [27] he gave a most unsympathetic description of Grinevitskaya, sister of the nihilist writer Pisarev, who appeared at the conference of the Caucasians in Geneva dressed as a man; and he disliked the idea of fictitious marriages.[28]

Yet he whole-heartedly accepted women as equals.

The Frichi, being even more puritanical than most radical women, tried to introduce celibacy as a condition for joint work, but the Georgians gently but firmly declined.[29] Vera Figner says that the alliance of the Frichi with the Georgians was most beneficial and "introduced a much more practical element into their plans"[30] and, one surmises, into their general outlook on life.

Having agreed on essentials, the new partners still had many practical problems to solve: to establish contacts with émigré printing presses, to arrange for the smuggling of books and journals into Russia, and to ensure funds for their activities in Russia. In this respect they could count on the Subotiny, who were rich, and on Tsitsianov—though his great wealth, consisting mainly in land, was not immediately available. Dzhabadari left for St. Petersburg to reconnoiter the situation at home, while Chikoidze and the Frichi remained abroad for a little longer. Bardina, after leaving Zurich, had tried but failed to complete her medical studies in Paris and had to be content with getting a midwifery diploma at Geneva, which took only a few months. The young people agreed to foregather and to start their work in Moscow, and most of the Frichi began to arrive there in November and December 1874. Some, however, did not get there before the new year; and Olga and Vera Lyubatovich were arrested at the frontier, accused of carrying letters from the émigrés, and imprisoned for several months. Vera Figner remained abroad, determined to complete her studies, and she had the sad task of winding up the affairs of her friends the Frichi and of their shipwrecked organization when she returned to Russia a year later.

The new organization called itself the All-Russian Social-Revolutionary Organization, and in later days it was sometimes referred to as the Moscow Organization for short. It was basically a continuation of the Chaykovist program, carried a little beyond what that group had had time to achieve. It operated well within the populist ideology, but it took account of two important experiences of the preceding years: firstly that without a well-organized conspiratorial society all efforts must fail, and secondly that the intellectuals were much less successful at propaganda in the villages than the workers who had kept their peasant roots. The Moscow Organization therefore intended to direct its propaganda first towards the industrial workers and only later, with the help of the workers, to carry it into the villages.

As only vague outlines of the proposed organization had been agreed upon at Geneva, Dzhabadari had to a great extent to use his own initiative in St. Petersburg. He met several of the Chaykovists, who were in hiding from the police, and was guided by their advice. Through them he also got in touch with workers who had been or still were their pupils. He found these workers so impressive, both intellectually and as personalities, that he promptly invited them to join the organization. In principle, the idea of a joint organization of intellectuals and workers had been advocated by Lavrov, but it had never before been realized. Apart from the workers (Mikhail Grachevsky, Pyotr Alexeev—a former pupil of Sofya Perovskaya—and Vassily Gryaznov), Dzhabadari also recruited from among the intellectuals the Caucasian Zdanovich, and Ivan Zhukov, who was a popular teacher of workers. And after his arrival in Moscow he recruited a student, Alexander Lukashevich, and a worker, Ivan Soyuzov—both Chaykovists and experienced propagandists.

When the St. Petersburg workers arrived in Moscow they settled in the factory district and immediately began to distribute illegal books and tracts and to spread propaganda. Soon they attracted, and co-opted into the organization, several local workers. Similarly, the Frichi plunged into revolutionary activities as soon as they reached Moscow, though by no means all "conspirators" had yet assembled and the form and shape of the future organization had not yet been agreed upon, or even discussed with all concerned. The impatience to act and the impulsiveness of youth were allowed to override the warnings of experience. In fact, contrary to all their intentions, they repeated the haphazard pattern of 1874. This could only lead to one result—another tragic and costly defeat for the revolutionaries.

But before the Moscow Organization went down, it achieved an astonishing amount—especially considering that it only existed for from three to six months. Not only did it prove the possibility of a harmonious and fruitful cooperation between intellectuals and workers in Moscow, it even expanded its activities to several more industrial districts (Tula, Ivanovo-Voznesensk, Kiev, and Odessa). The intellectuals mainly concentrated on the supply and distribution of books, the workers on establishing personal contacts within the factories. "Raw" workers, only recently arrived from the country, were the most susceptible to propaganda, but they were also the most illiterate and shockingly "unconspiratorial." Factory overseers and the police had no difficulty in catching them in possession of banned books and in tracing these to their source. Nor were the conditions of these workers' private lives such as to ensure secrecy: the inquisitiveness of their wives or mistresses, the sharing of lodgings with others—all encouraged indiscretions. When pressed by the police and threatened with prison, these workers usually crumbled at once and told all they knew and much that they invented.

It is thus a sad fact that the worker connection proved to be the Achilles heel of the organization. But in all fairness the Frichi could be equally blamed. Arriving from abroad with no knowledge or experience of Russian conditions, these overzealous young women insisted on going to work in factories like ordinary workers. Their male comrades, who knew the dreadful conditions of life and work at these factories, strongly opposed this, but, says Dzhabadari, one dared not try to dissuade them. "They would have laughed us to scorn, they were so proud and strong in their ignorance of life." [31]

The men always tried to learn something about the factory at which one or the other of the girls had found work and often pretended to be their brothers, so as to be allowed to visit them. Life at the factories was indeed made appalling by a fifteen-hour working day and only one free day per week. On their free day the workers could leave the factory but for the other six they were shut in behind the heavily guarded factory gates. There were separate dormitories for men and women—married couples could talk to each

other for ten minutes three times a week only. The sleeping
quarters were airless and the dirty mattresses and pillows, without
bed linen, were spread on overcrowded wooden bunks alive with
bedbugs and lice. The food was appalling, too: a plate of dirty thin
soup and a slice of bread per meal. It was hard enough for the men,
but for the Frichi it was sheer folly; indeed criminal folly, since
they were bound to attract attention. They sacrificed themselves for
nothing, since they could neither get a response from the grey mass
of illiterate factory women nor establish contact with male workers.

The first of the Frichi to go to work at a factory was Betya
Kaminskaya.

Well do I remember [writes Dzhabadari] that Sunday night, when
Grachevsky and I were to deliver Betya at the gates of the factory at
4 A.M. We had booked two rooms at an hotel the evening before—
one for Betya and Evgenia Subotina and another for us. None of us
. . . slept . . . Evgenia . . . dressed Betya . . . in a simple peasant girl's dress with wide sleeves, put a string of cheap glass beads
around her neck . . . ; she tended her like a . . . bride; . . . at
about 3 A.M. Subotina knocked at our door. . . . We had stretched
ourselves out on the beds without undressing. . . . We jumped up
and went out into the corridor, saw Subotina with a candle in her
hand—everybody in the hotel was still asleep. "Do take Betya,
hurry," she whispered. Then she embraced Betya and started to
cry. "Why are you crying?" I asked. . . . "Oh! you do not know
how hard it will be for her!"—"Then why let her go?" But Betya
hurriedly and silently walked towards the front door and we had to
hurry after her. It was a frosty January night; we walked for about
three versts, without a word. . . . The farewell between the two
girls had literally crushed me. . . . It seemed as if we were leading
this young woman to some dreadful execution. . . . At the gates of
the ramshackle old factory there was already a crowd of workers,
men and women. They hurried through the gates, where the guard
frisked them . . . as if it were a prison and not a factory. Involun-
tarily, Betya shrank back, but then she went resolutely forward, let
herself be frisked without a word, and quickly entered the yard.
. . . We remained outside the gates for a long while, thinking.
. . . We returned to the hotel, but an hour later Grachevsky, with
some buns wrapped in a kerchief, went again to the factory and
asked to see his sister Masha Krasnova (this was the name Betya

had assumed). Betya came out to see him and was terribly glad to be visited so soon.

Throughout the whole of this first week Grachevsky went daily to see his "sister" and "on Saturday evening . . . he brought her to us by hackney cab. We welcomed Betya as if she had been away for years. . . . She had changed considerably—usually so fresh and rosy-cheeked, she was now pale, thin, and worn out, but remarkably pleased with herself and very talkative." [32]

The sisters Lyubatovich, Lydia Figner, and Alexandra Khorzhevskaya also went to work in factories, but none of them lasted for more than a fortnight—either the supervisors became suspicious or the men pursued them with wolf whistles and obscenities. They left without having begun their propaganda. But it was just as well that they did not last longer as their health would not have stood the unaccustomed hardships; we know for instance that Betya Kaminskaya so abominated the vile food that she ate only bread.

Sofya Bardina also went to work at a factory and was rather more successful than her friends. Perhaps it helped that she was less pretty, or perhaps she was more careful and methodical. Having tried to talk to the women in her dormitory, she found their interests quite incredibly narrow—there was little she could do with them. It was not easy to get at the men, but she made friends with a married woman and through her with her husband. Entrusted one day with a message from the wife, Sofya boldly entered the men's dormitory and began to read out of a pamphlet. The men immediately surrounded her, suspicious but intrigued. Who was she, where did she come from, how was it that her voice and manners were so genteel, and how was it that she, a girl, could read, when most of the men could not? But she had her answers ready: she belonged to a sect (sectarians had to be literate, to be able to read the Bible) and she had been a servant in a genteel household. From that day on Bardina constantly found pretexts to visit the men and was soon held in such esteem by them that not a single obscenity was uttered in her presence. She was their pet, their mascot; they were proud of her and liked to show her off to other workers; on their free day they would take her along to their usual taverns to read the newspapers aloud so as "to impress the public." The next step was to select a few men for more serious studies, and Bardina was already thinking of that when she was surprised one evening in the men's dormitory by the factory manager. Books that she had distributed were seized, and she was lucky to escape before being handed over to the police.

It was somewhat easier for the men to make contacts inside the factories and to follow them up. Some (Lukashevich, Alexeev, and a few more) went to work in the factories, while others (Dzhabadari, Chikoidze, Grachevsky) frequented the taverns and snack bars in the factory districts. On the workers' free days they all met, as if by chance, in one of these places. After inviting people to their table and standing a few rounds of vodka or tea, they would talk or read extracts from books and pamphlets. All this attracted much interest. It was comparatively easy to pick out the most wide-awake among the listeners, and these were selected for more advanced propaganda and eventually organized into small groups. The results were very encouraging—after only two months there were groups of four or five men at over twenty factories and at several smaller workshops and on the railways. There was also an "inner" group of workers which was completely won over to revolutionary activities; its nucleus consisted of the St. Petersburg workers who were already full members of the organization and of some workers newly recruited in Moscow. An outstanding newcomer was Nikolay Vasilyev, an extremely energetic young worker, a born popularizer and agitator. Though he could not read or write he caught socialist ideas "on the wing," as it were, and immediately transmitted them to others, usually in a simplified and easily understood form.

All these activities were in full swing when the founders of the organization began to formulate the statutes. In February 1875, Dzhabadari was commissioned to prepare an outline of statutes on the basis of the tentative program sketched by the Frichi in Neuchâtel in the summer of 1873. His outline was then discussed in the presence of all members, save a few who were kept away by work;

and finally Bardina, Lukashevich, and Zhukov were entrusted with the composition of the final text.

It is a curious document: utopian and naive in its general outlook, yet practical in detail. The statutes are, in fact, mainly concerned with organizational problems; and for the broader implications we have to rely on personal comments of the memoirists. Vera Figner has described the view of the future underlying the statutes: "After the ground had been prepared by propaganda . . . local revolts would be encouraged, later to result in a general rising." [33] And Dzhabadari says that the moral basis of their statutes was "the rejection of the negative sides of the existing political and economic order." [34] He adds that when the proposed text was discussed, he and Bardina hotly opposed any attempt to lay down in advance the forms of the future social order—this the people must be allowed to choose for itself.

Both the political and the moral principles outlined in the statutes closely followed those of the Chaykovists, but there was greater emphasis on organizational matters. The Moscow Organization was to embrace several *obshchinas*, or local groups, under a central administration controlled by the whole membership. The administration was to consist of two or three persons elected unanimously for one month at a time and it was to contain both workers and intellectuals. The work of the administration was restricted to purely technical matters such as renting of rooms or flats for members; building up stores of books, passport forms and false documents, invisible ink; inventing secret codes and corresponding with local groups; and, of course, administering the funds.

All in all, and allowing for serious weaknesses, the Moscow Organization and its statutes represented a great step forward in the development of the revolutionary movement in Russia. All previous revolutionary bodies were basically groups of intellectuals clustering around a leading personality: Nechaevists, Dolgushinists, Chaykovists. The Moscow Organization made the transition to an anonymous conspiratorial organization (Vera Figner pointed out later that the Chaykovists were the last to be named after an individual). And more important still, the Moscow Organization had a mixed membership of intellectuals *and* workers.

The final text of the statutes was copied out on very thin paper which could be easily swallowed if necessary. The organization was thus formally, though belatedly, constituted. With twenty-one members at first (of which ten were women and five were workers), it soon grew to about twice that size, with local groups in several industrial centres. Unfortunately it grew too fast and people were allowed to join and to learn all about it before it was realized that they did not fulfill all the requirements of the statutes, or even of simple common sense. The most unfortunate choice proved to be the worker Nikolay Vasilyev, whom everybody had thought so wonderful. An enthusiast in all things, he was ready enough to swear to lay his life down for the cause, but he had no intention of breaking with his mistress, an illiterate and jealous woman. The presence of all these young women cannot have been welcome to her. When Vasilyev, probably through his own carelessness, was picked up by the police, she promptly denounced them all, in a stupid attempt to save him. The police raided the headquarters of the organization, where they arrested nine people, including Bardina, Dzhabadari, and other prominent members. That was in April 1875, and by early September all the rest were rounded up, in Moscow as well as in the provinces. In Moscow they had known that the police were closing in on them, yet failed to clear the headquarters or to dispose of incriminating material. They were surprised at the tea-table and while the search was being conducted pretended to go on with their tea while busily swallowing as many notes and addresses as possible. In Tula it was another newly recruited worker who caused the collapse; again it was his mistress who denounced the group to the police. The incriminating material seized was not very compromising, but a copy of the statutes of the organization was unfortunately found on Zdanovich, who was arrested at a railway station.

Lukashevich, who had several years of conspiratorial experience to his credit—first with the Chaykovists and later with the Moscow Organization—noted that forgetting about danger was "the abiding sin common to us all" [35]—work was always at fever pitch and there was no time to think of safety. Certainly those members of the organization who survived the April arrests did not take better precautions. The new administration, consisting of Tsitsianov and Vera Lyubatovich, lived quite openly in hotel rooms. As Vera Figner writes: "Masses of people were for ever coming for this or for that. . . . Books were stored here; passports were 'washed' in a chemical solution, which filled the whole building with its stifling smell; on the table false documents were fabricated and correspondence coded and decoded." [36] Money was also kept there and considerable sums eventually fell into the hands of the police. Such careless disregard of security is almost unbelievable. It can only be understood in terms of how these young people saw themselves: they had seen socialist propaganda conducted quite openly in western Europe and they meant to establish their right to do likewise in Russia. Also they meant to show that they were not afraid of the police. When the police came to arrest Tsitsianov, he pulled out a revolver and tried to shoot the police officer. He was overpowered and disarmed, thrown on the floor and beaten. Vera Lyubatovich, a thin slip of a girl, thereupon threw herself into the fray to defend him. When this incident was later brought up at the trial, the whole court exploded with laughter, in which Vera joined. This was, incidentally, the first instance of armed resistance to arrest, which was later much practised by revolutionaries.

It remains unpardonable that our heroes and heroines involved so many others in their downfall. Altogether 105 persons were arrested and investigated, and many more questioned, in what was officially described as "the case of various persons accused of crime against the State, to wit, the formation of an unlawful society and the distribution of criminal writings." [37] Finally, in the autumn of 1876, the investigating authorities recommended that fifty-one persons be tried, fifty-four exiled without trial, and the rest released. The trial itself did not take place until February 1877.

PRETRIAL DETENTION

During the next few years Russian prisons [1] bulged at the seams and several new ones had to be hurriedly built. In St. Petersburg the model House of Preliminary Detention was opened in 1875—it was promptly nicknamed, by the revolutionary Georgy Plekhanov, the House of Slow Strangulation (a play on the Russian words *zaklyuchenie* and *zadushenie**)—and in the Kharkov district three fortress prisons were erected that would nowadays be described as strict-regime prisons. There were also the notorious old

---

* *Zaklyuchenie* means detention and *zadushenie* means strangulation.

prisons: the Peter and Paul Fortress and the Lithuanian Castle in St. Petersburg, the Shlüsselburg Fortress on an island in the Gulf of Finland, and the Butyrka prison in Moscow with its tower where, according to legend, the rebel Pugachev was kept in a cage.

There were more than 800 prisons altogether in the whole of Russia and Siberia, ranging from brand new brick buildings to ruins in danger of collapse. The prison staffs were very badly paid and therefore usually open to bribery. Small-town policemen were often literally in rags—their swords suspended from thick cords twisted round their waists and their greatcoats threadbare and much patched. There were many kindly men among them who were sincerely sorry for the young *barye* (gentry) who got themselves into prison for some incomprehensible reason, but they could do very little for them without risking their jobs. The conditions in provincial prisons varied greatly, since everything depended on the characters of the men in charge—prison governors, the local chiefs of police, and the provincial governors. These men were often transferred to remote posts because of fraud, embezzlement, criminal negligence, or cruelty, though there were also a few who found themselves similarly demoted because of their honesty and humanity.

Before the newly arrested men and women were placed in regular prisons, they were usually kept for some time in the filthy lice-ridden cells of police stations or village detention huts. Though political prisoners were supposed to be kept in separate solitaries, those among them who deliberately refused to identify themselves were classed as vagrants and placed with the criminals. Katerina Breshkovskaya kept up her refusal for three months, until the threat to involve her aged parents in her affairs forced her to admit her name. But even in their solitary cells, the political prisoners could not help hearing, day and night, the screams of drunks and thiefs, brutally beaten by the police; or the screams of new arrivals whom the ''old hands'' thrashed, in keeping with prison traditions, until they surrendered money and other valuables to their cell-mates; or the shrieks of women criminals and their children during the ferocious fights that periodically broke out. The effect of these daily scenes on the political prisoners, many of whom were mere young-sters, was shattering. Breshkovskaya was to write in her memoirs: "a long solitary imprisonment at an early age had fatal effects. The youngest usually contracted typhoid fever or consumption and died, or they became insane." [2] And suicides, too, were frequent—among those involved in all the trials of 1877–78, seventy-five ei-ther became insane or committed suicide or died of illness in prison.

Most of those arrested between 1873 and 1875 were not brought to trial before 1877 and thus spent two to four, and in some cases five, years in solitary confinement. It must have been doubly hard on young women, most of whom were of noble birth and gentle up-bringing. However, men and women who survived the first impact of imprisonment usually recovered their strength of purpose. The more mature prisoners were as a rule better able to adjust to prison conditions and they helped the others to do likewise.

Workers presented a special problem. There were many "sea-soned" revolutionaries among them who hardly behaved differently from their intellectual comrades. But the illiterate new recruits could not bear complete inactivity and isolation. Nikolay Vas-ilyev, who, with his mistress, had proved the weak link in the Mos-cow Organization, was a case in point. In his solitary cell he suf-fered agonies of boredom. And yet he was luckier than most, since Captain Lovyagin of the gendarmes, the same whom Tsitsianov had tried to shoot, had taken great pains to teach him to read and write by setting him to copy letters from cigarette packets. Soon Vasilyev could write sufficiently well to address the following let-ter, in capitals, to the authorities: "Mr. Prosecutor, my dear Sir, here I am thrown into this hole, positively for no reason at all; am deprived of light, air, space, and the company of people; well—do you want me to hang myself—have you no God?! Never will I believe that it's the Tsar's wish to have men thrown positively for nothing into such holes; let me out, give me back light, air, and space!" [3] Since there was, of course, no response to this *cri de coeur,* he surrounded himself with books one night, set fire to them, and perished in the flames.

Intellectuals could at least devise some means to occupy their minds: Sofya Bardina and Sergey Sinegub, and later Vera Figner, wrote poetry; the scientists and scholars Pyotr Kropotkin, Alexander Tsitsianov, and others continued to work on their subjects; the rest taught themselves foreign languages, or they read. Books were usually allowed, though pen and paper were permitted only in very exceptional cases, so that prose and verse had to be memorized by frequent repetition. This helped to keep the mind nimble but there was no remedy for frayed nerves and troubled hearts. The prisoners were anxious about their families and their comrades outside; and they were harassed by nagging doubts about their own recent activities.

It was clear to all that something had gone wrong—but what was it? Many unpalatable truths presented themselves. They had gone on their mission with preconceived ideas borrowed from the West and with an inadequate knowledge of the Russian people. They had learned to their cost that their propaganda fell on deaf ears and that even those who seemed to respond enthusiastically, like Nikolay Vasilyev, had largely misunderstood the message. Living among peasants in remote villages, or among working people in the factories, or among unemployed and often unemployable casual labourers in the doss-houses of the large towns, the young revolutionaries had come to realize how much they had to learn from the people before they could teach it anything. And for their illusions and their ignorance they were now paying with their own and their followers' freedom; they were lost to the revolutionary cause for many years and perhaps for ever. Grief, bitterness, helpless rage at themselves and their captors—these were the prisoners' waking and sleeping companions.

But before long hope revived: surely, armed with greater experience and insight and with different tactics, the revolutionary "party" would rise again? Had not the Chaykovists of 1872–73 been followed by the tidal wave of 1874, and was not this in turn followed by the Moscow Organization of 1875? And in the years after that propagandists had not stopped going to the villages and working among factory workers. Nobody doubted that they would be followed by still others. This unshakable hope sustained the prisoners through the long years of prison and through years of hard labour and exile in Siberia.

From local police stations political prisoners were transferred to the nearest prisons and eventually to St. Petersburg for preliminary investigation. This was conducted by the gendarmes and could last for a very long time. Sergey Kovalik, for instance, was so uncooperative that his case alone took over a year to investigate. The investigating gendarme officer said of him, with admiration: "In one summer he found time to visit thirty-two provinces—what wonderful energy! He has organized groups of revolutionary youth everywhere!" [4]

The investigation concluded, the prisoners were sent to await trial in the Peter and Paul Fortress or the Lithuanian Castle (this old prison no longer stands near the Maryinsky Opera House—it was burned down by crowds in February 1917). Some few were released on parole to reside with their parents. By now most of the prisoners were already in poor health. In particular, many had developed scurvy or blindness from prolonged sojourn in damp and airless cells. Thus Pyotr Kropotkin was so weak after two years in the Peter and Paul Fortress that he could hardly walk. He was lucky in that he was transferred to a military hospital, where he recovered his strength and whence he made his daring escape. Leonid Shishko, who spent four years in the same fortress, suffered in his eyesight but received no treatment either then or later in Siberia, and by 1885 he was almost totally blind. The scholarly Felix Volkhovsky became deaf in prison and Katerina Breshkovskaya developed chronic bad sight in one eye. And yet the prisoners did try to keep up their health with daily exercise. Pyotr Kropotkin would walk the length of his cell a thousand times per day. Breshkovskaya found the cell in the House of Preliminary Detention—Predvorilka for short—too small for walking, so she performed instead the national Russian dance, with so much stamping, leg-kicking, and high jumping that the frightened warder thought she had taken leave of her senses. Since she invariably wore the clumsy and shapeless prison garb, even when this was not compulsory, she must indeed have presented a grotesque spectacle.

Perhaps the worst feature of solitary confinement was the lack of contact with one's comrades. But with time, prisoners overcame this handicap by learning to "talk" to each other by tapping on the wall. According to revolutionary tradition it was the Decembrist Bestuzhev who first invented the technique, for which later generations of Russian prisoners were to be profoundly grateful. By placing all the letters of the alphabet in six rows, five to a row, and then tapping the appropriate number of times to indicate first the row, and then the position of the letter in that row, regular telegram-style "conversations" could be conducted between cells, though they needed infinite patience and great powers of concentration. Neighbours usually began with the question: "Who are you?" repeated again and again until the newcomer mastered the rules. After names had been exchanged, personal histories and news from the outside or from other prisons followed. In the two-storied Fortress only few contacts could be made, but the five-storied Predvorilka offered almost infinite possibilities. A modern building with central heating, it had heat pipes passing from cell to cell throughout its five floors; in addition beds, chairs, and tables were all connected with those in the next cell by iron bars—and all these pipes and bars carried sound very clearly. This made "long distance" communication possible between nonadjacent cells, and tapping could be perfected to a high degree.

Katerina Breshkovskaya described how in the months preceding the trials "tapping grew daily bolder. . . . We tapped with our feet and hands or with objects. . . . We tapped on the window-sills, the walls, the water-closet seat" [5]—and all these various methods produced different sounds. By agreeing that prisoner A should tap with a pencil, B with a foot, C with a hand and so on, they could always identify the tapper, even when several people joined in the "conversation," which could then develop into a debate. Eventually it was discovered that when the bowl of the water closet, of which there was one in each cell, was emptied and they spoke into it, they could be heard in all cells above and below; in this way ten people could converse with each other at one and the same time.

Each such unit of ten was thereupon constituted as a "club" and the entire Predvorilka was divided into several clubs.[6] Soon these clubs engaged in regular symposia; it was decided to write jointly a history of the Russian revolutionary movement to date. All through the day the prison resounded with a cacophony of metallic and other sounds—the noise in the corridors was deafening, but inside the cells, with their ears glued to iron pipes or bars or water closets, the prisoners remained unaware of it.

Contact with their comrades greatly improved the morale and even the health of the prisoners. Sergey Sinegub records that his headaches and insomnia disappeared and that he enjoyed a healthy appetite and sound sleep.[7] The influence of some of the older comrades was beneficial to the younger: they inspired them with courage, rebuked them for hysterical or defeatist moods, and urged serious study. "If there had not been such people as 'granddad' [Mitrofan Muravsky],[8] Volkhovsky, Myshkin, Breshkovskaya . . . the prisoners could not have stood the oppression," [9] says Sinegub.

It is surprising that the authorities did nothing to stop all this. Tapping was, of course, forbidden and punishable with several days in the punishment cells on bread and water. But in the last months before the trials the authorities turned a deaf ear to worse things than tapping. Thus male prisoners in the Predvorilka removed the window-frames and shouted to each other across the prison yard; affixed strings along the outside walls from window to window, and passed notes to each other with the help of these strings. They even converted their daily walks in the yard into social occasions by simply climbing over the fences of their separate narrow walking cubicles and forming a happy group with other prisoners. Several attempts at escape were made with the help of warders, some of whom accepted money. And though the prisoners were recaptured, neither they nor the warders were seriously punished. On the other hand, the cells were frequently searched and all written material removed. This entirely unusual state of affairs can have only one explanation. By listening into the tapped conversations and confiscating the written material, the authorities were hoping to obtain the evidence which the Third Section was so desperately eager to find and which all the extensive and lengthy investigation had failed to bring to light: the evidence that a huge revolutionary organization existed in Russia.

In this the authorities did not succeed, for the prisoners talked and wrote only of a *future* organization. It was clear, too, that many of them had never met or known each other before and had certainly not shared beliefs or plans. What they did share was a spontaneous sense of solidarity which increased with every day in prison. The long years of captivity had, as one of them, Kvyatkovsky, was to say, "fused together, made known to each other a great mass of people. Having got into prison before they could properly be called revolutionary, being caught in the mesh often quite by chance . . . having spent several years in solitary confinement . . . the majority . . . emerged as fully fledged protesters." [10] Indeed, many were *now* ready to join a revolutionary party if one came into existence. The time in prison proved for many of them a time of political education. Later generations of Russian revolutionaries were wont to call prisons their universities, and in this instance it was certainly true, since many of the prisoners spent their most "teachable" period—between sixteen and twenty—in prison.

9
POLITICAL TRIALS, 1877-78

Long after the investigation period was over, the Third Section still hesitated to bring the accused to trial. To have arrested thousands of suspected conspirators and to be unable to provide proof of a conspiracy put the secret police in a quandary: should it arrange secret trials with as little noise as possible followed by a speedy dispatch to "distant parts," or even a speedy dispatch without a trial? This could be done by the simple expedient of an administrative directive—a method for which there was no legal justification but which was constantly practised. Yet this time it did not seem advisable to apply it to *all* the prisoners, even **127** though it could be, and was, applied to scores of them. The mass arrests had attracted so much public notice and interest that something must be *seen* to be done. On the other hand public trials invariably made martyrs and heroes of the accused revolutionaries—even in the case of the followers of Nechaev—while the government invariably emerged as the villain. And then again there was really not enough material for public trials. Only very few could be accused of incitement to rebellion and to the overthrow of autocracy; the hundreds that "went to the people" could be accused only of teaching and doctoring the peasants and sympathizing with them in their poverty and suffering—particularly as most of the propagandists had deliberately avoided attacking religion and the tsar.

The problem of trials was causing headaches at the highest level. The Grand Duke Konstantin advised the tsar to keep the trials small by limiting the number of the accused, but the tsar was afraid to give an impression of weakness and decided on big public trials. He hoped that these trials would demonstrate the wickedness of the revolutionaries and the strength and justice of the government. There was furthermore the matter of legality. Russia was supposed to have, since 1864, a brand new legal system, according to which political offenders were entitled to public trials. The tsar was justly proud of this. Yet the Third Section consistently disregarded the legal rights of Russian citizens and even the tsar went in fear of the all-powerful chief of gendarmes. It was time to show the country, and the Third Section, that the tsar was upholding the law of the land!

The year 1877 was to be the year of mammoth trials: first of the Moscow Organization ("the trial of the 50") [1] and then of the "going to the people" propagandists ("the trial of the 193").[2] This seems chronologically wrong, since the second case concerned those arrested in 1872–74 and the first those arrested in 1875, but the proposed order was deliberate, for in the case of the Moscow Organization there was proof, however slender, of the existence of an organization, while in the other case there was none. But before those two trials could begin, a few things occurred to raise the number of trials and to embarrass the government still further.

The first thing to happen was a street demonstration that took place in December 1876, in the centre of fashionable St. Petersburg, in front of the cathedral of Our Lady of Kazan.[3] There had been rumours that a special service was to be held at the cathedral—some said for those who had died in prison, others for Russian volunteers fighting on the Serbian side against the Turks. Since both causes were popular with the young, many of them forgathered in front of the cathedral or inside it. After the service the crowd did not disperse. Suddenly a young boy in a peasant sheepskin coat was seen to unfurl a red flag with the inscription *Zemlya i Volya* (Land and Freedom) and a young man swung himself onto a ledge and made a rousing speech against the persecution of "the best Russians" by the government. The boy, a sixteen-year-old worker called Potapov, had been a supporter of the Moscow Organization, and the young man was the future founder of Russian Marxism, Georgy Plekhanov. The demonstration was in fact organized by the newly founded revolutionary organization Land and Freedom. As police whistles sounded, the young people who had been listening to the speech formed themselves into a procession, headed by a sixteen-year-old girl, Felicia Sheftel.

Now, political demonstrations were a very new phenomenon in Russia. The police countered it with an ingenious new technique: instead of dispersing the demonstrators with its own forces, it incited illiterate townsfolk to beat them up. (This technique was later perfected during the anti-Jewish pogroms.) It was particularly easy for the police to use it in this case—the beautiful Kazan Cathedral stands quite near the Central Market, where there were many market porters, butcher boys, and apprentices about. It would seem that they were told that the students were stirring up trouble against the tsar—and at once they fell upon the unsuspecting students and bystanders, beating up and kicking men and women to the ground.*

---

* An almost identical technique was used on 3 April 1878, in Moscow: a crowd of local students which assembled in the street to greet a transport of students arrested in Kiev was brutally beaten up by small shopkeepers and their assistants. The police, which had spread malicious rumours about the students, arrived three hours late. (Bogucharsky, V. (3), pp. 47–51.)

The uniformed police arrived when the battle was in full swing and arrested thirty-two people, including eleven women—but from among the victims! Plekhanov managed to escape, but the boy Potapov was detained as he walked down the Nevsky Prospect between Vera and Evgenia Figner, still wearing his sheepskin coat and with the red flag carelessly tucked under his arm.

The demonstration enraged the government, which had believed itself safe from renewed revolutionary action. Twenty-two of the arrested men and women were tried almost immediately, without preliminary investigation and before their defending lawyers had time to acquaint them with the accusations. They were tried by a special court dealing with crimes against the state, and the sentences were severe out of all proportion. Five men received terms of from ten to fifteen years of hard labour, and the rest were exiled. Felicia Sheftel, on account of her tender age, was sentenced to six years and eight months in exile; and Potapov, for the same reason, to five years in the Solovki Monastery on an island in the White Sea.

The second event was even more significant, particularly in the long run: arrests in Odessa brought to light the existence of a South-Russian Workers' Union,[4] organized by the Lavrovist Evgeny Zaslavsky, consisting almost entirely of workers and numbering no fewer than 200 members! This was the first palpable indication of the success of revolutionary propaganda among workers. The South-Russian Union was formed in 1875 and it was followed, in 1878, by the Northern Union of Russian Workers—together they represented the beginning of the autonomous Russian working-class movement. This was perhaps not yet obvious in 1877, at the time of the trial of Zaslavsky and his friends, but it held an ominous threat to the government and by the same token gladdened the hearts of the revolutionaries. They concluded that the reserve of revolutionary energy in the country had not been exhausted by mass arrests, and they faced their trials with greater confidence.

There was little hope that their punishment would be mild, but it was not their personal fate that concerned them most at this moment. What they wanted above all was to be able to break down the wall of silence and secrecy built around them by the police. In the absence of free speech and a free press, their ideas and aspirations had either remained unknown to, or had been largely misunderstood by, the Russian public. The dock in a public trial was probably the only place from which they could hope to enlighten their compatriots. And this would make their past and future suffering easier to bear. For the rest, they did not expect a just trial. The legal reform of 1864 had raised great hopes that justice and legality would at last prevail in Russia, but these hopes were already fading. The government and the Third Section could still manipulate justice; the administrative method of exile was still used; and every expression of oppositional spirit was still classed as "state crime." By law, political trials had to be held in public and fully reported in the official *Government Gazette*. Yet the staging of these trials—whether they were or were not to be public, which senators should be chosen as judges, even what sentences should be passed by the court—was ultimately decided in advance or endorsed afterwards by the tsar. And he was known to reduce or increase the sentences in such an arbitrary fashion as to deprive political trials of every semblance of legality.

The "trial of the 50" opened on 21 February 1877,[5] before a special court of the Imperial Senate,* sitting in the Regional Court building on Shpalernaya Street (now renamed Street of I. Voinov). This building was connected by a long corridor with the Predvorilka, which occupied the building next to it on the same street. It was in this corridor that all the accused were lined up on the morning of their trial. One of their number was missing—Betya Kaminskaya had succumbed to melancholia in prison and had been handed over to the care of her father; the case against her was closed. Her fate was none the less tragic for that. When she recovered from her mental illness, she could not bear the thought of having been spared the ordeal undergone by her friends, and killed herself.

On the morning of their trial, the accused were far from feeling

---

* The Russian Senate was not a parliamentary body; it had various functions, acting as a court of appeal, as a special court for crimes against the state, etc.

tragic—they were delighted to be together again, even though they were spaced out in the corridor in such a way that gendarmes with drawn sabres stood at regular intervals between them. But the sabres did not impress them; they called noisily to one another and openly discussed points in their defence. The officer who arrived to take the roll call could not keep the excited prisoners in order, and there was loud laughter when he stumbled over the difficult Georgian names. In the end the prisoners were marched into the courtroom and distributed on both sides of the senator judges. Behind the judges sat several illustrious personages: Chancellor Prince Gorchakov, Minister of justice Count Pahlen, and even a member of the imperial family, the amiable Prince of Orenburg. Relatives of the accused were admitted to the gallery by ticket only; and so were a few members of the general public. During the tedious formalities—names, ages, etc.—and the reading of the indictment, which took several hours, the accused chatted happily and were in high spirits.

Theirs was the first major political trial in which the accused were composed of three almost equal parts: male intellectuals, female intellectuals, and workers. Theirs was therefore a new type of political group—one, moreover, in which there were no leaders. The accused were fully aware of the significance of all this and they were determined—since the trial was public—to explain to the world the true aims of Russian revolutionary youth. And the public was indeed impressed, even on that first day, by the dignity and proud bearing of these young men and women. Particularly the women created a sensation—they were so young and yet just as steadfast as the men! Of course there were many sympathizers in the public gallery who needed little persuasion, but even they were moved beyond their expectation. Valerian Osinsky, who was soon himself to become a legendary hero and to perish on the scaffold, "fell," he said, "so much in love with these women, these heavenly angels," that he decided to give more people the chance "to fall in love with them, too." [6] Having prepared several hundred fake entrance tickets, he and his friends distributed two hundred instead of the officially issued fifty. That was on the first day of the trial and passed unnoticed, but when on the second day *five hundred* tickets were presented at the door, the gendarmes smelt a rat. Osinsky found himself in a cell in the Predvorilka, shouting words of sympathy and encouragement to the accused through his window.

The trial lasted five weeks. A disproportionate time was given over to disentangling the names, nicknames, and aliases of the accused, who had lived under their own or each other's names, or under altogether assumed ones, and had even "fictitiously" married each other under borrowed names. A certain youthful levity had pervaded all their dealings with each other, and their correspondence, decoded, made comical reading in the courtroom. In the matter of distribution of "dangerous" books, the case rested mainly on the evidence of informers and so-called voluntary witnesses, but these were quickly discredited when most of them revoked their earlier statements. They were also shown to be illiterate—they could not identify the books with any certainty, and were ignorant of the meaning of such words as, for instance, revolution. The much more serious charge concerning the existence of an anti-government secret society rested on very inconclusive evidence, that is, the one copy of the "proposed statutes" found on Zdanovich. The prosecutor himself admitted that the organization appeared to have been formed *after* its "core" or "nucleus" had already been arrested. As for the accusation of being "mere emissaries from abroad" (that is, from Russian radicals abroad), not a shred of evidence to support it was offered at the trial.

The prosecutor and his indictment, his ·summing up, and his whole case made a most unfavourable impression on the public. There was much sympathy for the defendants. Not even the judges remained unaffected—certainly the sentences compared favourably with those passed in other recent trials. Alexander Tsitsianov and the workers Pyotr Alexeev and Gregory Alexandrov were each sentenced to ten years' hard labour, and Sofya Bardina and Olga Lyubatovich each to nine; and the others to less. Later the sentences were further reduced—Tsitsianov's by one year—while Bardina's and Lyubatovich's were converted to exile for life. Of course, the total extent of punishment was never expressed solely in terms of the formal sentence, since hard labour was automatically followed by exile for life or, in some cases, for twelve to fifteen years. Nor should we forget that fifty-four persons connected with this case had been exiled by the administrative method without being tried or formally sentenced.

At the very end of the trial the accused had their moment of triumph. The undoubted climax came when those of them who had refused defence lawyers were asked to say their "last words." Two of these—Bardina's [7] and Pyotr Alexeev's [8]—developed into full-length speeches and became famous. Alexeev, who was the first to speak, had a powerful voice which at times shook with passion. He had rehearsed his speech in advance with the help of his comrades, and when the time came he delivered it with maximum effect. He described the plight of the millions of working people who were given no schooling or any other chance to develop into proper human beings but, instead, were thrust at the tender age of ten into unhealthy, filthy factories, where with kicks and blows they were forced to work for seventeen hours a day at jobs that were beyond their young strength. Insufficient food, sleeping on bare boards among vermin—and all that for a miserable wage, often enough reduced to practically nothing by the savage system of fines practised in Russian factories. Under such conditions the mind was stifled and morals corrupted; no wonder that workers were considered to be no better than animals—what else could they be? Reading and learning were not encouraged even in the workers' few free hours; nor were there any books suitable for workers. "And yet," asked Alexeev, "are we, the workers, really . . . deaf, dumb, and blind . . . unaware of how . . . all around us other people get rich? Are we really such dullards as not to see . . . why *our* work is priced so low . . . and where *their* wealth comes from?" The working people were forever waiting for justice to come from above—Alexeev recalled the grateful feelings with which the Russian people had thanked the tsar for the abolition of serfdom. It proved an empty dream, the people were as poor as or poorer than before, and they were still bullied and humiliated, though now it was by the factory owner or the village policeman. The least complaint or attempt to argue was countered with a punch to the jaw and often with flogging, prison, exile to Siberia. Russian working people got no redress from anyone and "no help or sympathy except from our educated young people."

At this point the presiding judge jumped up and shouted "Silence! Be silent!" but Alexeev, described by Dzhabadari as a "man of strong character and stubborn energy," [9] only raised his voice: "They alone stretched out a brotherly hand to us. They alone . . . understood why the peasants were groaning all over the Russian Empire. . . . They alone . . . will walk shoulder to shoulder with us towards that day [he raised his arm] when the millions of working people will raise their strong arm [once again the judge, now in real alarm, shouted 'Silence! Silence!'] and . . . despotism, sheltering now behind soldiers' bayonets, will crumble into dust!" It was the first time that the voice of an ordinary worker had been heard, and it created a furore. "A true folk tribune!" could be heard from the corner where the lawyers were standing. Next day Alexeev's cell could hardly hold the gifts of fruit, tobacco, and food. [10]

After the uproar created by Alexeev's speech, the judge was nervous and interrupted more often. Zdanovich's "last word" [11] stressed the fact that young Russians had hoped for a peaceful transition to a more just social order in their country and had started out with peaceful aims. But they were met with suspicion, hostility, and persecution; and their peaceful socialism became revolutionary socialism. The present socialist movement was no accidental, passing phenomenon; it embraced the best part of the young generation, all the most vital forces. And no amount of brute force would kill it—however numerous the victims, young people would remain true to their convictions.

Chikoidze [12] spoke only briefly but his deep and melodious voice stirred the emotions to such an extent that when he finished both the public and the defendants were in tears.

Bardina's manner was very different. Indeed, if it had not been so, the presiding judge, thoroughly rattled by now, would have stopped her altogether. But she began so softly, seemed so sweetly reasonable that there appeared to be no need to interrupt her. And yet, as Kravchinsky was to write in her obituary, "never, either before or after, were the ideas and aims of the Russian socialist party of the day formulated more precisely, more clearly, or with greater logic." [13] She began with the humorous observation that she could not for the life of her understand the meaning of the accusation against her. She would not deny that she had been conducting propaganda in a Moscow factory, but as for belonging to an organization—that she could not make out. The prosecutor himself alleged that this supposed organization was founded *after* her arrest on 4 April, and that she and those arrested with her represented only a kind of "core" or a "germ" of a future organization. She was puzzled as to the exact article of the penal code under which "germs" of future organizations could be charged and punished. . . . But she was denying herself the honour of belonging to that future organization not for fear of punishment but because the whole accusation seemed to her illogical and legally untenable.

Personally, she considered herself wholly innocent, as she had neither intended nor inflicted any harm on society or the people. The accusation levelled against her and others, of wanting to destroy the foundations of property, family, religion, the state—all this was due to misunderstandings. She never wanted to do away with property, on the contrary she thought she was defending it by demanding that everybody should have a right to property, that is, to the product of his or her personal work. As to what should be done with it, that should be left to the producer to decide. And the family, who was undermining it more—the existing social order, under which women went into factories where both they and their children were debauched or forced into prostitution, or the accused, who were trying to end the poverty that was the main cause of almost all social evils, including the decay of family life? And religion—she personally thought that she had been and still was entirely true to the spirit of the founder of her religion.

There remained the state—and she could not think that any efforts by individuals could bring the state down; if it did collapse it would be because it carried the germ of decay in itself. If, for example, some state kept its people in slavery—political, economic, and spiritual slavery; if it drove its people, through all kinds of abnormal economic pressures, to penury, illness, and crime, then such a state, it seemed to her, would have only itself to blame for its downfall. There was, therefore, no sense in punishing and persecuting a few powerless individuals. Rebellion and revolution, a bloodbath—she and her friends did not desire them and would be sorry if it proved impossible to change the social order without them. She and her friends belonged to the type of young people known as peaceful propagandists, who aimed at spreading among the people the ideals of a better, more just society—a society that would abolish privileges and the division into haves and have-nots. But this could not be achieved by physically exterminating all the rich. Nor was it intended to promote a workers' class that would rule over other classes; rather one hoped for happiness and equality for all. These hopes might be thought utopian but certainly they were not bloodthirsty; moreover, in the West such ideas were commonly discussed and not considered particularly radical, perhaps because people there were used to discussing ideas in public, openly. In conclusion Bardina stressed that she was not asking for mercy, nor did she desire it. She belonged to a large movement, which had started several years back, and it could not be stopped by repression. It would revive with redoubled force, again and again, until it triumphed.

Disregarding the nervous interruptions by the judge, Bardina ended:

I am also convinced that a day will soon dawn when our sleepy and lazy society will wake up and be ashamed that it has allowed itself to be humiliated for so long; that it has not resisted when its brothers, sisters, and daughters were taken away and destroyed for no greater crime than being true to their convictions. And when this day comes, society will avenge us. Go on persecuting us, physical force is still on your side; but moral force and the force of historical progress is on ours; ours is the power of ideas, and ideas—you may regret it—cannot be impaled on the points of the bayonets. . . .

The effect of the speech was tremendous—without bombast Bardina had triumphantly demonstrated the moral truth of her and her comrades' convictions. Her restraint and occasional light humour broke down only at the very end when her deep passion and sincerity blazed forth. When the public was leaving the court, many were saying: "They are saints," "These are apostolic times." [14]

A pathetic "last word" was spoken by the peasant worker Filat Yegorov: "Our Saviour had said: judge not that ye be not judged—so how is it that you are judging us, though we are all Christians? I believe that you, too, will be judged . . . by the Lord . . . at his terrible Last Judgement!" [15]

The official *Government Gazette*, which had been publishing the stenographic report of the trial, did not print the texts of the last speeches. They were partly printed illegally in Russia (seven people were imprisoned for printing Bardina's speech) and eventually were reproduced in Lavrov's *Vpered!* abroad.

The government, court circles, and the tsar were extremely annoyed by the public acclamation of the trial. The imperial chancellor, Prince Gorchakov, was reported to have told the Minister of justice, Count Pahlen, that he regretted that a public trial had been decided upon: "You have merely persuaded everybody that they [the accused] were no children, no silly boys and girls, and no drunken peasants either . . . but men and women of mature intellect and strong, unselfish character, who . . . knew full well what they were fighting for." [16]

Exasperated, the government swung right over. The next important trial, that of "the 193," [17] which was due to open on 18 October 1877, would be held *in camera*, in the presence of only a few selected members of the public, to maintain the semblance of a public trial; and the *Government Gazette* would print only the indictment in full. Consequently on the first day of the trial there was not even an official stenographer present and the defence had to ask for permission to make its own shorthand record. All of which clearly indicated that the government had no intention of complying with the law.

On the day of the trial, 193 men and women accused of "revolutionary propaganda in the empire" were crowded into the hall of the Special Court of the Senate, which was only just big enough to hold them and had no room for the public even if it had been allowed in. The accused, looking pale and ill after their long imprisonment, realized that they were to be deprived of their chance to speak to the Russian public. They were already very angry over the indictment, which had reached them through their defence lawyers only just before the trial began, and which contained many accusations they considered slanderous. And indeed, though the indictment took many hours to read out, it offered no solid evidence of guilt. At later stages of the trial the examination of witnesses proved equally unproductive. Scores of frightened schoolboys, peasants, and bewildered landladies had been questioned during the preliminary investigation, but when called upon to testify at the trial most of them could no longer remember their own depositions. And only very few defendants had, as the official jargon termed it, offered sincere admission of guilt.

Throughout the first day of the trial the defendants talked excitedly among themselves—they had been keyed up for a public trial and they felt cheated and desperate. The presiding judge was quite unable to keep order; the more he admonished them, the louder the defendants became. Defence lawyers also found a lot to object to and protest against. The hearing ended in complete chaos and the court did not sit the next day owing, it was stated, to the indisposition of one of the senators. When it reassembled on the third day, the judges announced their decision to divide the defendants into seventeen groups and to try each group separately. This manoeuvre was greeted with great indignation—why should the accused be tried in separate groups if they were supposed to belong to the same organization? And how could any group defend itself if it was ignorant of what had been happening during its absence from the court? The majority of the accused decided to protest by refusing to participate in the trial. During the first few days they were taken to the courtroom by force, but this proved so difficult and the disorder was such that henceforth they were left unmolested in their cells and were tried *in absentia*. Only a few did not join in the protest—those who faced only very minor charges and did not want to make their case worse. There were also two other abstainers: Vera Rogacheva, chosen by the women to keep them informed of the course of the trial, and Ipolit Myshkin, who, by his own request, was to be the spokesman for the accused.

Myshkin discharged his self-appointed task brilliantly—he was the very man for the job. The son of a serf woman and a soldier, Myshkin had experienced from childhood all the frustrations and hardships that beset a gifted and ambitious son of the people. He never got beyond primary school, but study and reading at home made him intellectually equal to any student. He became first a government topographer and then a stenographer. Both were well-paid jobs, but Myshkin was not interested in financial security. Like so many young men of his generation he cherished the ideal of a life dedicated to the good of the people, and like so many others he progressed from dreams of peaceful activity in the service of the people to a realization that such dreams led nowhere in Russia. So he became a revolutionary, organizing, with his own hard-earned money and some help from Voynaralsky, an illegal printing press in Moscow. When arrests began in summer 1874, he vanished. But eventually he was caught in eastern Siberia, where he was making a daring attempt to help Chernyshevsky escape from exile.

From his cell in the Peter and Paul Fortress, Myshkin bombarded the Prosecutor of the Senate, Zhelikhovsky, who was preparing the indictment, with long letters even before the trial.[18] Nobody, he complained, seemed interested as to why he and his comrades had become "state criminals," what had driven them to it, and he felt it to be his duty to explain. These remarkable letters gave his personal story against a broad canvas of Russian life with all its barbarity and injustice. They infuriated the Prosecutor and after the second letter he forbade the prison governor to forward any more to him. At the trial itself, Myshkin—in full agreement with his comrades—opened his attack at once. The speech that made him famous [19] was, in effect, a series of interpolations, constantly interrupted by the presiding judge. Myshkin was not to be silenced; his vibrant voice rose above the hubbub until in the end he was forcibly removed from the courtroom—though only after he and his friends had fought the gendarmes, while all around them women fainted and sobbed. Back at the Predvorilka, Myshkin lifted out his window-frame and repeated his speech for the benefit of his comrades. The gist of his speech was not very different from Bardina's, and like hers it was a statement of the beliefs and intentions of the revolutionaries. Like hers, too, it had an enormous success, both with the radicals and with the general public, to which it seeped through by word of mouth—for, of course, it was not printed in the *Government Gazette*. Later it was published abroad.

The trial ran the rest of its course through five months of boredom. The accused remained consistently uncooperative, while defence lawyers grew ever bolder as the time went by, openly declaring their sympathies with the accused and treating the prosecution witnesses with the contempt they deserved. On the other hand the judges became more and more confused and, one feels, more doubtful about the whole case. Yet they knew, and the accused and the public knew, that they were expected to pass severe sentences; so they battled on, though neither their final verdict nor the sentences strike one as whole-hearted. The verdict stated that in 1872, under the influence of west European revolutionary teaching, several people had formed in Russia an unlawful society for the purpose of overthrowing, *in the more or less distant future* (my italics), the government and the lawful order of the Russian Empire. And so sixty-five defendants were found guilty of either founding or joining this unlawful society and circulating or printing or importing from abroad unlawful books; several were found guilty of circulating such books without belonging to the society; two were found not guilty of belonging to the society but guilty of knowing about it and not informing against it; and three others of knowing about the circulation of "criminal" books and not informing against that! In its final stages the verdict made less and less sense: a young peasant was found guilty of uttering a blasphemy on one occasion in 1874; Mrs. Subotina (mother of the three sisters sentenced in the "trial of the 50") was found guilty of uttering *without premeditation* (my italics) words disrespectful and insulting to the sacred person of the emperor. Finally, and most surprisingly, some ninety people were found altogether not guilty, including such well-known revolutionaries as Sofya Perovskaya, Olympiada Alexeeva, Vera Rogacheva, Martyn Langans, and Andrey Zhelyabov. Truly the mountain of conspiracy had given birth to a mouse—a mouse, however, that had upset the authorities of 37 Russian provinces and the central government itself.

The sentences included ten years of hard labour for Myshkin, Voynaralsky, Kovalik, Rogachev, and Muravsky, and from nine to three years of hard labour for many others; five years for Katerina Breshkovskaya. Many were sentenced to long terms of Siberian exile; and many to prison or penitentiary for one year, six months or even less—terms long exceeded by the length of pretrial detention. But it was evident that the judges themselves were aware of the absurdity of the situation, for in submitting all the sentences "to the merciful consideration of the monarch," they particularly stressed the extreme youth of some of the defendants and the great length of time they had already spent in prison, begging him to reduce the sentences. In fact they recommended milder sentences for almost everyone, except Myshkin. But Tsar Alexander felt that the Special Court of the Senate, which he regarded as his very own and obedient instrument, had let him down this time, and he did not feel merciful. The chief of the Third Section, Mezentsev, also advised against leniency. The tsar did not reduce the sentences; some he even increased.[20] Thus many went to serve terms of hard labour whom the court had not considered deserving of such punishment. And of the ninety people who had been declared not guilty, eighty were re-arrested by the secret police and sent into exile by the administrative directive, thus fittingly ringing down the curtain on the travesty of justice that went under the name of the "big trial," or the "trial of the 193."

APOSTLES INTO TERRORISTS

A sequel to the series of mammoth political trials of 1877 came early in the following year. A young woman, Vera Zasulich, shot and wounded the chief of the St. Petersburg police, General Trepov, in revenge for the flogging of a political prisoner in the Predvorilka.[1] It was widely understood to be an assertion of human rights and human dignity which the police so constantly violated. And it was also—apart from Karakozov's attempt on the life of the tsar—the first time that an act of terror was used as a gesture of protest.

The all-powerful General Trepov was an unscrupulous and un-   **143** savoury individual whom St. Petersburg "society" would not receive, even though it condoned his brutal and lawless methods of suppressing "those terrible revolutionaries." Perhaps society would have approved of him less if it had known, as we now know from police archives, that by his orders not only the revolutionaries but absolutely everybody, including the most illustrious personages, was spied upon by servants, house porters, and even waiters.

General Trepov was in control of all prisons and prisoners in St. Petersburg. In July 1877, he happened to cross the yard of the Predvorilka, where some of the prisoners were out on their walk. One of them was Bogolyubov, a young man arrested during the disturbances in front of the Kazan Cathedral and sentenced to fifteen years' hard labour in the Siberian mines. Trepov, being obviously in an irritable mood, noticed, or thought he noticed, that Bogolyubov failed to take his hat off to him. Whereupon he fell into a great rage and roared: "Have him flogged!" Prison officers dragged the unfortunate victim away and he was flogged later the same day.* [2]

Many of the prisoners witnessed the incident in the yard and the news soon spread throughout the prison. A pandemonium of howling, shouting, and banging broke out. The indignation was fully justified. Corporal punishment had been made unlawful since 1863, though flogging was retained for special cases, such as for the punishment of convicts. But Bogolyubov's case was up for appeal and he was not yet officially a convict, so that there was no legal justification for the flogging. And in any case flogging was felt to be particularly degrading when applied to an educated man, a student. The prison was soon in a state of uproar, the prisoners shouting for the public prosecutor and yelling: "Hands off Bogolyubov!" [3] The noise redoubled when the prisoners were told that Bogolyubov had already been flogged. Next, groups of twenty to thirty policemen broke into several cells and savagely trampled upon and beat up the inmates. This was done completely at random and among the victims were some who had made no noise at all—

---

* After Trepov had obtained the consent of the Minister of justice, Count Pahlen, who must have known that it was unlawful.

for instance Felix Volkhovsky, who had become deaf in prison and had been unaware of the whole incident. After the beating the prisoners were dragged along the corridor into the punishment cells, which were so foul that at the subsequent inspection the public prosecutor could not bear to stay inside even for a matter of minutes. Yet several prisoners were kept in them for three to four days—after which some were in a high fever. [4]

The whole affair was felt deeply by the political prisoners because it showed up their complete inability to counter the abuse of law by those in power. The implications reached far beyond the walls of the Predvorilka. It posed a basic problem—was any Russian citizen, imprisoned or free, innocent or guilty, safe from such abuses? And what should be done about it? This was a breaking point for the revolutionaries, and those who date the birth of Russian terrorism from the moment of Bogolyubov's ordeal (he died soon afterwards in prison) may well be right. [5]

Thoughts of revenge were in all their minds, but particularly strongly among those who were free and felt that it was a betrayal of their comrades in prison to remain inactive. Two young women took it upon themselves to avenge Bogolyubov and political prisoners in general: Maria Kolenkina, a former member of the Kiev commune and a close friend of Katerina Breshkovskaya, undertook to shoot Zhelikhovsky, the author of the indictment in the "trial of the 193," while Vera Zasulich, who had been implicated in the trial of the followers of Nechaev, was to deal with Trepov. They waited until the "big trial" was over so as not to prejudice its outcome, but the very next morning they presented themselves in the waiting rooms of the two officials. Kolenkina, in spite of a big bribe to the servant, was not admitted, but Vera Zasulich was. She was wearing a long, voluminous cloak—it was a cold January morning—and after stating her business (she asked for a permit to become a domestic teacher), she fired a revolver at Trepov from under her cloak and wounded him. [6]

Vera Zasulich was tried by jury at the main Criminal Court of St. Petersburg on 31 March 1878. The presiding judge was the famous jurist and legal reformer, Anatoly Koni; counsel for the defence was the able Alexandrov; the prosecutor was the colourless bureaucrat Kessel. The public was admitted by ticket only, and these had been issued mainly to high officials, senators, and social-ites who had "pulled strings" to get in; Dostoyevsky was also there.[7] Most of the spectators were sensation seekers. For weeks past the attempt on the life of General Trepov had been the main topic of town gossip, and though Vera Zasulich was talked of in the salons as "that vile woman" and "that paramour of Bogolyu-bov,"[8] she was also described as beautiful, a *femme fatale.**

The court room was packed. The defendant, pale and *plain* Vera Zasulich, spinster, noblewoman, twenty-eight years of age, was accused of shooting and wounding General Trepov with intent to kill. The general was not present at the trial and sent a medical certificate to the effect that he was too ill to attend—though he could be seen every day driving down the Nevsky Prospect![10]

The defendant admitted that she shot General Trepov but stressed that it did not matter to her whether she killed or only wounded him. She wanted to avenge Bogolyubov, whom *she did not personally know* (my italics).[11] But she had heard about him:

I had heard that . . . Bogolyubov was flogged until he stopped groaning . . . that soldiers broke into the cells and dragged the protesting prisoners into the punishment cells. . . . Furthermore among those imprisoned at that time in the House of Preliminary Detention many had already been in prison for three or three and a half years, many had become insane or killed themselves. . . . All this seemed to me to be not punishment but outrage . . . it seemed to me that such things should not be suffered to pass without conse-quences. I decided that even at the price of my own ruin I had to demonstrate that such degradation of human personality should not be allowed to be inflicted with impunity. . . . I could find no other way of drawing attention to what had happened. . . . *It is a terri-ble thing to lift a hand against a human being* [my italics], but I felt I had to do it . . . I fired without aiming. . . . [She had then im-

---

* "High society" invariably embellished political and terrorist acts with titillating detail. At the time of the "trial of the 193" the gossips had it that the defendants, crowded together on narrow benches, had sexual intercourse with each other through-out the hearings;[9] and later on, society ladies fought for convenient places for their carriages, from which to watch public executions.

mediately thrown the revolver down] I was afraid it might go off again. . . . I did not want this.* [12]

Vera Zasulich then gave a short history of her life. She had been educated at a *pensionat* in Moscow, and left at the age of seventeen with the certificate of a domestic teacher. For some time she had worked as a clerk in the provinces, and in 1868 she came with her widowed mother to St. Petersburg, where she attended a training school for teachers. It was there that she met Nechaev. She was not attracted by his theories but allowed him to use her address for correspondence from abroad. She was arrested in connection with his case in 1869 and from then on until 1875 she was given no peace. When first arrested she spent almost two years in solitary confinement, interrogated from time to time, but not told what she was arrested for. Released, she was almost at once re-arrested and sent into exile—without money, in just the clothes she was wearing, and without being able to notify her relatives. Nor was she left for long in the same place but was constantly shifted from one to another. She was brought back to St. Petersburg to appear as a witness in the trial of Nechaev's followers, and then again exiled— first to Tver and then to Kharkov, where she took a course in midwifery but could find no job. Finally, after six years, residential restrictions were removed and she again went to St. Petersburg and then to Penza in search of work. Throughout that time her mother, who was financially dependent on her, was practically destitute.

The testimony of General Trepov, in the form of a written document, contained such flights of fancy as, for instance: "Kurneyev had to grapple with her, she was going to shoot again!" [13] Major Kurneyev, a subordinate of the general, was in fact the man who, on his master's orders, had had Bogolyubov flogged and had later given to the investigating commission a completely distorted account of the incident.

---

* According to Vladimir Dubrovin, an officer and revolutionary, hanged in 1879, Vera Zasulich's revolver was an obsolete and inferior model; most of the terrorists, he says, knew next to nothing about fire-arms and most of their failures were due to ignorance and inexperience. (Bogucharsky, V. (3), pp. 473–474.)

The prosecutor's speech was uninspired and unconvincing, while that of the counsel for the defence was brilliant. He recapitulated the defendant's life story, which, he said, was typical of the harassment and humiliation to which perfectly innocent and decent young people were subjected; he stressed that the sympathy the defendant felt for the stranger Bogolyubov sprang from her own experiences—she, too, had known the deep despair induced by prolonged solitary confinement and the degradation of being bullied by an insolent investigator. The speech was not only eloquent but also very clever: it turned the defence of Vera Zasulich into an indictment of General Trepov, so that it seemed that it was he who was standing in the dock. This illusion was so strong that when the jury acquitted Vera Zasulich, it was generally understood to be a condemnation of Trepov and his police.

Such were the bare facts, but luckily we know much more about the background of this trial than about any of the preceding ones, owing to the fact that Anatoly Koni, the presiding judge, left extensive memoirs that offer a unique insight into the legal and political atmosphere of the times. Koni belonged to that generation of liberals who in the early days of Alexander II's reign sincerely hoped for drastic changes in Russian life; in particular, he belonged to that band of enlightened and erudite jurists who rightly considered that a basic precondition for any such changes was the introduction and the enforcement of a firm legal system. Russia was lucky in possessing several outstanding jurists who prepared the legal reform of 1864. This splendid reform incorporated all the best aspects of European jurisprudence, but it proved much too advanced for Russia. No legal system can function properly where there is no proper understanding of legality, of legal rights and duties, or where the concept of equality before the law is unknown. In Russia, lawlessness from above, from the tsar down, had permeated the entire fabric of public life. Neither the chief of police nor the factory owner nor the poor and the powerless could be made to understand that under law they had equal rights, and no more; and that when these rights were violated, they could be asserted.

One of the innovations of the legal reform was trial by jury, and the law reformers were particularly keen on it because they hoped that such trials would educate the public in legal matters. For that reason Koni and others of his mind had urged that it should be applied in the Zasulich case. But the ministry of justice, like the procurator's office, was populated with bureaucrats of the old school, hostile to the reform and incapable of understanding the legal implications of this new kind of trial. Since it was fashionable to profess liberalism—the tsar himself had started the fashion—Count Pahlen enthusiastically backed Koni's suggestion. At the same time he was confident that he could manipulate this trial as he had others, and he undoubtedly promised the tsar that the jury would condemn Zasulich. His rage at the acquittal was almost comical: "Why didn't he [Koni] suppress the jury's verdict! . . . Having read it, he should have picked up the inkstand as if by mistake for the sand, and poured it all over the paper." [14] Pahlen lost his job over the Zasulich trial—deservedly so, but for the wrong reasons.

The procurator's office was no better. When two of the procurators of the St. Petersburg district had refused to prosecute because they were told not to discuss the role played by Trepov, they were heavily penalized: one was forced to resign altogether, and the other was transferred to a small provincial court.[15] The job was then given to Kessel, a yes-man. Legal bureaucrats of the old school just could not understand how the new law functioned, and the same was true of the senators, from among whom judges for political trials were picked. Koni records the following conversation with one of them, involved in the "trial of the 50":

"So glad to meet you, Koni, I wanted a bit of advice. . . . Things are not going well at the trial. . . . What are we to do— there is absolutely no evidence against some. . . . What are we to do?"

"Well, if there is no evidence, you must acquit!"

"No, seriously, I am not joking, what must we do?"

"My answer is not meant as a joke," Koni exploded. "Your Excellency, you—a senator, a judge, how dare you ask me such a

question? . . . There can only be one answer—acquit!"
"But what will Count Pahlen say?" [16]

Such men of straw were the pillars of Russian justice even after the reform.

General Trepov was in fact hardly worse than his superiors. It is true that he was almost illiterate and had made a fortune from the bribes he accepted. Yet when he ordered a political prisoner to be flogged he was reflecting the outlook that prevailed at Court and in the highest circles. Koni records that during the winter of 1876–77, there was, in the salons, an orgy of demands for the reintroduction of flogging of political offenders, men or women. Faced with the unexpected spread of revolutionary agitation, few, it would seem, could think of any better remedy than flogging, and few could be bothered to look for the deeper reasons of discontent among the young. When the situation was discussed at the ministry of justice, Koni suggested changes in the school curriculum—more Russian history and less Latin and Greek. He also argued that improving the situation of the peasants and the administration of the law would win the sympathy of the young. But nobody was interested in winning the sympathy of the young.[17] Count Pahlen, unoriginal to the end, proposed to give school authorities the right to flog pupils for propagating revolutionary ideas, thus proving Nikitenko right, who had written: "The most dangerous enemies within our country are . . . statesmen, who turn people into nihilists and cause indignation and revulsion against the government." [18]

The acquittal of Vera Zasulich created a sensation. There is no doubt that the impassioned speech of her counsel and the impartial summing up by Koni—he had impressed upon the jurors that they must consider themselves as "the conscience of society" [19]—had altered the climate of opinion within the court. Dostoyevsky spoke for the majority, it would seem, when he said that "to punish this young woman would be inappropriate and superfluous." [20] He was afraid that she would be made into a heroine; others already saw her as one. The court room exploded into shouts of "Bravo!" even before the foreman of the jury had finished reading the verdict.

People cried and laughed, crossed themselves and embraced each other. Outside, the huge crowd that had been waiting for the result went wild with joy. When the defence counsel, Alexandrov, appeared on the front steps, he received an ovation, was lifted shoulder high and carried off in triumph. Probably only two people felt deflated: Koni and the defendant. Koni considered the verdict juridically wrong—one could *morally* excuse the act but could not *legally* condone it—and he would have preferred one of "guilty of wounding . . . without intent to kill." [21] This would have made it possible to pass a light sentence; as it was, he foresaw a lot of trouble ahead for himself and for his cherished trial by jury. While one of the spectators at the trial said to him: "This is the happiest day of my life," Koni's reaction was: "It might yet turn out to be a fatal day!" [22] He meant that the repercussions of that verdict could endanger the institution of trial by jury and even the entire structure of the new justice, and he was not far wrong. As for Vera Zasulich, she had expected to be executed "after the comedy of the trial was over" [23] and had inwardly so completely prepared herself for death that she felt almost let down. It took her a long time to readjust.

Koni was convinced that to let Vera Zasulich step out a free woman through the front door of the court would cause a public demonstration, and this in turn would inevitably lead to clashes with the police. To avoid this he sent her back to the Predvorilka to collect her belongings, and gave orders that she should then be released through a side gate where the crowd would not expect her. His carefully thought-out plan was frustrated, however, by Trepov's underlings, who were eager for a confrontation with the crowd. Immediately after the announcement of the verdict, an order signed by the tsar had gone out to re-arrest Vera Zasulich, and the police obviously intended to do so in full view of the crowd so as to provoke disturbances which it would then have the pleasure of suppressing. In any case Koni's orders were not obeyed: Vera Zasulich was allowed to leave prison through the main gate, which was next to the courthouse, and was enthusiastically received by the waiting crowd. But her supporters either already knew of the plans for her arrest or else simply mistrusted police intentions. She was whisked away in a carriage, the police gave chase, the crowd helped the carriage to get away, and there was a street battle, with one dead and several wounded, and many more arrested. On balance, nevertheless, the episode must count as a humiliating defeat for the police—the defendant had got away, was kept safely hidden for a time, and then smuggled abroad by her friends.

But Koni was left to face the full blast of indignation and resentment "in high places." A special meeting of ministers, presided over by the tsar himself, branded him as the main culprit for the acquittal; and he and his two fellow judges were hauled before the senate and severely reprimanded, without being given a chance to speak in their own defence. It was even suggested that Koni should stand trial. Pressure was put upon him to resign his chair at the Law School and his position as the presiding judge of the district criminal court of St. Petersburg. He resigned his chair, thus losing a considerable part of his income; but he would not resign as a judge, in spite of the fact that the tsar himself wished him to do so. The irremovability of judges was one of the most important, most basic tenets of the legal reform, and Koni would not surrender it. He continued as judge for another three years, disregarding the tsar's displeasure and the malicious intrigues that surrounded him on all sides. He was practically ostracized by society. Seeing him at the memorial service for a senator, a society lady exclaimed: "How dare he show his face in church, after acquitting Zasulich and accusing poor Trepov!" [24] The exclusive English Club decided that the increase in revolutionary feelings was due to the new-fangled courts—and who but Koni was to blame for them? A lesser man would no doubt have been broken in a short time, and indeed Koni wrote to a fellow lawyer that he would gladly quit his job if he were not afraid that the whole trial procedure would then fall into what he called "unclean hands." [25] But he was a strong man, he persevered, earned for himself the approval of the new minister of justice, and eventually became procurator, senator, and member of the state council.

Throughout this time the general public behaved in its characteristically ambivalent manner. At first everybody, from old courtiers to university professors and writers, both conservative and liberal, was delighted with what was felt to be the first manifestation in Russia of a truly civilized, European-style legality, and the victory of public conscience over the lawless authorities. But soon people began to be afraid of their own courage—after all, the tsar had shown his support for Trepov by visiting him the day after the shooting, and had later expressed his disapproval of the verdict and of Koni. It was rather intoxicating to hail all this modern legality, but where would it lead, how far would it go? Conservatives were the first to recover, the liberals wavered for a little longer, but soon Russian society as a whole regained its usual uneasy equilibrium, sympathizing with new ideas while being subservient to the old. In spite of the gallant stand of its defenders the legal reform was systematically attacked from above and practically destroyed towards the end of the century.

The Zasulich case thus provided an outstanding example of what Koni's friend, the enlightened jurist Boris Chicherin, called "the outrageous inconsistency in Russian life—that is, legality and reformed jurisprudence in principle and complete illegality and arbitrariness of the police and the administration in practice." [26] The government was the most inconsistent of all in that it had no firm will and no clear thinking; it had no moral authority either. No wonder that Russian society had lost all sense of direction.

11
PRISON
AND
EXILE

The arrests that began in 1873, and the subsequent trials in 1877 and 1878, represented the first mass exercise of tsarist terror since the suppression of the Decembrists, and it involved much bigger numbers. Again it effectively stifled a whole generation of educated Russians and caused untold suffering to their families and friends. The poet Nekrasov dedicated a poem to the participants of the "trial of the 50," in which he spoke of them as if they were dead:

> Silenced they lie on the field of honour,
> silenced are their lonely voices
> raised for the suffering people. . . .[1]

155

And "buried alive" and "dying a slow death" were other ways in which their contemporaries spoke of those condemned in the trials. And indeed none of them could have much hope of a return to normal life. If insanity or death did not claim them, they would be settled permanently in Siberian exile after their term of hard labour had expired, or shifted from one place of exile to another, and ever after kept under constant police supervision. Very few managed to escape and fewer still were able to resume their former activities.

Tsarist terror was much more amateurish and haphazard than that of the Soviet secret police, and torture was not generally applied (though it was suspected in a few cases). But in some respects it was almost as bad. For instance political prisoners were often put in chains; they might even be chained to wheelbarrows when working in the mines; some of them were kept in solitary confinement for up to twenty-five years or for life. Moreover—and here indeed there is a parallel—the innocent were as liable to be punished as the guilty. It was for good reasons that the tsarist secret police was feared and hated by Russians of all classes.

The sufferings of the condemned men and women before, during, and after the trials of 1877–78 have been described by themselves in the numerous memoirs that have survived, and by several observers. The picture that emerges is sad enough. After years of pretrial detention they had to wait many more dreary months after the trials, before being transported to the "distant and not so distant" places specified in their sentences. The first to be moved were those sentenced to *katorga*. This term could mean hard labour in the gold and silver mines of eastern Siberia; or solitary confinement in fortresses such as Peter and Paul and Shlüsselburg, or the new prisons in the Kharkov area.

It was in the latter that first Alexander Tsitsianov, Ivan Dzhabadari and Pyotr Alexeev and then Myshkin, Voynaralsky, Rogachev, Muravsky and others were incarcerated for many years. The conditions in these prisons were so harsh [2] that for criminal offenders, but seemingly not for political ones, each year was counted as two; and so unhealthy that a high percentage of inmates died of scurvy and other diseases. The prisoners were kept in shackles day and night; the solitary cells were dark and dank; books and paper, visitors and correspondence were all forbidden; and for the least complaint or protest the prisoners were severely beaten and then thrown into punishment cells. When eventually a government inspector was sent to investigate the reasons for the high number of dead and insane in these prisons—six political prisoners, including Muravsky, died there—he reported that the prisons were unfit for human habitation. After several years spent there, the political prisoners were transferred to the *katorga* prisons in eastern Siberia, where most of their comrades already were.

The authorities were extremely nervous about attempts to free the condemned men as they were transported from St. Petersburg, and they took all possible precautions. Such attempts were indeed made but all were foiled by the vigilance of the police. The prisoners were practically smuggled out of town and driven away at dawn in *troikas* under strong guard, chained hand and foot, and sometimes even chained to the side of the carriage.

The first woman political prisoner to be sent to *katorga* in Siberia was our old friend Katerina Breshkovskaya. Several other women had been sentenced to *katorga*, for instance Sofya Bardina and Olga Lyubatovich, but their sentences had been converted to terms of exile. Breshkovskaya was obviously considered to be a particularly hardened state criminal and her sentence was allowed to stand. She made the journey [3] in a party of ten to fifteen fellow convicts, among whom she mentions the Chaykovists Shishko, Sinegub, and Charushin. The wives of the latter two, Larissa Chemodanova and Anna Kuvshinskaya, had been politically active themselves, but had been acquitted in the big trial and were claiming now the privilege of following their husbands to Siberia voluntarily. These "free wives," so called, were transported at the expense of the government provided they submitted to the same rules and restrictions as the convicts themselves. Breshkovskaya noticed that the authorities were often particularly vindictive towards the relatives of the convicts—thus the mother and sister of Timofey Kvyatkovsky, who had come all the way to Tomsk in order to see him, were allowed a bare half-hour of visiting time.

Breshkovskaya's party left St. Petersburg in July 1878 and travelled first by rail to Nizhny Novgorod and then by convict barge to Kazan and Perm. These barges, several of which were usually drawn by one steamer, resembled nothing so much as huge floating animal cages, the decks being thickly covered with close wire netting. Inside, the barges were divided into several large sleeping quarters where criminals and politicals, men, women, and children, were all herded together. They were unventilated, overcrowded, and filthy. There was sometimes, but very rarely, a special deck space reserved for the nobility, but it was almost as sordid and dirty and contained no washing facilities. In fact Breshkovskaya's party had their first wash in over two months in the Krasnoyarsk prison in Siberia; and as usual a gendarme was present when the women washed themselves in the bath house.

From Perm the party travelled by *troika* to Tyumen and thence again by convict barge to Tomsk, 2,700 miles from St. Petersburg. On the overland journey all convicts and exiles, political and criminal, had to spend the nights at the so-called *étapes,* or rest houses. These *étapes* consisted of a few primitive barracks surrounded by a stockade—one barrack for the guards and one or more for the prisoners. The unheated and unventilated barracks were locked up for the night and the prisoners left to find a place for themselves either on the raised wooden platforms or on the dirty floor. There were no blankets or pillows, the windows were permanently nailed up and the air foul with the sweat of bodies, fumes of cheap vodka, and the stench of the lavatory pail. The language of the criminal convicts was foul, too; and fights, often with knives, alternated with sexual orgies. The guards tolerated anything for a bribe, and indeed expected one for anything and everything, even for starting the convict party off in the mornings. There was no provision for cooking food or even for boiling water, though some of the convoy soldiers would sell jugs of hot water and procure illicit vodka—at a price! Food was not supplied by the authorities; instead each convict received several kopeks per day, which was barely enough to keep body and soul together. Usually, local peasant women came to the

Exiles marching through the snow (The Mansell Collection)

gates to sell black rye bread, hard-boiled eggs, cold cooked meat, or pies to the prisoners.

Katerina Breshkovskaya's party reached Tomsk after almost two months and still they had covered only two-thirds of their journey. They travelled on to Irkutsk, capital of eastern Siberia, and thence to the mining centre of Kara, where they arrived in September. Breshkovskaya—though she had deliberately trained herself to bear physical hardship—found the journey almost unbearable. Even the drive in the *troika*—a great innovation and privilege, since the Decembrists were made to walk all the way to eastern Siberia and criminal convicts continued to do so—soon became an agonizing torture: the unsprung, unpadded horse carriage bumped and jolted over the bad roads and the gendarmes seated on both sides of the prisoner practically smothered their charge between them, while their boots and rifles inflicted heavy bruises on shins and arms. The American George Kennan (whose journey to Siberia I shall describe later on) was travelling in his own well-sprung, well-padded carriage and had no gendarmes as companions, yet he, too, complained that the jolts gave "incessant shocks to the spinal cord and the brain," [4] making the journey almost unendurable.

Throughout the journey several prisoners in Breshkovskaya's party—Shishko, Charushin, and the anarchist Sazhin—were kept in hand and foot irons by special order from the tsar. By law noblemen were not put in irons until they reached their ultimate place of *katorga*, but the tsar disregarded the law. And his order was so strictly observed that the irons were not removed from Charushin even when he fell ill with typhus. Nor was a doctor called for him, and he was forced to travel on with the rest of the party, until eventually he was left behind in a hospital. But at least his wife was allowed to stay with him, and her nursing no doubt saved his life.

Vladimir Korolenko, on his way to exile in Siberia in 1881, witnessed [5] in Perm the arrival of a specially important convict barge—it carried the survivors of the famous trials, from the Kharkov prisons to Kara. They were to be put aboard the train to Yekaterinburg (the railways did not yet extend farther into Siberia), which was leaving at 8 o'clock in the evening. Shortly before its departure, a double file of armed guards stationed itself all the way from the quay to the platform, and soon the melancholy din of chains was heard and the weary and pale figures emerged from the bowels of the barges. Korolenko recognized Dzhabadari, Pyotr Alexeev, Tsitsianov, Lydia Figner, Zdanovich, Dmitry Rogachev and Vera Rogachova, Myshkin, and others. Soon afterwards he was to meet the same party and several others in the comparative "comfort" of the Irkutsk transit prison, where they had to spend quite a long time before being dispersed to their various final destinations. Here the cell doors were kept open by day, the prisoners were allowed to move about and to talk to each other, and even to congregate in the prison hall on special occasions. This unexpected freedom went to their heads to such an extent that when they were assembled in the hall for the funeral of their elected elder, Myshkin felt inspired to make an oration. When this was reported to higher authorities, he received fifteen additional years of *katorga*. He reflected bitterly that he had only made two speeches in his whole life and that the first had cost him ten and the second fifteen years of hard labour.[6]

For political convicts the journey ended at the mines of Trans-Baikalia.[7] Nothing could be more depressing. The gloomy valleys were hemmed in by bare mountain ridges, there was not a tree in sight, and the earth was black with the dross of the mines. Originally Nerchinsk and Akatuy had been the main centres of mining. The Decembrists had worked there, as well as some 7,000 out of the 19,000 Poles sent to Siberia after their risings. But at the time of our story, it was to Kara that political convicts were sent.

All mines belonged to the tsars (though some were sold by them to private individuals) and all labour employed at the mines was convict labour. The mining methods were extremely primitive and unsafe; when dynamite was used, it was handled so inexpertly that convicts were often injured. The walls of the mines dripped with water and the wooden supports were rotten with age. Convicts were lodged in prisons for half their term of *katorga*, after which they were allowed to live in the so-called "free commands" or "free settlements"[8] before being moved for the rest of their lives to some other part of Siberia. Mothers, sisters, wives, and children who had followed convicts to Siberia also lived in the free settlements. These were shantytowns clustering around the prisons and composed of barely habitable shacks and huts with leaking roofs and broken windows. The authorities did nothing to repair them and the majority of the convicts cared little how or where they lived, as they were later moved elsewhere in any case.

And there was always a hope of escape. In spite of the presence of troops, the isolation of the settlements, and the dangers of the surrounding mountains and forests, great numbers of convicts did try to escape each spring,[9] and it was estimated that each year in the whole of Siberia as many as 30,000 succeeded. Sometimes they remained unreported for a considerable time, while the dishonest prison officers continued to draw and resell the escaped men's rations; but in the end they were always recaptured, unless they had already perished in the wild. And still, though the punishment for escaping was flogging and four additional years of *katorga*, each spring the call of "General Cuckoo" proved irresistible. All the powers of passion and imagination left in the wretched convict centred on his dream of freedom, and some of the most haunting and beautiful Russian folksongs are those of the convict escaping from the Siberian mines.

The prison complex of Kara (the Tartar word for black) stretched for some twenty miles and comprised seven or eight separate prisons, each with its free settlement. Two of the newer prisons were for political convicts, one for men and the other for women.[10] The officer of the gendarmes in command of the political prisons was particularly unsympathetic, and by his orders several men were kept day and night in foot irons. At first, when the men were taken out daily to work in the mines with the criminals, he also had some of them chained to their wheelbarrows. Fortunately the officer in command of the whole district, Colonel Kononovich, was a humane and decent man who made all kinds of concessions to political prisoners. He had a sick bay and a fairly good library installed in the men's prison and arranged for the men to be exercised every day in the prison yard or to work in small carpentry and cobbling workshops. Prisoners were allowed to wear their own clothing, which was particularly pleasing to the women, and above all to write and to receive letters, parcels, and money from relatives. In spite of the great delay in getting news from home, the link with their families was the most cherished of all privileges. Colonel Kononovich was also very good to the wives of the political convicts living in the free settlements, and he allowed Katerina Breshkovskaya to live there until the women's prison had been opened.

However, the benevolent colonel was eventually dismissed and political convicts in the Kara were deprived of most of their privileges, including correspondence. They were no longer to work in the mines—many of them had liked it as a respite from their cells—

but were kept permanently in prison and in chains. Those already transferred to free settlements were returned to prison. Living in the derelict shacks on very little money and food—one had to queue up for it every morning at the prison gates—had been miserable enough, but a return to the cells seemed so unbearable that two of the prisoners killed themselves.

Henceforth the desire to escape, which was strong at all times, became an absolute obsession with most prisoners. It was "freedom or death" from now on. Some indeed had always been determined to escape at the first opportunity. Katerina Breshkovskaya and Ipolit Myshkin were perhaps the most persistent among them. Myshkin had even tried to break out of the impregnable prison near Kharkov, but failed. Breshkovskaya all but succeeded in escaping from the Predvorilka in St. Petersburg. She never gave up hope— indeed she wrote later that it was only that hope that sustained her in her sixteen years in Siberia. She saw a chance in 1880,[11] when she was moved from Kara to Bargusin, on the east shore of Lake Baikal. There she persuaded three young and energetic political exiles to flee with her. Their attempt seemed to succeed at first but the complexities of the mountainous and perilous terrain and their ignorance of the old tribal paths led to their recapture. The three young men were administrative exiles and were punished by being moved to remote native hamlets in the Yakutsk region. But Breshkovskaya was a convict and the usual punishment for convicts was forty lashes and four years of *katorga*—and to that she was promptly sentenced. Her sentence had to be confirmed in St. Petersburg, however, and for nine anxious months she waited in jail; in the end flogging was cancelled, probably because of the uproar that would certainly have broken out among other politicals.

In the spring of 1882 eight men at last succeeded in breaking out of the Kara prison, but were all recaptured and brought back.[12] Myshkin with his companion got farthest away and was arrested as he was about to board a steamer to America in Vladivostok. The retribution was swift and terrible. Some 300 to 400 Cossacks rushed into the men's prison in the middle of the night of 11 May, dragged the prisoners from their bunks, stripped them of their outer clothing, and drove them, with the help of rifle butts, some ten miles to neighbouring criminal prisons. They were given no food and on arrival were put into punishment cells. These so-called "secret" cells were small and dark with floors of stone, with the inevitable "pail" as the only furniture. In these cells the prisoners were kept for two whole months, on black bread and water only, with a very occasional thin prison soup. In the end some were nearly dead. The wives living in the free settlement were not allowed to see their husbands, and anxiety over their fate drove one of them, Vera Rogacheva, to suicide. Women prisoners were also made to pay for the men's escapes, though they had known nothing about them. One day gendarmes invaded their cells and ordered them to take off their clothes—they had been wearing their own dresses—and put on prison clothing. When they demurred and asked for the reasons for this order they were forcibly stripped and beaten with rifle butts. In protest one of them, Sofya Leshern von Hertsfeld, tried to kill herself.

After two months those of the men who had tried to escape and several others were taken to St. Petersburg and incarcerated in the island fortress of Shlüsselburg. Myshkin, realizing that no escape was possible from there, made a bid for another kind of freedom: he deliberately insulted the prison governor and was executed in the old yard of the fortress.

The men who remained in Kara were eventually returned to their own political prison. They found it much changed: the cells had been made smaller, tables and benches and all bedding had been removed, and books and correspondence no longer allowed. The prisoners were warned that they would be flogged at the least sign of disobedience. As we know, there was quite a tradition of protest against corporal punishment among Russian revolutionaries and this time, too, the reaction to the warning was immediate—the prisoners went on a hunger strike. After thirteen days the prison governor gave in and withdrew his warning.

Meanwhile there was a tragic little sequel to the "pogrom of May 11th." A young woman revolutionary, Maria Kutitonskaya, who had already finished her term at Kara and had been settled in a small village some distance away, escaped from it and made her way to Chita, where she shot and wounded the governor of Trans-Baikalia in revenge for the pogrom. She was twenty-four years old and pregnant at the time. She was tried and sentenced to death by hanging, but the sentence was commuted to *katorga* for life; her child was born dead in prison.

During the reign of the next tsar, Alexander III, conditions in the Russian *katorga* and in exile grew steadily worse. A circular of 1888 abolished all distinctions between criminal and political convicts, as a result of which two male political prisoners were flogged on Sakhalin, the new island penal settlement in the Far East. And in November 1889, Nadezhda Sigida,[13] a young woman political prisoner, a noblewoman, was flogged at Kara; she received a hundred lashes and died a few days later. The whole women's prison was in revolt and three women poisoned themselves. Five days later, when the news reached the men, twenty of them also took poison in protest, but only two died, owing to the fact that the poison had deteriorated.

Personal reminiscences apart, by far the fullest and fairest account of prison, exile and *katorga* conditions in Siberia came from a complete outsider. An American writer and lecturer, George Kennan—a relative of the distinguished diplomat and writer of to-day—came to Russia in May 1885, that is, at a time when most of those sentenced in the trials of 1877–78 were still serving their sentences. Accompanied by his artist friend George A. Frost, he came on a fact-finding assignment for *Century Magazine*. (His dispatches were first serialized in *Century Magazine* and later came out in book form.) Both men had been to Russia before and spoke good Russian. Kennan arrived, by his own admission, with a strong prejudice against the revolutionaries; in his lectures in America he had referred to them as "unreasonable and wrongheaded fanatics".[14] But he was prepared, with rare impartiality and thoroughness, to investigate and see both sides of the question. He intended to travel all the way to the farthest corners of eastern Siberia to see for himself the conditions under which political convicts and exiles were living and to hear their story from their own lips if possible. He also interviewed the officials, many of whom, he noticed, "manifested a disinclination [to give information] or made . . . transparent and preposterous attempts to deceive" [15] him; read many official reports and statistical data on the prison and exile administration; and even studied pertinent parts of the Russian legal code.

He found that there was an almost willful lack of an overall system of prison and exile administration and almost no control from above. Some prisons were crumbling, others were brand new; but all were overcrowded and extremely insanitary; and hardly any had a hospital attached. One of the most important Siberian transit prisons, at Tyumen,[16] was meant to hold 850 prisoners but there were actually 1,741 on the day Kennan visited it. In its unventilated overcrowded cells the air was foul to the point of nausea. About 300 prisoners were said to die there annually, mainly from typhus. Convicts were issued with one coarse linen shirt every six months, and every twelve months with one coarse linen caftan or coat with a black or yellow diamond-shaped patch on the back. All prison garments deteriorated very rapidly because they were of very poor quality and because the prisoners wore them day and night. When prisoners were taken to the communal bath house, they had to wash their clothes at the same time as themselves and put them on again all wet.[17] Prison buildings, food, and clothes were all of the poorest quality because the state money allocated for their purchase or repair always found its way into the pockets of officials or contractors.[18] And no wonder—prison officers and warders were miserably paid and all took bribes. Prison governors were also often corrupt and ready to bend the law to their own advantage. Though both Kennan and Korolenko met with a few decent and humane administrators, these usually did not last long in their posts. Kennan came across some who warned him that official statistics were often "cooked," [19] and others who expressed sympathy with political exiles and tried to help them. One of them said that "these were men and women who under other circumstances might have rendered valuable service to their country." [20]

The state of Siberian prisons was well known to the tsars, for from time to time they received quite accurate official reports. George Kennan quotes at length from the two reports submitted to Alexander II in 1880 and to Alexander III in 1882 by the Governor General of eastern Siberia, Anuchin. The Governor reported that with the exception of two new ones all the prisons were in a "lamentable condition." [21] The *étapes* and some transit prisons were tumble-down buildings, freezing cold in winter and stifling hot in summer and at all times "saturated with miasma." [22] From the point of view of the state, the prisons were too easy to escape from and the *étape* system too costly even though the convicts were starved and died off like flies. On arrival at the mines the convicts were too weak to work. The political convicts usually arrived in such poor health that they, too, had to be kept idle in local prisons. Years of solitary confinement had reduced many of them to physical and mental wrecks and further detention in prison resulted in frequent suicides and outbreaks of insanity. The insane had to be kept together with the sane, as there were no mental hospitals in Siberia.

The reports also dealt, very realistically, with the dilemma of those political prisoners who, after finishing their term of *katorga,* were settled in various remote parts of eastern Siberia. In most of these places they could find no work and had to subsist on the official allowance, which was quite insufficient for survival. It was doubtful, the Governor pointed out with rare acumen, whether these state criminals had been "brought to their senses" [23] by the harsh punishment they had suffered—if anything they had become more obdurate. And not infrequently these settlers exercised a highly dangerous political influence on the local population. Thus it had to be admitted that the government, at great expense to itself, was helping to spread "anarchistic" [24] ideas in remote places where they had not penetrated before. The reports must have made depressing reading, as the tsar scribbled on the margin: "a sad but familiar picture! . . ." [25] but nothing was done to improve matters.

Kennan's itinerary largely coincided with the notorious Great Road to Siberia, which stretched for 3,000 miles from the Urals eastwards and along which countless convicts had walked to *katorga*. Kennan was told that in the years between 1878 and 1885 no less than 170,000 had done so. By far the greater part of these were not criminals in the usual sense of the word, but peasants whom the village *mir* or the rural police wanted to get rid of.[26] Winter and summer, across endless flat deserts and over mountains and swamps, the walking parties of convicts could be seen slowly trudging along the Great Road. In summer they could be dimly discerned from afar as an enormous, barely moving cloud of dust; next one would hear the melancholy clanging of chains; and nearer still, some 200 or 300 men in long shapeless grey coats would be seen shuffling along in their heavy leg irons, flanked by armed guards. Behind them walked a hundred or more women and children. Last of all came some twenty *telegas*—that is, open one-horse carts, which carried luggage and the very sick or the very young of the party. To be jolted about on these *telegas* was so painful that most of the sick preferred to "die on their feet."

The walking parties could make approximately 1,000 miles in three months; it took them sixteen months to get to Yakutsk province. Every third night the convoy was changed while the party rested, for twenty-four hours, at an *étape*; other nights were spent at the so-called *semi-étapes*, which were even more primitive. The convicts set off on their day's march without breakfast, and no supper or hot drink awaited them at night, even when they came in drenched from snow or rain. Instead there were two breaks during the day, when they halted by the roadside and ate the food that they had purchased from the peasant women. But often when a village was sighted, the walking party stopped and its elected elder asked the convoy officer for permission to sing for alms. Permission granted, the column shuffled forward again and intoned a mournful dirge (called in Russian *miloserdnaya*—a song to please the heart), that once heard was sure to haunt one for the rest of one's days. A mixture of chanting and wailing, "like a crude fugue," it struck Kennan as being "a half-articulate expression of all the grief, the misery, and the despair that had been felt by generations of human beings in the *étapes*, the prisons, and the mines." [27] A striking counterpart to that other great Russian "half-articulate" dirge—the song of the Volga boatmen.

Political prisoners and exiles also followed the Great Road to Siberia, though no longer on foot. They saw the walking parties churn up the mud, or raise the dust of the road. They saw them munch their scanty crusts of bread when resting at the side of the road, and heard them chanting their *miloserdnaya*. At night they shared their barracks at the *étapes*. What a panorama of human suffering and degradation! It was as if "abandon all hope" were hourly dinned in their ears as they were nearing their own ultimate hell.

Kennan succeeded, not without some difficulties, in reaching the silver and gold mines of Nerchinsk, Kara, Akatuy, and Algachi. He found the whole district unutterably dreary and gloomy. The mining village of Algachi appeared to him quite God-forsaken—the prison was falling down and was supported by rotting wooden planks. In the dark and dismal cells he noticed a continuous, broad, blood-red dado around the walls which turned out to consist of squashed bedbugs.[28]

At Kara, Kennan was shown the political prison for men but was not allowed to speak to the inmates. He was shown several criminal prisons and found them among the worst he had seen anywhere. There was a hospital attached to one of them where, he was told, more than a thousand had died in one year of illness and general debility. He was not allowed to visit the political prison for women but was told that it was tidier and less crowded but neither more sanitary nor more comfortable than the criminal prison for women; the latter, on inspection, turned out to stand over a swamp visible through the rotting floor-boards. Inside the free settlements Kennan managed to evade the strict supervision of the local authorities and to meet and talk to several political convicts and "free wives." He was particularly impressed by some of the women: Natalya Armfeld,[29] Anna Korba,[30] Katerina Breshkovskaya,[31] and others.

Outside the mining district Kennan was much less restricted and travelled throughout many parts of Siberia seeking out and, when possible, talking to exiles, including former convicts. Of the politi-

A prison in Kara (The Mansell Collection)

cal offenders the convicts formed the smallest group, those tried and sentenced to exile were more numerous, and those exiled without trial, by the administrative method, by far the biggest group. All exiles were at the mercy of the local police and administrators, who could deprive them of the right to work and earn, and subject them to all kinds of petty persecution and punishment. The rules governing the status and supervision of exiles were extremely vague and were generally disregarded. Thus the sore question of whether the state or the exiles paid for the return journey from Siberia—most exiles could not afford it—was never resolved and caused conflicts and mutinies right into the twentieth century. Those exiled to small villages or towns and to the native hamlets in the extreme north suffered most—both from isolation and from physical hardships. In the hamlets of the Yakutsk region of north-eastern Siberia, where winter is nine months long, exiles had to live in the same tents as the native tribesmen and their deer. But even in European Russia some places of exile were so remote and primitive that it was almost impossible to live and work there.

Exiles sent to larger towns were luckier. In Siberia there were several prosperous cities where interesting contacts and occupations could be found. On his journey Kennan was pleasantly surprised to find that Yekaterinburg possessed a museum of natural history, a society of friends of natural sciences, and two newspapers (though unfortunately news in Siberian newspapers was over three weeks old, since everything had to be submitted to the censor in Moscow before publication). Irkutsk was the capital of eastern Siberia and the residence of the governor general. It had a certain elegance and there were many official visitors, but exiles could not be happy under the stern eye of the authorities. They felt much freer in Minusinsk, a small town somewhat off the beaten track, which had a splendid museum of natural history, archeology, and ethnology. It had been founded by a local chemist in 1876 and expanded by political exiles, Alexander Kropotkin, Pyotr's brother, and Dmitry Klements among them.

There were many very rich people in Siberia—merchants and factory and mine owners—who built palatial mansions for themselves and laid out parks and greenhouses full of palms and orange trees and orchids.[32] These people were not averse to employing the exiles as tutors for their children and as accountants, engineers, and technical staff in their enterprises. But most exiles were less lucky and found it difficult to earn their living.

Exile by the administrative method, without trial or right to appeal, was abhorrent to all right-minded people in Russia and legal reformers tried repeatedly to abolish it. Their efforts proved futile and the method survived right up to 1917. It has a long and interesting history.[33] In the early part of the eighteenth century the right to send anyone belonging to the nonprivileged classes into exile, to confiscate his property, to have him tortured, branded, and flogged, had been invested in no less than twenty different types of persons:

governors and vice-governors of towns, military commanders, various ecclesiastical authorities, chief foresters, postmasters, stationmasters, masters of the mint, managers of state salt mines and many more. The right to exile or imprison noblemen belonged in principle to the tsar alone, but when all these rights were concentrated in the hands of the secret police, the endorsement by the tsar and, in the case of exile, the minister of justice became a pure formality. Anybody in Russia could be arrested without a warrant, kept in prison for up to two years, and then exiled, for from one to five and later ten years, by the simple stroke of a pen.[34]

Arrests were often made completely at random. Thus Korolenko records that during one of the periodical fits of police hysteria everybody by the name of Gordon or Kayransky was arrested in St. Petersburg; also everybody present at a private evening party, on suspicion that the guests were "dancing with some revolutionary purpose." [35] Long-haired students were the most usual targets of police persecution; they were often arrested in the streets for "presenting a suspicious appearance." [36] But quite ordinary and respectable citizens were also likely to be arrested and administratively exiled for no better reason than that they had been acquainted with "suspects." In fact the words "suspect, suspicious" were the key to it all: one could define the whole institution of administrative exile as punishment on suspicion. Most of the unfortunates were sent to some more or less remote parts of European Russia or the less remote parts of Siberia, where they remained under overt or secret police supervision. But it rarely stopped at that—irritated by petty chicanery and as often as not knowing themselves innocent to begin with, such exiles soon found themselves in some conflict with the local police, with the result that their term of exile was extended and/or they were moved farther east, usually to the desolate Yakutsk region.

Of the administrative exiles the Poles formed a truly colossal group, including a fair proportion of women. Bervi-Flerovsky wrote that he learned from the exiled Polish insurgents "how to die silently . . . without a moan," [37] but others found that they could also learn from them how to survive, to adapt themselves to even the most unpropitious surroundings, and earn a living as small traders or craftsmen. The Polish exiles also had a great intellectual influence on the local youth. Though the authorities kept them separated from the Russian population as far as possible and the Poles themselves were not keen on mixing with it either, their more civilized manners and way of life could not pass unnoticed. The fact that they were martyrs for the cause of freedom lent them an additional glamour. It was yet another example of how the Russian government, by its own policies and at its own expense, helped to spread those very same "pernicious" ideas which it was so afraid of.

Kennan found the whole system of prison and exile "a chaos of injustice, accident and caprice." [38] Though he was not allowed to talk to the inmates of prisons and met those outside by stealth, it was enough to change all his preconceived ideas. He realized that Russian revolutionaries were not the bloodthirsty monsters he had imagined but "ordinary men and women exasperated to the pitch of desperation" [39] by the suppression of free speech and free thought in their country. He was deeply moved by meeting some young women aged only seventeen or eighteen. He "experienced for the first time something like a feeling of contempt for the Russian government. . . . The idea that a powerful government like that of Russia could not protect itself from schoolgirls and Sunday-school teachers without tearing them away from their families and [sending them into] the middle of the great Asiatic desert seemed to me not only ludicrous but absolutely preposterous." [40]

Kennan found political exiles "intelligent, well-informed men and women . . . with warm affections, quick sympathies, generous impulses, and high standards of honour and duty." [41] In short, he thought them the cream of the nation and "not . . . lacking in the virtue and the patriotism that are essential to good citizenship. . . . If, instead of . . . serving their country, they are living in exile, it is . . . because the government, which assumes the right to think and act for the Russian people, is out of harmony with the spirit of the time." [42] He found it unbearable to think of them perishing slowly in the prisons and the hamlets of Siberia. He could not have given a better proof of his sympathy and friendship than by publishing his dispatches and, in 1891, his two-volume book *Siberia and the Exile System*.

TOWARDS TERRORISM 12

In the years before the big trials of 1877–78 St. Petersburg swarmed with the relatives of the detained men and women. Their presence cast a gloom over the city, as if there were sickness in its midst. Heart-broken parents, wives, and sweethearts thronged the offices of police and gendarmerie officials and the waiting rooms of ministers and other important personages. Some few parents succeeded in getting their sons and daughters off on parole and carried them away to their country homes, there to await their trial. The rest continued their petitions and enquiries, cold-shouldered by high officials and treated rudely by their subordi- **175** nates. As months stretched into years of pretrial detention, and as news of sickness and death, of suicide and insanity, filtered through from the prisons, relatives and friends became more and more desperate and their despair was echoed throughout Russia among the thousands of their acquaintances.

The revolutionaries, too, were like a stricken family. Those who had slipped through the police net drifted to St. Petersburg to be near their unlucky comrades in prison and to see who else was still free. They knew that it was risky to remain in St. Petersburg, under the very nose of the Third Section, and so they went "underground," living under assumed names and with false passports.

By 1876 that indefatigable organizer Mark Natanson, having escaped from his latest exile, began to gather all the remnants into one organization. The greatest possible secrecy was observed, so that Dmitry Klements nicknamed it the "society of troglodytes"— cave-dwellers. This nickname somehow became known to the police, which gave rise to the following curious report to the tsar: "Troglodyte was the name given in ancient times to wild Ethiopian tribes. . . . These tribes lived in herds. Women and children were shared. To-day in Africa, the name 'troglodytes' is given to races of chimpanzees, extremely intelligent and so well-trained that they can sometimes replace servants, but also extremely irritable, changing quickly from high spirits to ferocity." [1]

The new organization called itself Zemlya i Volya (Land and Freedom) after the short-lived group of 1862. It was formed under the shadow of the impending trials and its emotional involvement with the trials showed in all its activities. It materially supported the prisoners through the illegal Red Cross and planned their escapes—Kropotkin's successfully, and Kovalik's, Voynaralsky's, and Breshkovskaya's unsuccessfully. It organized street demonstrations at the funerals of those who had died in detention, and also on other occasions. The most dramatic was the demonstration in front of the Cathedral of Our Lady of Kazan, at which, as we have seen, the organization first announced its existence to the public.

It was a moment of crisis for populism. The "going to the people" and the "peaceful propaganda" campaigns had been defeated twice over—by the indifference, even hostility of the people and by the intervention of the police. Some populists were beginning to think that until there was freedom of speech, of press, and of assembly in Russia and until the arbitrariness of the police was curbed, no such campaigns could succeed. Thus the position was again reversed—just as the liberals were settling down to the performance of "small deeds" in the *zemstvo* and other civic movements, so the radicals were turning their thoughts to problems of political freedom.

At this stage, however, most populists were still secretly hoping that a dialogue with the tsar was possible. This was a hope salvaged from the early years of Alexander II's reign, and even from further back. Beneath all the revolutionary jargon, the age-old patriarchal bond with the tsar still held. When one reads the depositions of the imprisoned revolutionaries, their letters to the prosecutor, their addresses to the judges, and their speeches in court, one cannot escape the impression that they were still hoping for a reconciliation. And not only with the tsar but with the whole of Russian society. If only they were listened to, if their point of view, their motives, were understood—then, surely, they could all work together for the good of the country!

When at last the trials began, the savage sentences inflicted on the participants of the "Kazan demonstration," and endorsed by the tsar, came as a tremendous shock to the revolutionaries. But their spirits soared when the speeches of Sofya Bardina, Pyotr Alexeev, and Ipolit Myshkin won such admiration and sympathy throughout Russian society. There was further jubilation when the judges in the "trial of the 193" passed comparatively mild sentences and even released great numbers of the accused. The latter— "revenants from the dead"—were enthusiastically received by their friends and their rooms were crowded with well-wishers. We are told that as many as a hundred visitors called daily, transforming the premises into veritable revolutionary clubs.[2] The political climate again seemed favourable to change. Even the secret police seemed somewhat subdued. The only unknown factor was the attitude of the tsar himself.

The tsar soon made his position clear. With peevish disregard for public feeling, he refused to endorse the recommendations of the judges to reduce the sentences; in some cases he even increased them. By this act the tsar identified himself with the secret police. Thus he broke the link that still held the Russian revolutionaries to him; he also signed his own death-warrant.

The revolutionaries were left with a burning sense of injustice, and also with a deep craving for revenge. Revenge was the motive of Vera Zasulich's attempted assassination of Trepov in January 1878, and of Sergey Kravchinsky's successful assassination of the chief of gendarmes Mezentsev in August of the same year. These terrorist acts were a warning that the revolutionaries were resolved to defend their honour and human dignity.

In southern Russia a whole series of revenge killings of spies and informers and police officials was carried out. Based on the new concepts of "revolutionary justice" and "a life for a life," they were a spontaneous answer to mass arrests and trials and to the treatment of prisoners in detention. "As long as the present regime is based on the abuse of power by *individuals*, from the tsar down to the lowest watchman," wrote the secret journal *Zemlya i Volya*, ". . . we shall continue the most merciless fight against such individuals." [3]

The most active terrorist group, led by Valerian Osinsky, operated in Kiev and Odessa. In proclamations pasted on the walls of houses by night, the group announced "the execution" of such and such a spy or official. These proclamations bore a seal with a crossed revolver, dagger, and axe encircled by the legend "Executive Committee of the Social Revolutionary Party." [4] The committee was a complete fabrication and the term "executive" was used in the sense of executing, killing, the man found guilty. The group frankly admitted that it could not resist "teasing the police" and pretending to be omnipresent. The authorities were thoroughly alarmed and the wildest rumours circulated among the public. The "red-peril" scare spread over the whole country and indeed to other countries. In western Europe the exploits of Russian terrorists, or "nihilists" as they were mistakenly called, were eagerly followed in the newspapers.

The Russian government retaliated by handing over political trials to military tribunals, reviving the death penalty, and prohibiting the carrying of arms by civilians. There were sixteen executions of revolutionaries in quick succession. The earliest to be condemned to death, for armed resistance to arrest, was Kovalsky in Odessa.[5] It was the first execution for a political crime since Karakozov's in 1866. Also in Odessa one of the most selfless and saintly of Russian revolutionaries, Dmitry Lizogub, was hanged with two others, for no better reason than that he intended to donate his immense fortune to Zemlya i Volya. The handsome and intrepid Valerian Osinsky, a true hero of romance, was in the end caught and hanged with two comrades in Kiev in 1879.[6] Among those arrested and tried with him were two remarkable women: Natalya Armfeld, who deeply impressed George Kennan when he met her in the free settlement at Kara, and Sofya Leshern von Hertsfeld.[7] The latter was sentenced to death and she exulted at the thought of being the first woman revolutionary to die on the gallows. When she was told on the eve of the execution that her sentence had been commuted to exile for life, she was inconsolable. Osinsky spent the last night of his life comforting her. He also dictated to her his political testament, which was later smuggled out of the prison.

The executions, carried out with full military turn-out and much beating of drums, were meant as an awful warning to the public and to other revolutionaries. In the event, the calm and steadfast bearing of the condemned men impressed the public and inspired the terrorists with even greater courage. At the same time the terrorists recognized how little political impact they had made so far. These assassinations were mere self-defence, the rearguard action of a small and threatened band of revolutionaries. The random killing of underlings did not rock the political order. The core of that order was the tsar and only his death could make a difference. Such seemed the inescapable conclusion. Valerian Osinsky himself had arrived at it, as he hinted in his testament. And in April 1879, Alexander Solovyev acted upon it. He had been one of the peaceful populists who lived and worked in the countryside. He became exasperated by the lack of political freedom and convinced himself that the tsar should die. So he went to St. Petersburg to kill him.[8] He was unsuccessful and was executed. But the shock of his attempt finally aroused the ranks of the revolutionaries.

Zemlya i Volya had only a short span of life. Natanson was soon arrested again and though his wife, Olga Shleysner, carried on his work with remarkable energy for a little longer, she and many other prominent members of the organization were apprehended in 1878.* And in the following summer, in the course of two momentous secret meetings—at Lipetsk and at Voronezh [9]—Zemlya i Volya split over terrorism. The purists of populism took the name of Cherny Peredel (Black Repartition, meaning redistribution of agricultural land) and carried on the tradition of "going to the people," preaching a gradualist form of agrarian socialism. Their activities were soon stopped by the police; their secret press was seized; many were arrested, and others fled abroad. Later on, some of them revived the populist tradition in the Social-Revolutionary party, while others became Marxists and founded the Social-Democratic party.

The other half of Zemlya i Volya formed a terrorist organization under the name of Narodnaya Volya. This name is usually translated as The People's Will, which does not allow for the ambiguity of the word *volya*, which means both will and freedom. In retrospect both meanings are appropriate: in the beginning the word *freedom* was in all good faith taken over from the parent Land and Freedom, and indeed the cause of the people's freedom remained as important as ever. But in the immediate struggle against autocracy

---

* The treatment of political prisoners, and particularly women, was markedly more brutal from now on. Olga Shleysner and two of her comrades, Malinovskaya and Kolenkina, were forcibly stripped in the presence of male doctors and gendarmes, to have their "distinguishing marks" recorded; Olga Shleysner, who defended herself, was beaten and died a month later; Malinovskaya became insane. Olga Lyubatovich had to submit to a similar indignity some time later. (Bogucharsky, V. (1), part 2, pp. 121, 317–318.)

Narodnaya Volya saw itself also as the bearer of the people's will. The patient teacher, helper, and friend of the people thus became the avenger and the executioner in the name of the people.

The transition to terrorism did not come easily to Russian revolutionaries. Most of them had to overcome a deep resistance to violence, which involved them in a painful inner struggle. If they did join the new organization, it was only because they saw no other way of advancing the cause of political freedom in Russia. They argued that in killing the tsar they would be eliminating not a human being but an abstract principle—the autocracy. But they remained reluctant assassins and repeatedly expressed their revulsion from bloodshed. Vera Zasulich spoke for them all when she said that it was a terrible thing to lift a hand against a human being.

After Solovyev's attempt on the life of the tsar, the government had appointed, in six main regions, military officials with practically dictatorial powers and had delegated to them the task of putting down sedition. These men employed the most ruthless methods. When the students of the Medical Academy in St. Petersburg complained that they were being deprived of more and more rights, such as a mutual aid fund and so forth, detachments of mounted and foot police bore down on students gathered at the gates of the Academy, whipped them savagely, and arrested 130 of their number. The students at the Kharkov University were beaten in the same way. The Council of the St. Petersburg University sent a protest to the minister of education, criticizing the persecution of students by the Third Section and suggesting that the autonomy of the universities and corporate student organizations, which had been banned since 1863, should be restored.[10] This was a courageous gesture on the part of the professors, but it had no effect at all.

Russia was in a state of siege. The disproportion between the few revolutionaries still at large and the entire mobilized might of the Russian empire was never so blatant. The revolutionaries realized that their backs were to the wall. They had to act quickly and decisively before they perished; and they had to ensure that they did not perish too soon. To that end they tightened up their conspiratorial methods and imposed a much stricter discipline. The

Alexander Mikhaylov
(A. P. Priblyeva-Korva and
V. Figner, *A. D. Mikhaylov*,
Leningrad, 1925)

Andrey Zhelyabov
(*Byloe*, No. 7, 1906, St. Petersburg)

Sofya Perovskaya
(*Byloe*, No. 8, 1906, St. Petersbu

Vera Figner
(New York Public Library)

Vera Zasulich
(Culver Pictures, Inc.)

Terrorists

members were pledged to obey absolutely, to carry out orders promptly, and to learn to avoid being shadowed or pursued. If they were caught they had to deny all connection with the organization, or to admit only to being "a third-degree agent." They expected no mercy once caught—they were what nowadays would be called a suicide squad, and some of them did, indeed, prefer suicide to arrest. They lived on false passports, constantly changing their names and lodgings; they carried at all times a dagger and a revolver; they became artists of impersonation and disguise.

Narodnaya Volya took over from the southern terrorists the name and the seal of the "Executive Committee." It suited its purposes well to mystify the police and the public, to make them believe that this dreaded body had survived the arrests and executions and had now extended its activities to northern Russia. But it used the name more precisely to denote the central body of the "party," as they liked to call it. The police and the public were not to know that the membership of that party was so small that the Executive Committee was in effect nearly all there was.

Narodnaya Volya was centred on St. Petersburg. The Executive Committee consisted at first of twenty-eight and later of thirty-seven members, of which about one-third were women.[11] Supporting groups were later formed among workers ("workers' brigades") and among army and navy officers ("military organization"). For specific tasks helpers were sometimes recruited from among sympathizers, but these helpers usually knew only the person who had recruited them.

Small though it was, Narodnaya Volya was strong in talent and its members had stature. Outstanding among them were two men and two women—Andrey Zhelyabov and Alexander Mikhaylov, Sofya Perovskaya and Vera Figner. Of these Sofya Perovskaya [12] was the veteran—in experience though not in years—having already played a cardinal role among the Chaykovists. Arrested with most of them in 1873, she was fortunate to be allowed to await her trial on her parents' estate in the Crimea, and more fortunate still to be acquitted in the "trial of the 193." Wisely, she at once went "underground" and so escaped being re-arrested. Yet the fate of her less fortunate comrades did not allow her to rest, and for a whole year she devoted all her energies to organizing their escapes. She went to Kharkov, the centre of the new prison district, collected money, men, horses, carriages—but all attempts to intercept the transport of the prisoners failed and she and her friends had to flee from the town.

Soon afterwards she was arrested at her mother's home in the Crimea and put on the train to St. Petersburg in charge of two gendarmes. She was resolved to escape at the first opportunity, but characteristically did not try it while the gendarmes guarding her were "decent, kindly men," [13] whom she did not want to get into trouble with their superiors. But when, at the very end of the journey, her guards happened to be brutish and unfriendly, she immediately started looking for her chance. This came when she was taken off the train to spend the night at a railway station. She was put into a small room and her two "Cerberuses" composed themselves for the night: one stretched at full length on the floor just inside the room across the threshold and the other in front of the window. As soon as they were both asleep, Sofya Perovskaya calmly examined window and door and found that the latter opened outwards—a circumstance obviously overlooked by her watchdogs. Gently she pushed the door open, stepped over the snoring gendarme, walked unhurriedly through the station and on to the end of the platform. There she waited in the thick bushes for the next train, which luckily arrived before the law woke up. She had of course no ticket, but that was easily solved. She put on her dumb-peasant-girl act—she had never been on a train before, she did not know about tickets—to such good effect that the guard let her be. She was a most convincing actress and she knew no fear. In his moving profile of her, Sergey Kravchinsky said that "this small, graceful, ever-laughing young girl possessed a fearlessness that amazed the bravest of men." [14]

Sofya Perovskaya was one of those who had taken a lot of persuading before joining Narodnaya Volya. But it was characteristic of her, as perhaps of all women revolutionaries, that once they were convinced of the rightness of a course of action, they followed

it with absolute single-mindedness. Sergey Kravchinsky speaks of
Perovskaya's deep sense of duty and also of the "divine spark"
which glowed so richly in her and which "women possess in a
much greater measure—let us admit it—than men." And he adds—
"That is why the Russian revolutionary movement owes its almost
religious fire above all to them, and why, as long as there are
women in it, it will remain invincible." [15] Through the Narodnaya
Volya Sofya Perovskaya met her death, at the age of twenty-seven,
and her one short spell of personal happiness. She and Zhelyabov
lived as man and wife for six months before they went to die
together on the gallows in 1881. It was the first and only love of
her life.

Andrey Zhelyabov [16] was the son of a serf and himself a serf
until his owner noticed his exceptional ability and sent the boy to
school at his expense. Later he went to the university in Odessa,
but was expelled during student disturbances. At Odessa he pursued a rather cautious political path, until he was asked to join the
Narodnaya Volya. A convinced populist and an opponent of terrorism, Zhelyabov did not immediately agree. But in the end he was
persuaded to join and went to St. Petersburg. Here he came into his
own. Vital, even exuberant, energetic, and a born orator, he soon
acquired the stature of a leader.

By comparison Alexander Mikhaylov [17] seemed a cool, calcu-
lating administrator and strategist. He was a comparative newcomer, but he had been present at the "trial of the 50" and "went
to the people" in 1877 and 1878; he had known the Osinsky group
in Kiev and had helped to organize Zemlya i Volya. And when most
of its leadership was arrested in October 1878, he rebuilt the organization almost single-handed. [18] From the experiences of those
years he had learned one lesson—that no political group or party
had a chance of surviving in Russia without fool-proof conspiratorial techniques. Indeed almost every past lapse could be attributed
not to the efficiency of the police—it was laughably inefficient—
but to the carelessness and lack of discipline of the revolutionaries.

This was unpardonable even in the early stages, when those involved in socialist propaganda could still believe that they were

doing nothing criminal (since it was not considered criminal in western Europe) and therefore did not try to conceal it. They should have known that things were very different in Russia. Now, hundreds of police agents were hunting for the terrorists, and the terrorists knew that they would die on the gallows or rot in prison if caught. Their number being so small, they could not afford losses. Alexander Mikhaylov made the safety of the organization his particular task. He did not allow anybody to run unnecessary risks; he became the "shield" and the "eye and ear" of Narodnaya Volya, personally checking and rechecking all plans; wisely he also placed a trusted man as a clerk in the Third Section to signal any hint of danger. He knew by heart the map of St. Petersburg with its warren of interconnected courtyards, some with double exits, and he insisted that all his comrades should know it too. He was a tyrant, but a much loved one.

Vera Figner [19] was also a comparative newcomer. Though she had been one of the original Frichi, she did not return to Russia with them and so escaped the results of their fiasco. When she did return she wound up their affairs and gave what help she could to her imprisoned sister Lydia and the others. Then, in the spring of 1877, she went "to the people." In accordance with the prevailing populist tactics, she intended to settle for a longer period in the same place, working as midwife and not trying to foist any propaganda on the peasants. Vera Figner had not previously worked in the countryside and she was much shaken by the poverty and ignorance of the peasants. Yet she found them responsive to kindness and was gratified to see them eager to learn. Only the local officials were hostile and suspicious from the start and after barely three months she had to leave to escape arrest.

Undaunted, she went, accompanied by her younger sister Evgenia,[20] to another district where they soon became very popular among the peasants, who flocked to Vera's surgery (there was no doctor in the district) and to Evgenia's classroom (there was no school in the district either). In the evenings the two young women often went to one or other of the peasant homes, where neighbours assembled to hear them read aloud or talk. They let the villagers tell them their troubles without imposing their radical views upon them; Evgenia even taught children prayers so as not to offend religious feelings. Nevertheless it was the local priest who denounced them to the authorities * and once again the sisters only just escaped being caught. The peasants lamented their departure and assured them that their work had not been in vain. The experiences of the two sisters were typical of this late stage of populism: there was greater response from the peasants, who had come to realize that the young people who came to live among them were on their side. But however modest and legal the work of the populists might be, the authorities would not leave them alone, and there was no sense persevering along those lines.

Vera Figner and her sister had no liking for terrorism, but they joined Narodnaya Volya nevertheless. Vera had previously met Sofya Perovskaya and the two young women immediately liked each other. In contrast to the natural and unassuming Perovskaya, Vera Figner had a reserved manner with just a touch of hauteur. She was twenty-seven years old and strikingly beautiful. The writer Gleb Uspensky, who though not a member was a close sympathizer of Narodnaya Volya, admitted to an almost religious adoration for that "young woman of a strong and silent, almost nunlike type"; she combined, he said, high intelligence and great energy with warm responsiveness to human suffering—"she understands all sorrow," she has "a truly great heart." [21] She was said to be "all fire and energy . . . an apostle of the revolution." [22] At a later stage Vera Figner emerged also as a brilliant writer. Her memoirs are not only a unique and moving record of her twenty years of solitary confinement in the Shlüsselburg Fortress, but also a most perceptive account of the revolutionary movement of her time.

Altogether Narodnaya Volya made up in quality what it lacked in numbers, as Mikhaylov had already said of Zemlya i Volya. It was a most varied and colourful band of people. Kibalchich,[23] the man responsible for the manufacture of dynamite and bombs, was a

---

* This was not an isolated instance—many of the peaceful propagandists (Dmitry Klements and Ivanchin-Pisarev among them) were denounced to the police not by peasants but by the village priests.

very able scientist and inventor. As a student he did not meddle in politics. But a friend happened to leave propaganda material in his room, the police found it, and he was arrested. It was during his two years in pretrial detention that he became a socialist. Later he wrote one of the most persuasive texts in defence of regicide. Aaron Zundulevich [24] was unsurpassed as an organizer of secret printing presses and as a smuggler of books and people out of the country. The fearless Mikhail Frolenko [25] helped three revolutionaries to escape from prison by entering the prison service as a warder, and then escaping with his friends. Alexander Kvyatkovsky,[26] whose brother was already in Siberia, and Nikolay Sukhanov, the leader of the military organization, were both uniquely attractive human beings. Of Sukhanov Vera Figner wrote that he was a wholly unselfish and honest man whom it was impossible not to love—"it was a puzzle how such a personality, clear as crystal, could have been formed among the surrounding lies, deceit, and hypocrisy . . . happy is the party that a Sukhanov chooses for his own. . . ." [27]

It can be truly said of all members of the Executive Committee that they were remarkable for either high courage or intelligence or strong will, some combining all these qualities. This was true of the workers Stepan Khalturin, Presnyakov, and Grachevsky,[28] as it was of Anna Yakimova, Sofya Ivanova, Tatyana Lebedeva, Maria Oshanina, Anna Korba,[29] and our old friends from the Moscow Organization—Olga Lyubatovich [30] and Gesya Gelfman,[31] who had both escaped from their places of exile. Each one of them was to play a difficult and dangerous part later on.

It took Narodnaya Volya just over a year to organize itself and to agree on its aims. Zundulevich provided it with a particularly efficient printing press,[32] and when this was captured by the police, replaced it by another. These presses printed the periodical *Narodnaya Volya,* and also occasionally *Leaflets of the Narodnaya Volya.* The periodical was printed in some 2,500 to 3,000 copies which were widely distributed and read. The two publications fully reflected the ideological problems that faced the group. It was not easy to justify regicide, but in the end a more or less coherent view emerged which can be summarized as follows. The reforms of Alexander II had failed to bring political freedom to Russia and the tsar himself had become the greatest obstacle to liberalization. But neither the liberals, who were still hoping for a constitution, nor the weak bourgeoisie, which had been lately encouraged and even financed by the government, had any immediate intention to fight for political freedom. The upper strata of society had been frightened by the bogey of red peril and dared not move in any direction, and the peasants, though discontented, were not ready to rise against tsardom. The revolutionary party was the only force capable of political action, and it must act quickly while there was still widespread discontent in the country and before capitalism had grown too strong.

If the government after all agreed to convene a freely elected Constituent Assembly, in which the peasants were represented, the revolutionary party would suspend its activities and submit to the will of the people. But under Russian conditions it was more realistic to think that only a revolution could change the situation. Should a revolution occur, the revolutionary party would be only a holding force that would defend it against all enemies until the Constituent Assembly was convened and the people declared its will. Under no circumstances should the revolutionary party assume a dictatorial role and force "a despotic utopia" [33] on the people. The immediate aim of the revolutionary party was the destruction of despotism and the only effective way of achieving this was to kill the despot.

The survey of the situation was in many ways quite realistic, but the conclusions drawn from it were absurd. Here was a revolutionary party embarking on the murder of the tsar in the name of a people that—as the party itself admitted—clung to their faith in the tsar and would not rise spontaneously against him. Yet the same party repeatedly vowed not to go against the will of the people.

But it would be futile to look for logic at that stage. A sympathizer from Moscow who visited St. Petersburg at the time said that most members of the Executive Committee seemed to have become a little stupid—meaning probably that they were no longer capable of reasoning. And, indeed, they had become too obsessed to reason. They had but one thought: the tsar must be killed. Among the many motives, resentment was perhaps the strongest—he had failed as a reformer and he had failed as a patriarch—"there would have been no blood spilt," said Kibalchich at his trial, "if the revolutionaries had been treated more patriarchally." [34] This was indeed a case of love turning into hatred.

REGICIDE 13

On 26 August 1879, the Executive Committee of the Narodnaya Volya solemnly condemned Alexander II, Tsar Emperor of All the Russias, to death. From then on it was a desperate race against time—to carry out the sentence before the police discovered and crushed the conspiracy. Between August 1879 and March 1881, no less than eight assassination plots were hatched, each involving most elaborate preparations. With one exception they were all aimed at intercepting the tsar's carriage or train and most of them failed because the route or the time-table of the tsar's journey was changed.

Several failures were due to the inexperience of the plotters. It would seem that the inspiration to use dynamite had come to them from a widely reported case in western Europe, in which ship owners had deliberately blown up several of their old ships in order to collect insurance money. But the invention and the manufacture of explosive devices was still in an experimental stage and Narodnaya Volya could not afford the time to develop them properly. Transport presented further problems—the unpaved and deeply rutted Russian roads made the carrying of explosives by road a harrowing experience. And, of course, there was the constant danger of detection, which made the plotters sometimes rush their plans unwisely.

The first three attempts were made in the late summer of 1879, when the tsar was expected to return to St. Petersburg from his holidays in the Crimea. The railway tracks were mined at three points: at Odessa, at Alexandrovsk near Kharkov, and at Moscow. Dressed up as a society lady, Vera Figner went to ask the head of the Odessa railways to give employment to her servant and his sick wife who "needed healthy country air." [1] The official readily granted the request of the beautiful petitioner, and Mikhail Frolenko was soon installed as a signalman in a hut near Odessa, along with his "wife" Tatyana Lebedeva. It was from that hut that the mining of the tracks was done. However, the tsar went by another route and the whole enterprise had to be abandoned.

The second attempt, at Alexandrovsk, [2] was organized by Andrey Zhelyabov, masquerading as a leather merchant and manufacturer looking for a suitable site for his business. He and his assistants dug a hole under the railway line out in the country, and mined it. Later he used to say that it was a wonder that they were not blown up as they drove about in an open cart over the roughest roads, sitting on top of sacks of explosives. [3] This time the tsar did come their way and Zhelyabov joined the wires to set off the fuse at the proper moment—but nothing happened, owing apparently to a faulty connection. Clearly, the terrorists had not yet learned their craft, or were perhaps still too jittery.

The third attempt, [4] organized by Alexander Mikhaylov, took place the very next day, 18 November, and was more successful though not entirely so. This time it was Lev Gartman and his "wife" Sofya Perovskaya who went to live in a house in a Moscow suburb situated close to the railway line. From this house a tunnel was dug that ended right under the tracks. Twice Sofya Perovskaya averted the discovery of the tunnel. First, when a merchant came to survey the property—the "owners" had applied to him for a mortgage. Perovskaya did not let him enter, standing in the door with her arms folded over her stomach, and repeating over and over again: "I know nothing about it and himself is not at home!" [5] with a mien of such impenetrable stupidity that the exasperated merchant went away. On another occasion a fire broke out in a house nearby and everybody in the street rushed to help with getting the furniture out—Russian houses being built of wood, fire usually spread very rapidly. How to prevent these kindly people from entering the house? Perovskaya rushed out with an icon held high over her head and shouted: "Desist! Desist! Let God's will prevail!" [6] She had counted on the piety of her neighbours, who were sectarians—and they did indeed desist. But in case the police arrived to search the house, a bottle of nitroglycerine was kept ready; it would be Sofya Perovskaya's duty to fire at it with her revolver and so blow up the house with everybody in it.

It took altogether two months to prepare for this third attempt, and on the day on which the tsar was due, everything was ready and everybody gone, leaving Shyryaev and Perovskaya to set off the mine. The imperial train was due to reach Moscow between ten and eleven in the evening, but somewhat before that time the conspirators heard a train approaching. They were puzzled but decided that it must be the advance coach that sometimes preceded the main train. And so they let it pass and blew up the second train which, in fact, contained only the tsar's servants, while he himself had gone unharmed in the advance coach.

Thus all three attempts miscarried, but the whole country was by now aware of the threat to the tsar's life. The government was frantic. What more could it do, if the state of siege, the military tribunals, the executions all failed to avert this threat? The tsar, when told of the railway explosion, said bitterly: "Am I such a wild beast that they should hound me to death?" [7]

The Executive Committee could at least be glad that the organization as a whole had survived undetected. But before the end of 1879 Kvyatkovsky and Evgenia Figner, Zundulevich and Shyryaev were all arrested. And in January 1880 the clandestine press was discovered.[8] Nikolay Bukh with "wife" Sofya Ivanova had occupied a set of rooms in a central part of St. Petersburg. The respectable and friendly "couple" made a point of asking their neighbours in from time to time to show them how innocent their flat looked; meanwhile in one of the back rooms a press was operated by two compositors, who never left the house. On the night of 17 January 1880, the bell of the flat was rung violently, as only the police rang. Sofya Ivanova did not open the door until she had destroyed all compromising papers. Then an armed battle started. To warn comrades outside, they broke the panes of the windows and the wind blew the lamps out. In total darkness the five revolutionaries defended themselves against a combined attack by police and soldiers until their ammunition gave out; then one of the printers shot himself with his last bullet. The loss of the press was a calamity, but by May a new press had already been set up.

Meanwhile a further and more spectacular attempt on the life of the tsar was being prepared by Narodnaya Volya.[9] On 5 February 1880, the worker Stepan Khalturin, who had got himself employed as a carpenter in the Winter Palace, detonated what proved to be an insufficient amount of dynamite under the dining room of the palace—the floor shook but did not collapse. The tsar happened in any case to be late for lunch on that day and was not in the dining room at the time. There were, however, many victims among the soldiers whose guardroom was immediately below.

Though the attempt failed it spread great alarm in government and court circles—there was something particularly sinister about death stalking the Winter Palace. The public endowed the terrorists with almost superhuman powers and seemed mesmerized by them, awaiting the outcome of the "duel" with fatalistic passivity.

Even the tsar himself was becoming weary of his existence. His private life was unhappy and his family divided. He was tired out by the long struggle over the reforms and as disillusioned with the results as most of his critics. Of the few statesmen of integrity who had supported him at the beginning of his reign, none remained; he was surrounded by men of straw. From time to time a flicker of the old reforming zeal returned and in 1880 he entrusted the task of preparing a constitutional reform to his new minister of the interior, General Count Loris-Melikov. Strictly speaking there was never any question of introducing a constitution such as existed, for instance, in England.[10] Neither the tsar nor any of his advisers envisaged anything like it and the liberals indulged in wishful thinking when they expected it to be introduced. The two projects laid before the tsar—by Valuyev in 1863 and by the Grand Duke Konstantin in 1866—suggested simply that on specific occasions a few elected representatives from the *zemstvos* and the bigger cities should be summoned to take part in discussions—and then only in a consultative capacity. Loris-Melikov's new proposal did not go beyond the two earlier ones. And he warned the tsar that "popular representation" (at ministerial level one spoke of "popular representation," not of "constitution") was not only useless but actually untimely and therefore dangerous. He merely recommended that the State Council (a consultative body) should include a few elected representatives from the *zemstvos* and the cities. Yet modest as this proposal was, it met with strong opposition from the heir to the throne and his party and had to be shelved for the time being as too liberal. The future Alexander III was an autocrat to the core and had the greatest contempt for the liberals, whom he called "chatterboxes and lawyers." [11]

Loris-Melikov was a newcomer to politics and was bold enough to point out to the tsar that no good came of reforms if they were not properly implemented. That was what had happened to the reforms of the 1860s—"the peasant question fell into a rut . . . reformed law courts became isolated from social life . . . *zemstvos* . . . were not supported by the government." [12] In short, the bureaucracy had systematically sabotaged the reforms. This diagnosis was correct, but Loris-Melikov himself failed to act on it. His administration, proclaimed as a "dictatorship of the heart," offered a few crumbs to the liberal public while intensifying the persecution of the revolutionaries and introducing a stricter regime in the Kara political prisons.

Narodnaya Volya would have reacted favourably to real changes of policy, but since it saw none and distrusted the "dictatorship of the heart," it continued on its course. The next two attempts on the life of the tsar were, however, again costly failures. In the spring of 1880,[13] Sofya Perovskaya and Nikolay Sablin rented a shop in one of the main thoroughfares of Odessa, through which the tsar usually passed on his way to the Crimea. The plan was to dig a tunnel from the shop to the middle of the street; but while they waited for the dynamite to arrive, the tsar passed by before the expected date. Later on, in the summer of the same year, a bridge in St. Petersburg which the tsar frequently crossed to catch a train to Tsarskoe Selo was heavily mined. Zhelyabov and the worker Teterka were to light the fuse on the appointed day, but Teterka failed to arrive on time, because, as he explained, he "did not own a watch." [14]

Fortunately the police never knew of either plot and indeed the organization was much helped by the inefficiency and stupidity of the police. Most of the secret activities could hardly be concealed. Dynamite was manufactured in an ordinary private room and the fumes and the stink of the chemicals filled the whole house. The printing press could not be operated without considerable noise, nor the bulky bundles of printed material spirited out of the house unobserved. Yet all this escaped detection for an astonishingly long time.

In October 1880 the first trial of Narodnaya Volya—that "of the 16"—took place. Kvyatkovsky and Presnyakov were hanged and others received heavy *katorga* sentences. The executions took place on 4 November. The losses to the small organization were in themselves heavy enough, and they were aggravated by the arrest, on 28 November, of the irreplaceable Alexander Mikhaylov.[15] It was due entirely to his imprudence, the only one he ever committed. He went into a photographer's shop to order copies of the photographs of his two friends—Kvyatkovsky and Presnyakov—but the owner of the shop was a police agent and the police were waiting for him when he returned to collect the prints. The wife of the photographer tried to warn him of danger, his comrades had implored him not to go—one wonders what impulse made him disregard all warnings? Was it loyalty to his dead friends and desire to share their fate, or simply overconfidence? He was sentenced to death, but the sentence was commuted to *katorga* for life, to be served in the Peter and Paul Fortress; he died there in 1884.

The Executive Committee was meanwhile preparing the next coup. The sense of urgency was greater than ever and to ensure success the attempt was planned in three stages: a mine to be placed under the pavement of the street through which the tsar was expected to pass, bombs to be thrown by hand at close range, and if both failed, attack by dagger or revolver. This plan had been masterminded by Zhelyabov, and it was he who was to stab or shoot the tsar if all else miscarried.

Alexander II invariably took the parade at the Michael cavalry barracks on Sundays and he usually drove through the Malaya Sadovaya street to get there. Accordingly a suitable shop was rented in that street and a "cheese merchant" (Yury Bogdanovich) and "wife" (Anna Yakimova) moved in.[16] Apparently they did not act their parts very convincingly, for neighbours became suspicious and denounced them to the police. However, a search revealed nothing beyond a goodly supply of cheeses; a small pile of fresh soil discovered in a corner was explained away by Bogdanovich as being essential for keeping the cheeses fresh. If the police had looked more closely they would have uncovered the tunnel which the conspirators were digging. They were working under the most difficult conditions, bent double and suffocating in the narrow damp passage, but digging in feverish haste. Soon after the police search the tunnel was completed.

There was indeed need for haste. There had been more arrests and—a terrible blow—the man who had been planted in the Third Section had been discovered in January 1881. In addition, one of the arrested terrorists, Goldenberg, cracked under interrogation and disclosed all he knew about the organization. The police had now so much information that they could be expected to pounce at any moment. The first blow fell on 27 February, when Zhelyabov was arrested. This was a calamity of the first order since Zhelyabov held all the threads of the complex triple plan in his hands.

The Executive Committee decided to put the date of the assassination forward to the very next Sunday, March first.[17] The command was entrusted to Sofya Perovskaya. Headquarters were established in one flat, occupied by Sablin and Gesya Gelfman, while the bombs were being hurriedly prepared in another, occupied by Isayev and Vera Figner. Early on the morning of the fatal Sunday, Perovskaya took two of the bombs to the headquarters and Kibalchich brought two more. Soon after, she met the bomb-throwers in a café and handed over the bombs in an inconspicuous brown-paper parcel. Meanwhile Mikhail Frolenko was lounging in front of the cheese shop, ready to detonate the mine lodged under the street. He was expected to perish in the explosion, yet Vera Figner saw him calmly unpack a bottle of wine and a piece of salami and eat a hearty breakfast.[18] The bomb-throwers, too, were expected to be killed, since the bombs, specially invented by Kibalchich, were effective only at very close range. There were four of them, all very young men and all volunteers. They were not members of the organization but had been specially recruited for the job.

All now depended on whether the tsar would venture out, and if so, whether he would take his usual route. The tsar had been warned of danger by Loris-Melikov who implored him to stay at home. But the tsar laughed and said that he would not be kept prisoner in his own palace. He had resisted the attempts of the secret police to surround him with its agents, but had accepted in the end an escort of six Cossacks who were to accompany him whenever he rode out. On Sunday, March first, he set out for the parade as usual, only going by way of the Catherine canal instead of the Malaya Sadovaya street. The cheese shop was thus rendered useless and the "shop keepers" quietly decamped next day, Anna Yakimova leaving some coppers on the counter "for the meat the butcher had sent for our cat Vaska.'' [19]

Sofya Perovskaya had been watching the tsar's cortège go by way of the canal and decided that he was likely to return the same way. She therefore placed her bomb-throwers at intervals along the railings of the canal embankment and herself crossed over to the other side. From there she would be able to see the tsar's sleigh as soon as it turned into the canal embankment and would alert the throwers by waving a white handkerchief. The waiting was nerve-racking; there were not many people about and nothing could appear more peaceful than the ice-bound canal and its snow-covered banks. But at last, at 2:15 P.M., the sleighs and the escort of Cossacks came into view going at full speed; the handkerchief fluttered, and Rysakov threw the first bomb. It was obviously thrown a fraction too late and blew up the back of the sleigh without hurting the tsar. The whole cortège stopped, the tsar descended and walked back to the spot where a passer-by lay wounded on the snow. As he stood there he said, "Thank God, I am safe!" Rysakov, who had been seized by soldiers, said, "It may be still too early to thank God"—and almost immediately the second bomb exploded. [20]

When the smoke cleared, the tsar and the second bomb-thrower, Grinevitsky, could both be seen lying on the ground among several other bodies, blood and debris spattering the snow all around. The tsar was wounded in the stomach and legs and was bleeding profusely. In a faint voice he said: "It's cold . . . cold," and then— "Quick . . . to the palace . . . die . . . there." [21] He was lifted up and driven away. It would seem that the tsar's suite behaved with extraordinary stupidity—no attempt was made to stem the blood and much time was lost in getting him to his room and into the doctor's hands. He died the same night.*

The tsar was dead, but his death led neither to a popular revolt nor to political concessions from above. Narodnaya Volya's work-

---

* Not all accounts of the tsar's death agree with each other, and one, at least, maintains that he died in the street before being moved to the palace.

The wounded tsar being driven to the Winter Palace (The Mansell Collection)

ers' brigades and military organization which were supposed to start the revolution proved far too weak. A ripple of emotion—fear, expectation, surprise—passed over the country and died away. The peasants were confused, the townspeople mainly indifferent. In the capital, black shrouded in deep mourning, the authorities, the court circles and "loyal" society were confirmed in their ultraconservative, uncompromising attitude.

To Narodnaya Volya the reaction of the country came as a terrible anticlimax. Had the assassination achieved nothing, had it been just an empty gesture? Not being able to see into the future, the terrorists could not know that in fact they had dealt a blow to the charismatic image of tsardom and had thus prepared the way for a future revolution. What they could see was that the people did not rise, that the educated society was not roused to political action, and that in short, the state of affairs remained unchanged. In desperation the remnants of Narodnaya Volya planned the assassination of the new tsar, Alexander III. Surely, two assassinations in rapid succession would disturb the political order? But the Executive Committee was in no position to carry out the plan. The first of the bomb-throwers, the inexperienced Rysakov, cracked under interrogation and divulged all that he knew. He did not know very much, but enough to enable the police to arrest almost all the conspirators. Gesya Gelfman and the third bomb-thrower, the worker Timofey Mikhaylov, were arrested and Sablin shot himself to forestall arrest; a few days later Sofya Perovskaya and Kibalchich were also detained. The authorities hurriedly set about preparing a spectacular trial. With young Rysakov as the chief accused, they were hoping to be able to downgrade the importance of the plot and of the plotters. That would have frustrated the purposes of Narodnaya Volya, which was intent on demonstrating the deep political meaning of the assassination. So Zhelyabov, from his cell, declared himself to be the chief organizer of the plot and demanded to be tried together with the bomb-throwers.[22]

The trial took place on 26 March 1881 and ended in death sentences for all the accused. They all reaffirmed their beliefs and, except Rysakov, showed no sign of remorse. Poor, gentle Gesya Gelfman, who was pregnant, was told that her execution would be postponed until after the birth of her child. She waited for it many miserable months in the Peter and Paul Fortress. When her baby was born, it was immediately taken away from her and soon died in a foundlings' home; she herself died a little time later in prison.[23]

The others—Zhelyabov, Kibalchich, Timofey Mikhaylov, Rysakov, and Sofya Perovskaya—were hanged on 3 April 1881.

Most of the arrested members of Narodnaya Volya were sentenced either to death or to long terms of *katorga*, death sentences being in most cases converted to *katorga* for life. They served their sentences in the fortresses of Peter and Paul [24] or of Shlüsselburg.[25] In the former they were usually kept in cells below ground level, where it was almost completely dark and the mildewed walls ran with water; the floors were full of deep holes through which rats swarmed. Anna Yakimova, who like Gesya Gelfman was pregnant at the time of her arrest, gave birth, like Gesya Gelfman, in just such a cell. She refused to give up her child and watched over it day and night so that the rats could not get at it. There were two gendarmes posted in every cell, allowing the prisoners not a moment's privacy; books and correspondence, extra food and tobacco were banned, lice were everywhere; and a bath was granted only once a month. Dysentery and scurvy were general; there was no sick bay; and the insane were not removed to mental hospitals. The treatment of women was particularly brutal and they were put into a kind of straitjacket and tied to their beds for the least complaint. When in 1883 some of the prisoners were transferred to Kara,[26] they were so weak that they had to be carried out of their cells by soldiers. And some, Proskovya Ivanovskaya among them, were mentally sick. On their way to Kara both men and women were shackled hand and foot, including wives who were following their condemned husbands of their own free will. Among those there was one young woman with a small baby—she, too, was shackled.

Narodnaya Volya lay in ruins. The discovery of the dynamite workshop and of the second printing press (where Ivanovskaya and Grachevsky had been working) in St. Petersburg was followed by arrests in the provinces. From 1882 onwards the only member of the Executive Committee still at large was Vera Figner. With characteristic stubbornness she refused to flee abroad, as some others had done, and persevered in "retying the broken threads," [27] as she put it—looking for new people, new printing type, and above all new funds. But none of her efforts was enough to resuscitate the organization and she herself was denounced by a traitor and arrested in 1883. She was tried with two other women and a group of army officers in the "trial of the 14." [28] During the twenty months of her pretrial investigation she was allowed to write her deposition, which passed from hand to hand in the official circles and—so she was told—"read just like a novel." [29] At the trial itself, though dispirited and physically exhausted, she roused herself to make a long speech, in which she described her party's and her own transition from "social altruism"[30] to regicide. She and seven of her codefendants—all army officers—were sentenced to death; and, though some of the officers petitioned to have their sentences commuted, she scorned to do likewise. As it turned out, only two officers were executed and she and the rest were imprisoned in the island fortress of Shlüsselburg. Vera Figner spent twenty years in solitary confinement on this remote island, so completely cut off from the outside world that her mother was told not to expect any news of her daughter until the latter was in her coffin. She became a living legend, idolized as a martyr by some and abhorred as a bloodthirsty monster by others. She was able to crown her remarkable record by writing and publishing her invaluable memoirs in 1926.

After the last trial Narodnaya Volya virtually ceased to exist, though for several years small groups continued to claim to belong to it. As late as 1887 one such group made an unsuccessful attempt on the life of Alexander III and five young men were hanged, including Lenin's elder brother. But soon afterwards a very different stage of the revolutionary movement began in Russia. The first stage culminated in the assassination of Alexander II and died with him.

Some time after the assassination of March first, the moribund Executive Committee issued two impressive public statements in the form of letters. The first was addressed to Alexander III.[31] Couched in respectful and courteous words, the letter urged the tsar not to yield to his personal grief. "There is something higher than natural human feelings and this is duty towards one's native land." And this duty demanded full understanding of the situation in Russia. After ten years of persecution "the bloody tragedy of the Catherine canal . . . was inevitable"—the revolutionary movement was not halted by persecution—"irresistibly it grew in size and strength. . . . Sire, the revolutionary movement does not depend on a few individuals, it is a function of the national organism . . . created by the discontent of the people, by the desire of the country for new social forms. The whole people cannot be exterminated nor can its discontent be subdued by repression; that only strengthens it. . . .'' If government policies were to remain unchanged, a revolution would inevitably break out. The Russian government had never governed in accordance with popular wishes and its reforms had not benefited the people. As a result it had lost its moral influence over the people; even regicide had become acceptable in Russia. "In the interest of our native land, in order to avert . . . those terrible calamities which always accompany revolutions," the letter urged the tsar to make "a voluntary approach to the people." In that case the terrorists would abandon their activities and devote themselves to cultural work for the good of the people; and a peaceful exchange of ideas would replace violence. The letter went on to formulate the essential conditions for a peaceful solution: a general amnesty for all political prisoners; the summoning of a National Assembly, consisting of representatives of the entire Russian nation, elected by universal suffrage on the basis of free electoral programs; the recognition of freedom of press, of speech, and of assembly. "This is the only way that would allow Russia to embark on a fair and peaceful development. We solemnly declare, before our country and before the world, that our party will unconditionally submit to the decisions of the National Assembly."

The letter reached the Palace at a critical moment. Unbeknown to the public, Alexander II had, on the very morning of his death, at last signed Loris-Melikov's so-called constitutional proposal. Several ministers urged the new tsar to honour his father's last decision. But Alexander III was made of sterner stuff. He never wavered in his determination to hold on to his personal absolute powers and he surrounded himself with men who encouraged him in this. In the course of his reign he withdrew most of the concessions made by his father to the liberal aspirations of Russian citizens. His character and his political opinions had not been widely known before, and it is understandable that the Executive Committee tried to influence him. It is one of the ironies of fate that it was his father, a much more liberal tsar, who was assassinated; Alexander III deserved it more.

The second letter, dated September 1881, was addressed by

Narodnaya Volya to the American people on the occasion of the assassination of their president, James Abram Garfield.[32] After offering condolences, the letter protested against the use of political murder in such a case: "In a country in which the freedom of the individual allows an honest contest of ideas, where the will of the people determines not only the forms of law but the actual persons of the rulers—in such a country political murder . . . is an expression of the same despotic spirit which we feel it our duty to combat in Russia. Despotism, whether of a person or a party, is always reprehensible, and violence is justifiable only when it is directed against violence."

There could be no better summing up of the essence of Narodnaya Volya. And it would serve well as its epitaph.

NOTES
BIBLIOGRAPHY
INDEX

NOTES

For further information, refer to the Bibliography

INTRODUCTION
1. Nekrasov, N., vol. III, p. 153.
2. Florinsky, M., p. 315.
3. Quoted by Meijer, J., p. 226.
4. Itenberg, B. (1), p. 163.
5. Milyukov, P., p. 39.
6. Hingley, R., pp. 30–36.
7. Ibid., p. 35.
8. Grosman, I., pp. 683–736.
9. Hingley, R., pp. 44–47; also Burtsev, V., part 1, pp. 15–18.
10. Kropotkin, P. (1), p. 118.
11. Flerovsky, N. (Bervi), pp. 19–20, 22–23.

CHAPTER 1: **The Nihilist Protest**
1. Turgenev, I., p. 325.
2. Kravchinsky, S. (1), p. 20.
3. Nikitenko, A. (1), vol. II, p. 450.
4. Herzen, A., p. 126.
5. Nekrasov, N., vol. I, pp. 111–129.
6. Ibid., p. 125.
7. Bogdanovich, T., p. 11.
8. Ibid., p. 95 (quoted from Chernyshevsky's diary, in *Literary Remains,* vol. I, pp. 580–581).
9. Ibid., pp. 20–34, 67–263, 95, 144 (quoted from Pypina, V. Lyubov v zhisni Chernyshevskogo, p. 33).
10. Ibid., pp. 37–50, 264–420; also Shelgunov, N., Shelgunova, L., Mikhaylov, M.
11. Bogdanovich, T., pp. 296–299.
12. Ibid., pp. 280, 284, 276, 280.
13. Ibid., pp. 58–64, 421–438.
14. Ibid., p. 422.

15. Ibid., p. 421.
16. Ibid., p. 428 (quoted from an unpublished manuscript by Pypina, V. Vospominania o I. i M. Sechenovykh).
17. Mikhaylov, M., vol. III, pp. 369–430.
18. Ibid., p. 374.
19. Ibid., pp. 678 f.
20. Burtsev, V., part 1, p. 43.
21. Likhacheva, E., vol. II, pp. 2–3.
22. Ibid., vol. II, p. 3.
23. Ibid., pp. 17, 456.

CHAPTER 2: **Alexander II and Reform**

1. Shelgunov, N., Shelgunova, L., Mikhaylov, M., vol. I, pp. 76 f.
2. Zhukovsky, V., vol. I, pp. xl–xlviii; 299–344; 361–384.
3. Lermontov, M., vol. I, p. 20.
4. Zaionchkovsky, P. (1), pp. 41–49.
5. Pertsev, E., p. 132.
6. Burtsev, V., part 2, p. 53.
7. Ibid., p. 52.
8. Shtakenshneyder, E., p. 291.
9. Nikitenko, A. (1), vol. II, p. 530.
10. Burtsev, V., part 1, pp. 35–40.
11. Ibid., part 2, p. 49.
12. Ibid., part 1, pp. 25–33.
13. Ibid., pp. 40–46.
14. Tocqueville (de), A., p. 259.
15. Nikitenko, A. (1), vol. I, p. 520.
16. Ibid., vol. II, pp. 35–43.

CHAPTER 3: **Feminism and Women's Education**

1. Shtakenshneyder, E., p. 187.
2. Bulanova-Trubnikova, O., p. 73.
3. Ibid., pp. 67–134; also Likhacheva, E., vol. II, p. 384.
4. Stasov, V.; also Likhacheva, E., vol. II, p. 485.
5. Bulanova-Trulnikova, O., pp. 77 f.; also Likhacheva, E., vol. II, p. 484.
6. Kropotkin, P. (1), pp. 244–245.
7. Likhacheva, E., vol. II, p. 15.

8. Ibid., pp. 22–23.
9. Ibid., p. 38.
10. Ibid., p. 209.
11. Ibid., p. 227.
12. Ibid., p. 474.
13. Ibid., p. 478.
14. Ibid., p. 477.
15. Ibid., pp. 501–509.
16. Ibid., p. 609.
17. Ibid., p. 526.
18. Ibid., p. 515.
19. Ibid., pp. 517–518.
20. Ibid., pp. 604, 612–613.
21. Chudnovsky, S., p. 227.
22. Kovalevskaya, S.; also Leffler, A.
23. Stasov, V., p. 87.
24. Likhacheva, E., vol. II, p. 394.
25. Ibid., p. 398.

CHAPTER 4: **Early Radical Groups**

1. Itenberg, B. (1), p. 207.
2. Burtsev, V., part 1, p. 29.
3. Quoted in Krishan Kumar, p. 26.
4. Kravchinsky, S. (1), p. 21.
5. Korolenko, V., vol. II, pp. 271–272.
6. Nekrasov, N., vol. I, p. 111.
7. Korolenko, V., vol. II, p. 346.
8. Burtsev, V., part 1, p. 24.
9. Ibid., p. 32.
10. Korolenko, V., vol. II, p. 115.
11. Itenberg, B. (1), pp. 206, 236.
12. Burtsev, V., part 1, p. 114; also Itenberg, B. (1), p. 206.
13. Korolenko, V., vol. II, p. 107.
14. Nikitenko, A. (2), vol. III, p. 55.
15. Korolenko, V., vol. II, p. 294.
16. Itenberg, B. (1), pp. 210–240.
17. Ibid., pp. 215–216.
18. Shishko, L. (1), p. 5.
19. Itenberg, B. (1), p. 212.

20. Ibid., p. 229.
21. Ibid., pp. 229–230.
22. Korolenko, V., vol. II, p. 265.
23. Itenberg, B. (1), pp. 216–217.
24. Ibid., pp. 219 f.
25. Ibid., p. 235.
26. Lavrov, P. (1).
27. Dan, F., pp. 86, 94–96.
28. "Iz parizheskogo arkhiva Turgeneva," vol. II, p. 10.
29. Titov, A., p. 55.
30. Itenberg, B. (1), p. 217.

CHAPTER 5: **The Chaykovists**

1. Itenberg, B. (1), pp. 210–211; also Figner, V. (2), vol. V, pp. 204–216.
2. Itenberg, B. (1), pp. 239–240.
3. Ibid., pp. 233–234.
4. Sinegub, S. (1,2,3).
5. Kravchinsky, S. (1), pp. 54–61.
6. Ibid., pp. 69–74.
7. Kropotkin, P. (1), pp. 301–305; also Shishko, L. (1).
8. Volkhovsky, F., pp. 1–46.
9. Kropotkin, P. (2), p. 107.
10. Volkhovsky, F., p. 2.
11. Kornilova-Moroz, A.; also Perovsky, V.; also Asheshov, N.; also Kravchinsky, S. (1), pp. 88–111; also Kropotkin, P. (1), pp. 299–300; also Axelrod, P., p. 154; *et al.*
12. Breshkovskaya, K., p. 168.
13. Kravchinsky, S. (1), pp. 92–93.
14. Axelrod, P., p. 153.
15. Tsederbaum, S., p. 42.
16. Ibid., p. 43; also Breshkovskaya, K., pp. 135–136.
17. Figner, V., and Korba, A., pp. 198–201.
18. Tsederbaum, S., p. 44; also Shishko, L. (2), pp. 51–52.
19. Sinegub, S. (1), pp. 39–80.
20. Itenberg, B. (1), p. 226.
21. Shishko, L. (1), p. 11.
22. Itenberg, B. (1), p. 225.

23. Kravchinsky, S. (2), p. 196.
24. Shishko, L. (2), pp. 51–52.

CHAPTER 6: **"Going to the People"**
 1. Burtsev, V., part 2, p. 81.
 2. Itenberg, B. (1), pp. 134, 411.
 3. Corti, E., pp. 214–215.
 4. Burtsev, V., part 1, p. 187.
 5. Nikitenko, A. (2), vol. III, p. 352.
 6. Nikitenko, A. (1), vol. I, p. 495.
 7. Ibid., p. 506.
 8. Flerovsky, N. (Bervi), p. 315.
 9. Itenberg, B. (1), pp. 435, 464.
10. Ibid., p. 464.
11. Ibid., pp. 318–326, 426.
12. Ibid., pp. 345–349; also Ivanchin-Pisarev, A.; also
    Figner, V. (2), vol. V, pp. 199–204.
13. Itenberg, B. (1), pp. 422–423.
14. Kravchinsky, S. (1), pp. 74–79; also Bogucharsky, V. (1),
    part 1, pp. 226–233.
15. Axelrod, P., p. 102.
16. Ibid., p. 119.
17. Ibid., p. 114.
18. Burtsev, V., part 1, pp. 113–123.
19. Ibid., p. 113.
20. Ibid., p. 114.
21. Ibid., p. 115.
22. Ibid., pp. 115–116.
23. Ibid., p. 116.
24. Ibid., p. 117.
25. Ibid., p. 119.
26. Itenberg, B. (1), pp. 317–318, 466.
27. Burtsev, V., part 1, p. 119; part 2, p. 83.
28. Breshkovskaya, K., pp. 60–62; also Itenberg, B. (1),
    pp. 271–272, 469.
29. Itenberg, B. (2), pp. 388 f.
30. Ibid., pp. 387 f; also Nikitenko, A. (1), vol. II, p. 35.
31. Itenberg, B. (2), p. 389.

32. Nikitenko, A. (2), vol. III, p. 349.
33. Ibid., p. 352.

CHAPTER 7: **Towards Revolutionary Organization**

1. Meijer, J.
2. Kropotkin, P. (1), pp. 253–254.
3. Figner, V. (1), p. 116.
4. Ibid., p. 117.
5. Ibid., p. 49.
6. Burtsev, V., part 1, p. 106.
7. Kravchinsky, S. (3).
8. Dzhabadari, I. (2), p. 182.
9. Figner, V. (3), p. 54.
10. Dzhabadari, I. (2), p. 182.
11. Figner, V. (2), vol. V, pp. 41–42.
12. Figner, V. (3), pp. 76–77.
13. Kravchinsky, S. (3).
14. Figner, V. (3), p. 97.
15. Dzhabadari, I. (2), p. 183.
16. "Nekrolog Marii Dmitrievny Subotinoy."
17. "Nekrolog Beti Kaminskoy."
18. Figner, V. (2), vol. V, p. 35.
19. Bogucharsky, V. (2), part 1, pp. 252–253.
20. Meijer, J., p. 142.
21. Figner, V. (3), p. 65.
22. Ibid., pp. 124–125.
23. Dzhabadari, I. (2), pp. 177–179.
24. Ibid., p. 182.
25. Ibid., p. 183.
26. Dzhabadari, I. (1), p. 14.
27. Ibid., pp. 15–16.
28. Dzhabadari, I. (2), p. 177.
29. Figner, V. (3), pp. 97–98.
30. Figner, V. (2), vol. V, p. 114.
31. Dzhabadari, I. (3), p. 170.
32. Ibid., pp. 170–171.
33. Figner, V. (2), vol. V, p. 117.
34. Dzhabadari, I. (3), p. 172.
35. Lukashevich, A., p. 42.

36. Figner, V. (2), vol. V, p. 119.
37. Bogucharsky, V. (2), part 2, pp. 128–326.

CHAPTER 8: **Pretrial Detention**
1. Gernet, M.
2. Breshkovskaya, K., p. 109.
3. Dzhabadari, I. (3), pp. 186–187.
4. Breshkovskaya, K., p. 100.
5. Ibid., p. 108.
6. Itenberg, B. (1), pp. 392–399.
7. Sinegub, S. (3), pp. 33–34.
8. Lemke, M.
9. Sinegub, S. (3), p. 68.
10. "Zayavlenie A. Kvyatkovskogo," pp. 164–165.

CHAPTER 9: **Political Trials, 1877–78**
1. Bogucharsky, V. (2), part 2, pp. 128–326.
2. Ibid., part 3, pp. 1–302.
3. Ibid., part 1, pp. 345–346; also ibid., part 2, pp. 1–127.
4. Bogucharsky, V. (2), part 2, pp. 334–344.
5. Dzhabadari, I. (3), p. 189.
6. Ibid., pp. 191–192.
7. Bogucharsky, V. (2), part 2, pp. 327–331.
8. Ibid., pp. 331–333; also Dzhabadari, I. (3), pp. 193–194.
9. Dzhabadari, I. (3), p. 193.
10. Ibid., p. 194.
11. Itenberg, B. (1), pp. 357–363.
12. Dzhabadari, I. (3), p. 195.
13. Kravchinsky, S. (3), p. 19.
14. Kravchinsky, S. (1), p. 35.
15. Dzhabadari, I. (3), p. 195.
16. Ibid., p. 193.
17. Bogucharsky, V. (2), part 3, pp. 1–302.
18. Itenberg, B. (1), pp. 181–201, 415–416.
19. Ibid., pp. 371–391.
20. Bogucharsky, V. (2), part 2, p. 302.

CHAPTER 10: **Apostles into Terrorists**
1. Koni, A.; also Kravchinsky, S. (1), pp. 82–88.
2. Koni, A., pp. 11, 36, 38.

3. Sinegub, S. (3), pp. 52–53.
4. Ibid., p. 54.
5. Koni, A., p. 45.
6. Ibid., p. 506.
7. Ibid., p. 97.
8. Ibid., p. 65.
9. Ibid., p. 57.
10. Ibid., p. 98.
11. Ibid., p. 105.
12. Ibid., pp. 138–139.
13. Ibid., p. 120.
14. Ibid., p. 287.
15. Ibid., p. 285.
16. Ibid., pp. 17–18.
17. Ibid., p. 25.
18. Nikitenko, A. (2), vol. III, p. 90.
19. Koni, A., p. 209.
20. Ibid., p. 523.
21. Ibid., p. 212.
22. Ibid., p. 220.
23. Ibid., p. 523.
24. Ibid., p. 300.
25. Ibid., p. 547.
26. Ibid., p. 377.

CHAPTER 11: **Prison and Exile**

1. Nekrasov, N., vol. II, p. 411.
2. Bogucharsky, V. (3), pp. 377 f.; also Dzhabadari, I. (4), pp. 39–62.
3. Breshkovskaya, K., pp. 181–189.
4. Kennan, G., vol. I, p. 406.
5. Korolenko, V., vol. IV, pp. 169–170.
6. Ibid., p. 244.
7. Kennan, G., vol. II, pp. 130–165.
8. Ibid., pp. 166–190.
9. Ibid., p. 153.
10. Gekker, N., pp. 69–88.
11. Breshkovskaya, K., pp. 213–259.
12. Kennan, G., vol. II, pp. 229–245.

13. Ibid., pp. 263–273; also Osmolovsky, G., pp. 67–80.
14. Kennan, G., vol. I, p. iv.
15. Ibid., p. viii.
16. Ibid., pp. 84–92.
17. Ibid., vol. II, pp. 13–14.
18. Ibid., vol. I, p. 388.
19. Ibid., p. viii.
20. Ibid., p. 170.
21. Ibid., vol. II, p. 544.
22. Ibid., p. 546.
23. Ibid., p. 552.
24. Ibid., p. 552.
25. Ibid., p. 555.
26. Bogucharsky, V. (3), p. 73.
27. Kennan, G., vol. I, pp. 491–502.
28. Ibid., vol. II, p. 293.
29. Ibid., pp. 183–195.
30. Ibid., pp. 245, 248–249.
31. Ibid., pp. 119–122.
32. Ibid., vol. I, pp. 125, 358–359; vol. II, p. 323.
33. Ibid., vol. I, p. 254.
34. Ibid., p. 242.
35. Korolenko, V., vol. III, pp. 144–146.
36. Ibid., p. 140.
37. Flerovsky, N. (Bervi), p. 214.
38. Kennan, G., vol. I, p. 247.
39. Ibid., p. 257.
40. Ibid., p. 183.
41. Ibid., p. 186.
42. Ibid., p. 187.

CHAPTER 12: **Towards Terrorism**
1. Venturi, F., p. 562 (quoted from Kunkl, A. *Obshchestvo Zemlya i Volya*. Moscow, 1928, pp. 10–11).
2. Figner, V. (1), vol. I, p. 156.
3. Bogucharsky, V. (3), p. 124 (quoted from *Zemlya i Volya*, no. 1, of 15 October 1878).
4. Ibid., p. 469 (quoted from *Listok Zemli i Voli,* no. 5, of 8 June 1879).

5. Ibid., pp. 54–57 (quoted from *Nachalo*, no. 2, April 1878); also ibid., pp. 201–206 (quoted from *Zemlya i Volya*, no. 2, of 15 December 1878); also ibid., p. 415 (quoted from *Zemlya i Volya*, no. 5, of 8 April 1879); also Grinberg-Kon, Kh., pp. 160–162.

6. Bogucharsky, V. (1), part 1, pp. 67–76 (quoted from *Narodnaya Volya*, no. 2, of 1 October 1879).

7. Ibid., pp. 73–76 (quoted from the same number of *Narodnaya Volya*).

8. "Pokushenie A.K. Solovyeva na tsareubiystvo 2 aprelya 1879 g," pp. 133–150.

9. Frolenko, M. (1).

10. Bogucharsky, V. (3), pp. 225–226, 306–309.

11. Figner, V. (1), vol. I, p. 302; also Bogucharsky, V. (4), pp. 41–42.

12. Kravchinsky, S. (1), pp. 96–98.

13. Ibid., p. 98.

14. Ibid., p. 98.

15. Ibid., p. 107.

16. Footman, D.; also *Andrey Ivanovich Zhelyabov;* also Figner, V. (2), vol. V, pp. 217–221.

17. Figner, V., and Korba, A.; also Figner, V. (1), vol. I, pp. 229–230.

18. Figner, V., and Korba, A., p. 69.

19. Figner, V. (1); also Figner, V. (2).

20. Figner, V. (2), vol. V, pp. 303–313.

21. Uspensky, G. (1), vol. III, p. 569; also Uspensky, G. (2), vol. XIII, p. 630.

22. Bulanova-Trubnikova, O., p. 154.

23. Kravchinsky, S. (4).

24. Figner, V., and Korba, A., pp. 201–202; also Footman, D., p. 256.

25. Footman, D., p. 246.

26. Ibid., pp. 249–250.

27. Figner, V. (1), vol. I, pp. 237, 239.

28. Footman, D., pp. 248, 253, 246–247, respectively.

29. Ibid., pp. 255–256, 248, 250, 252, 249, respectively; also Tsederbaum, S., pp. 103–105 and 115–123, 55–56, 126, 107–109, 105–107, 124, respectively.

30. Lyubatovich, O.
31. Tsederbaum, S. pp. 32–39.
32. Ivanova-Boreysha, S.
33. Bogucharsky, V. (1), part 1, p. 103 (quoted from
    Narodnaya Volya, no. 3, 1 January 1880).
34. Bogucharsky, V. (4), p. 4.

CHAPTER 13: **Regicide**
1. Figner, V. (1), vol. I, pp. 211–212.
2. Footman, D., pp. 113–119.
3. *Andrey Ivanovich Zhelyabov,* pp. 29–30.
4. Kravchinsky, S. (1), pp. 112–118.
5. Ibid., pp. 98–99.
6. Ibid., p. 99.
7. Corti, E., p. 262.
8. Bogucharsky, V. (1), part 1, pp. 139–140 (quoted from
   Listok Narodnoy Voli, no. 1, of 1 June 1880); also
   Ivanova-Boreysha, S., pp. 9–11.
9. Footman, D., pp. 130–137.
10. Shchegolev, P., pp. 262–288; also "Zasedanie
    Gosudarstvennogo Soveta 8 marta 1881 goda," pp.
    194–199.
11. Shchegolev, P., p. 269.
12. Tatishchev, S., vol. II, pp. 636 f.
13. Footman, D., pp. 141–142.
14. "Protses 20-ti narodovoltsev v 1882 godu," p. 259.
15. Figner, V. (1), vol. I, pp. 228–229.
16. Ibid., pp. 247–248, 262–264; also Footman, D., pp.
    171–172.
17. Figner, V. (1), vol. I, pp. 265–267.
18. Ibid., p. 267; also Folenko, M. (2), p. 296.
19. Figner, V. (1), vol. I, p. 307.
20. Bogucharsky, V. (5), pp. 1–32.
21. Ibid., p. 11; also Tyrkov, A.
22. Kravchinsky, S. (1), p. 164.
23. Ibid., pp. 79–82.
24. Bogucharsky, V. (1), part 2, pp. 313–320, 321–329.
25. Figner, V. (1), vol. II; also Volkenshteyn, L.
26. Bogucharsky, V. (1), part 2, pp. 118–119, 120 f.

27. Figner, V. (1), vol. II, p. 355.
28. Ibid., vol. I, pp. 376–390.
29. Ibid., p. 365.
30. Ibid., p. 385.
31. Bogucharsky, V. (1), part 2, pp. 304–307.
32. Burtsev, V., part 1, p. 180.

BIBLIOGRAPHY

Andrey Ivanovich Zhelyabov. London, 1882.

Aptekman, O. *Obshchestvo "Zemlya i Volya" 70-ikh godov [The Society "Land and Freedom" of the Seventies]*. Leningrad, 1924.

Asheshov, N. *Sofya Perovskaya*. Petrograd, 1920.

Axelrod, P. *Perezhitoe i peredumannoe [Past Experiences and Thoughts]*. Berlin, 1923.

Benua, A. *Zhisn khudozhnika [The Life of an Artist]*. New York, 1955.

Black, C., ed. *The Transformation of Russian Society: Aspects of Social Change since 1861*. Cambridge, Mass., 1960.

Bogdanovich, T. *Lyubov lyudey shestidesyatykh godov [The Love Life of the People of the Sixties]*. Leningrad, 1929.

Bogucharsky, V. (1) *Literatura partii Narodnoy Voli [Publications of the Party of the People's Will]*. Rostov-on-Don, no date.

————. (2) ed. *Gosudarstvennye prestupleniya v Rossii v XIX veke [State Crimes in Russia in the Nineteenth Century]*. St. Petersburg, 1906.

————. (3) *Revolutsionnaya zhurnalistika semidesyatykh godov [Revolutionary Journalism of the 1870s]*. Paris, 1905.

————. (4) *Iz istorii politicheskoy borby v 70-kh i 80-kh gg [Contributions to the History of Political Struggle in the Seventies and Eighties]*. Moscow, 1912.

————. (5) "1 marta—3 aprelya 1881 (Petersburg 25 let tomu nazad)" ["March 1—April 3, 1881 (St. Petersburg Twenty-five Years Ago)"]. *Byloe* 3 (March 1906): 1–32. Reprinted, The Hague, 1968.

Breshkovskaya, K. *Hidden Springs of the Russian Revolution*. Stanford, Calif., 1931.

Broido, E. *Memoirs of a Revolutionary*. London, 1967.

Bulanova-Trubnikova, O. *Tri pokolenia [Three Generations]*. Moscow-Leningrad, 1928.

Burtsev, V. *Za sto let (1800–1896) [One Hundred Years (1800–1896)]*. London, 1897.

Charushin, N. *O dalekom proshlom (1878–1895) [About the Distant Past (1878–1895)]*. Moscow, 1931.

Chernyshevsky, N. *What Is to Be Done?* New York, 1961.

Chudnovsky, S. "Iz dalnikh let" ["From the Distant Past"]. *Byloe* 10 (October 1907): 218–240. Reprinted, The Hague, 1969.

219

Corti, E. *The Downfall of Three Dynasties.* London, 1934.

Dan, F. *Proiskhozhdenie bolshevisma* [*The Origins of Bolshevism*]. New York, 1946.

Dobrolyubov, N. "Luch sveta v temnon tsarstve" ["A Ray of Light in the Kingdom of Darkness"]. *Literaturnaya Kritika,* 1961, pp. 608–677.

Dubenskaya, E., and Bulanova, O. *Tatyana Ivanova Lebedeva.* Moscow, 1930.

Dzhabadari, I. (1) "Protses 50-ti (Vserosiyskaya Sosial-Revolutsionnaya Organizatsia 1874–1877 gg)" ["The Trial of the Fifty (The All-Russian Social-Revolutionary Organization of 1874–1877)"]. *Byloe* 8 (August 1907): 1–26. Reprinted, The Hague, 1969.

――――. (2) Ibid. *Byloe* 9 (September 1907): 169–192.

――――. (3) Ibid. *Byloe* 10 (October 1907): 168–197.

――――. (4) "V nevole" ["In Prison"]. *Byloe* 5 (May 1906): 39–62. Reprinted, The Hague, 1968.

――――. (5) Ibid. *Byloe* 6 (June 1906): 157–177.

Fedosov, I. *Revolutsionnoe dvizhenie v Rossii vo vtoroy chetverti XIX veka* [*The Revolutionary Movement in Russia in the Second Quarter of the Nineteenth Century*]. Moscow, 1958.

Figner, V. (1) *Zapechatlenny trud* [*Work Recorded*]. Moscow, 1964. An abridged English translation was published in New York in 1927 and reprinted in 1968 under the title *Memoirs of a Revolutionist.*

――――. (2) *Sochinenia* [*Works*]. Moscow, 1932.

――――. (3) *Studencheskie gody* [*Student Years*]. Moscow, 1924.

Figner, V., and Korba, A. *A. D. Mikhaylov.* Moscow-Leningrad, 1925.

Fischer, G. *Russian Liberalism: From Gentry to Intelligentsia.* Cambridge, Mass., 1958.

Flerovsky, N. (Bervi). *Tri politicheskie sistemy: Nikolay I, Alexandr II, Alexandr III* [*Three Political Systems: Nicholas I, Alexander II, Alexander III*]. Geneva or Paris, 1897.

Florinsky, M. *Russia.* New York, 1960.

Footman, D. *Red Prelude: A Life of A. I. Zhelyabov.* London, 1944.

Frolenko, M. (1) "Lipetsky i Voronezhesky syesdy" ["The Lipetsk and Voronezh Meetings"]. *Byloe* 1 (January 1907): 67–86. Reprinted, The Hague, 1969.

――――. (2) "Dopolnitelnye svedenia o protsese 20-ti" ["Supplementary Information on the Trial of the Twenty"]. *Byloe* 6 (June 1906): 296–300. Reprinted, The Hague, 1968.

Garvi, P. *Vospominania sotsial-demokrata* [*Memoirs of a Social-Democrat*]. New York, 1946.

Gekker, N. "Politicheskaya katorga na Kare: Vospominania" ["Prisoners in Hard Labor at Kara: Memoirs"]. *Byloe* 9 (September 1906): 69–88. Reprinted, The Hague, 1969.

Gernet, M. *Istoriya tsarskoy tyurmy* [*The History of Tsarist Prisons*]. Moscow, 1960–1963.

Grinberg-Kon, Kh. "K protsesu I. M. Kovalskogo" ["On the Trial of I. M. Kovalsky"]. *Byloe* 10 (October 1906): 160–162. Reprinted, The Hague, 1969.

Grosman, I. "Grazhdanskaya smert Dostoyesvskogo" ["The Civic Death of Dostoyevsky"]. *Literaturnoe Nasledstvo* 22–24 (1935).

Herzen, A. *Byloe i Dumy* [*Past Life and Thoughts*]. Leningrad, 1946.

Hingley, R. *Russian Secret Police*. London, 1970.

Itenberg, B., ed. (1) *Revolutsionnoe narodnichhestvo 70-kh godov* [*Revolutionary Populism of the 1870s*]. Moscow, 1964.

———. (2) *Dvizhenie revolutsionnogo narodnichestva* [*The Revolutionary Populist Movement*]. Moscow, 1965.

Ivanchin-Pisarev, A. *Khozhdenie v narod* [*The Going to the People*]. Moscow, 1929.

Ivanova-Boreysha, S. "Pervaya tipografia 'Narodnoy Voli' " ["The First Printing Press of the People's Will"]. *Byloe* 9 (September 1906): 1–11. Reprinted, The Hague, 1969.

"Iz parizheskogo arkhiva Turgeneva" ["From Turgenev's Paris Archive"]. *Literaturnoe nasledstvo* 2 (1964).

Kennan, G. *Siberia and the Exile System*. London, 1891.

Kolosov, A. *Alexandr II*. London, 1902.

Koni, A. *Vospominania o dele Very Zasulich* [*Memoirs of the Case of Vera Zasulich*]. Moscow-Leningrad, 1933.

Kornilov, A. (1) *Obshchestvennoe dvizhenie pri Alexandre II* [*The Civic Movement in the Time of Alexander II*]. St. Petersburg, 1907.

———. (2) *Obshchestvennoe dvizhenie pri Alexandre II*. Moscow, 1909.

Kornilova-Moroz, A. *Perovskaya i kruzhok chaykovtsev* [*Perovskaya and the Chaykovsky Group*]. Moscow, 1929.

Korolenko, V. *Istoria moego sovremennika* [*The Story of a Man of My Time*]. Moscow, 1965.

Kovalevskaya, S. *Vospominania i pisma* [*Memoirs and Letters*]. Moscow, 1951.

Kravchinsky, S. (Stepnyak). (1) *Podpolnaya Rossia* [*Underground Russia*]. Moscow, 1960.

———. (2) "Letter to Vera Zasulich, dated 24 July 1878." *Krasny Arkhiv* 19 (1926).

———. (3) *Sofya Illarionovna Bardina*. Geneva, 1883. Published anonymously.

————. (4) *Nikolay Ivanovich Kibalchich.* Geneva, 1899. Attributed to Kravchinsky.

————. (5) *A Female Nihilist.* Boston, 1885. Biography of Olga Lyubatovich.

Krishan Kumar, ed. *Revolution.* London, 1971.

Kropotkin, P. (1) *Zapiski revolutsionera* [*Reminiscences of a Revolutionary*]. London, 1902.

————. (2) "Letter on the Occasion of the Funeral of L. Shishko." In *Pamyati L. E. Shisko.* London, 1910.

Lavrov, P. (1) *Istoricheskie pisma* [*Historical Letters*]. St. Petersburg, 1906.

————. (2) "Narodniki-propagandisty 1873–1877 gg" ["Populists-propagandists in 1873–1877"]. *Materyaly dlya istorii ruskogo sotsial-revolutsionnogo dvishenia* 10 (1895). Reprinted in Leningrad, 1925.

Leffler, A. *Sonia Kovalevsky.* London, 1895.

Lemke, M. "Molodost 'Otsa' Mitrofana" ["The Youth of 'Father' Mitrofan"]. *Byloe* 1 (January 1907): 188–233. Reprinted, The Hague, 1969.

Lermontov, M. *Sobranie sochineniy* [*Collected Works*]. Moscow-Leningrad, 1948.

Likhacheva, E. *Materyaly po istorii zhenskogo obrazovania v Rossii* [*Materials for a History of Women's Education in Russia*]. St. Petersburg, 1899.

Lowenthal, R. "Unreason and Revolution." *Encounter* (November 1969).

Lukashevich, A. "V narod!" ["To the People!"] *Byloe* 3 (March 1907): 1–44. Reprinted, The Hague, 1969.

Lyubatovich, O. (1) "Dalekoe i nedavneye. Vospominania iz zhisni revolutsionerov 1878–81 gg ["The Remote and the Recent Past. Memoirs from the Life of Revolutionaries of the Years 1878–81"]. *Byloe* 5 (May 1906): 209–245. Reprinted, The Hague, 1968.

————. (2) Ibid. *Byloe* 6 (June 1906): 108–154. Reprinted, The Hague, 1968.

Martov, Yu. *Zapiski sotsial-demokrata* [*Notes of a Social-Democrat*]. Berlin, 1922.

Meijer, J. *Knowledge and Revolution: The Russian Colony in Zurich* (*1870–1873*). Assen, 1955.

Mikhaylov, M. *Sochinenia* [*Works*]. Moscow, 1958.

Milyukov, P. *Outlines of Russian Culture*: II (Literature), edited by M. Karpovich. Philadelphia, 1970.

Moser, C. *Antinihilism in the Russian Novel of the 1860s.* The Hague, 1964.

Narodovoltsy posle 1-go marta 1881 goda: Sbornik statey i materyalov, sostavlennye uchastnikami narodovolnicheskogo dvizhenia [*The People's Will after March, 1, 1881: A Collection of Essays and Materials Prepared by Participants of the People's Will*]. Moscow, 1928.

————. *Sbornik III*. [*Collection III*]. Moscow, 1931.

Nekrasov, N. *Sobranie sochineniy* [*Collected Works*]. Moscow, 1948.

"Nekrolog Beti Kaminskoy" [Obituary of Betya Kaminskaya]. *Obshchina* 6–9 (1878).

"Nekrolog Marii Dmitrievny Subotinov" ["Obituary of Maria Dmitrievna Subotina"]. *Obshchina* 6–7 (1878).

Nikitenko, A. (1) *Zapiski i dnevnik* (1804–1877) [*Notes and Diary*]. St. Petersburg, 1904–1905.

————. (2) *Dnevnik* [*Diary*]. Leningrad, 1956.

Osmolovsky, G. "Kariyskaya tragedia (Iz vospominaniy)" ["The Tragedy at Kara (from Recollections)"]. *Byloe* 6 (June 1906): 59–80. Reprinted, The Hague, 1968.

"Pamyati A. Yakimovoy" [To the Memory of A. Yakimova]. *Katorga i Ssylka* (1927).

Perovsky, V. *Vospominania o sestre* [*Memories of My Sister*]. Moscow-Leningrad, 1927.

Pertsev, E. "Zapiski o 1861" ["Notes on 1861"]. *Krasny Arkhiv* 3 (1926): 118–164.

Pipes, R. "Narodnichestvo: A Semantic Inquiry." *Slavic Review* XXIII: 3 (September 1964).

"Pokushenie A. K. Solovyeva na tsareubiystvo 2 aprelya 1879 g" ["A. K. Solovyev's Attempt to Kill the Tsar on April 2, 1879"]. *Byloe* 1 (January 1908): 133–150.

"Protses 17-ti narodovoltsev v 1883 godu" ["The Trial of Seventeen Members of the People's Will in 1883"]. *Byloe* 10 (October 1906): 193–258. Reprinted, The Hague, 1969.

"Protses 20-ti narodovoltsev v 1882 godu" ["The Trial of Twenty Members of the People's Will in 1882"]. *Byloe* 1 (January 1906): 233–308. Reprinted, The Hague, 1968.

Radkey, O. *The Agrarian Foes of Bolshevism*. New York–London, 1962.

Sapir, B. "Peter Lavrov." *International Review of Social History* 17 (1972): 441–454.

Schapiro, L. *Rationalism and Nationalism in Russian Nineteenth-Century Political Thought*. New Haven, Conn., 1967.

Shashkov, S. *Istoria ruskoy zhenshchiny* [*History of the Russian Woman*]. St. Petersburg, 1879.

Shchegolev, P. "Iz istorii 'konstitutsionnykh' veyaniy v 1879–1881 gg"

["From the History of 'Constitutional' Trends in the Years 1879–1881"]. *Byloe* 12 (December 1906): 262–288. Reprinted, The Hague, 1968.

Shelgunov, N., Shelgunova, L., and Mikhaylov, M. *Vospominania [Memoirs]*. Moscow, 1967.

Shishko, L. (1) *Kravchinsky i kruzhok chaykovtsev [Kravchinsky and the Chaykovsky Group]*. No city, no date.

———. (2) "Iz vospominaniy proshlogo" ["From Recollections of the Past"]. In *Pamyati L. E. Shishko*. London, 1910.

Shtakenshneyder, E. *Dnevnik i zapiski (1854–1886) [Diary and Notes (1854–1886)]*. Moscow-Leningrad, 1934.

Simmons, E., ed. *Continuity and Change in Russian and Soviet Thought*. Cambridge, Mass., 1955.

Sinegub, S. (1) "Vospominania chaykovtsa" ["Memoirs of a Chaykovist"]. *Byloe* 8 (August 1906): 39–80. Reprinted, The Hague, 1969.

———. (2) Ibid. *Byloe* 9 (September 1906): 90–128. Reprinted, The Hague, 1969.

———. (3) Ibid. *Byloe* 10 (October 1906): 31–79. Reprinted, The Hague, 1969.

Starik [Sergey Kovalik]. "Dvizhenie semidesyatykh godov po Bolshomu protsesu (193-kh)" ["The Movement of the 1870s According to the Big Trial (of the 193)"]. *Byloe* 10 (October 1906): 1–30. Reprinted, The Hague, 1969.

Stasov, V. *Vospominania o N. V. Stasovoy [Memories of N. V. Stasova]*. St. Petersburg, 1899.

Szamuely, T. *The Russian Tradition*. London, 1974.

Tatishchev, S. *Imperator Alexandr II, ego zhisn i tsarstvovanie [The Emperor Alexander II, His Life and Reign]*. St. Petersburg, 1903.

Titov, A., gen. ed. *Nikolay Vasilyevich Chaykovsky, Religiosnye i obshchestvennye iskania [N. V. Chaykovsky, His Religious and Social Search]*. Paris, 1929.

Tocqueville, de, A. *L'ancien Régime et la Révolution. Oeuvres*, vol. 4. Paris, 1886.

Tsederbaum, S. *Zhenschina v ruskom revolutsionnom dvizhenii, 1870–1905 [Women in the Russian Revolutionary Movement, 1870–1905]*. Leningrad, 1927.

Turgenev, I. *Sobranie sochineniy [Collected Works]*: XII (Letters 1831–1833). Moscow, 1958.

Tyrkov, A. "K sobytiyu 1 marta 1881 goda" ["To the Event of March 1, 1881"]. *Byloe* 5 (May 1906): 141–162. Reprinted, The Hague, 1968.

Uspensky, G. (1) *Sobranie sochineniy* [*Collected Works*]. St. Petersburg, 1906.
_____. (2) *Sobranie sochineniy* [*Collected Works*]. Moscow, 1951.
Venturi, F. *Roots of Revolution.* London, 1960.
Volkenshteyn, L. "13 let v Shlüsselburgskoy Kreposti" ["13 Years in the Schlüsselburg Fortress"]. *Zapiski.* Purleigh, England, 1900.
Volkhovsky, F. "L. Shishko." In *Pamyati L. E. Shishko.* London, 1910.
Weidlé, W. *Russia—Absent and Present.* New York, 1961.
Yakimova, A. "Iz dalekogo proshlogo." ["From the Distant Past"]. *Katorga i Ssylka* (1924).
Zaionchkovsky, P. (1) *Provedenie v zhizn krest'ianskoi reformy 1861 goda* [*The Implementation of the Serf Reform of 1861*]. Moscow, 1958.
_____. (2) *Krizis samoderzhavia na rubezhe 1870–1888 gg* [*The Crisis of Autocracy, 1870–1888*]. Moscow, 1964.
"Zasedanie Gosudarstvennogo Soveta 8 marta 1881 goda" ["The Session of the State Council of March 8, 1881"]. *Byloe* 1 (January 1906): 194–199. Reprinted, The Hague, 1968.
"Zayavlenie A. Kvyatkovskogo" ["The Declaration of A. Kvyatkovsky"]. *Krasny Arkhiv* 14 (1926): 159–175.
Zazhivo-pogrebennye [*Buried Alive*]. St. Petersburg, 1878. Reprinted, Leningrad, 1921.
Zhukovsky, V. *Sochinenia* [*Works*]. Edited by Alferov. St. Petersburg, 1902.

INDEX

Peter and Paul Fortress. *See* Prisons, in Russia
Petrashevsky, Mikhail, 12-13
Pirogov, Nikolay I., 30-31
Pisarev, Dmitry, 18, 30, 42, 68, 75, 109
Plekhanov, Georgy, 119, 129-30
Police, 9, 10-14, 17, 33, 37, 43, 156, 178; and feminists, 52-53; hatred of, 156; organization of, 11; powers of, 11-14, 153, 172, 177; and propaganda activity, 70, 77, 79, 80, 83, 88, 89, 90, 92-93, 95-96, 98, 112, 115, 142; provincial, 120, 135, 168; raids Moscow Organization, 117, 118; seeks evidence of conspiracy, 126, 127; and students, 11, 41, 57-58, 62, 64, 172, 181; suppression of books, 64-65, 77, 112; and terrorists, 186, 194, 196, 197-98; and "troglodytes," 176; uniformed, technique with demonstrators, 129-30, 181; and Zasulich verdict, 151-52. *See also* Corps of Gendarmes, Third Section
Polish insurgents, 52, 63, 161, 172-73
Political Red Cross, 76, 77, 176
Political trials: enlightenment of public through, 131, 132, 134-38, 141; "of the 14," 202-203; "of the 16," 196; "of the 50," 118, 128, 131-38, 141, 149, 155, 185; "of the 193" (Great Trial), 96, 128, 138-42, 145, 146*n*, 177, 183; *in camera*, 138-39; of Kazan Cathedral demonstrators, 130, 177; of Narodnaya Volya (the accused of March 1, 1881), 201; of Nechaev group, 66, 145, 147; of radical writers, 42-43; of students, 65; of Zasulich, 145-53
Popular Vengeance. *See* Narodnaya Rasprava
Populism, v, vii; apostolic and revolutionary forms of, 97; of Chaykovists, 77-83; crisis of, 177, 180; evolution of, 61-64, 67, 68; as "going to the people," 70, 77, 83, 85-98, 107, 128, 177, 180, 185, 186; illusions of, 122; Lavrov theory of, 69, 86, 101, 107; moral conviction, 87, 137-38; of Moscow Organization, 110-18; and terrorism, 180, 185, 189, 203-205; and Zemlya i Volya split, 180
Possessed, The (Dostoyevsky), 66
Potapov (demonstrator), 129-30
Predvorilka. *See* House of Preliminary Detention
Presnyakov, Anton, 188, 196, 197
Pretrial detention, 96, 119-26, 142, 156, 176

Printing presses: clandestine, 88, 90-91, 93-94, 96, 140, 180, 188, 194, 196; émigré, 101, 110
Prisons, in Russia: Butyrka (Moscow), 120; communication in, 124-25; conditions in, 120-25, 144-45, 156-57, 202; infiltration of, 188; *katorga* served in, 156-57, 196, 197, 201; in Kharkov district, 119, 156, 160, 163, 184; Lithuanian Castle (St. Petersburg), 120, 123; number of, 120; Peter and Paul Fortress (St. Petersburg), 13, 41, 66, 120, 123, 124, 156, 197, 201; Shlüsselburg Fortress, 120, 156, 164, 187, 201, 203. *See also* House of Preliminary Detention
Prisons, in Siberia, 120; escape from, 161-62, 163-65; Irkutsk transit prison, 159, 160; Kara complex, 159-65, 169, 179, 196, 202; *katorga* in, 157-69; Kennan on, 173-74; Krasnoyarsk transit prison, 158; Tomsk transit prison, 157, 158, 159; Tyumen transit prison, 158, 166
"Problems of Life" (Pirogov), 31
Proclamations, radical, 27, 40
Propaganda: "book work" as, 64-65; lack of discipline in, 118, 185-86; Lavrov on role of, 69; mass arrests for, 96-97, 118, 128, 130, 139; Pahlen on, 93-95; peaceful, 66, 67, 69, 85-98, 128, 135, 137, 177, 180, 186-87; among peasants, 64, 78-79, 88, 90, 94, 96-97, 98, 111, 128, 186-87; popular texts for, 88; three groups in, 94-95; among workers, 64, 79-82, 93, 111-15, 122, 130. *See also* All-Russian Social-Revolutionary Organization, Chaykovists, "Going to the People"
Pushkin, Alexander, 8, 12, 22, 23

Radicalism, vi-vii; accepts equality of women, 19-20, 25, 30, 109; attitude toward peasant reform, 39-40; bureaucracy fosters, 14; Decembrist sources of, 10; of 1840s and early 1850s, 16; and feminism, 45, 46, 47; first foothold with workers, 82; Herzen and, 12; imprecise terms of, 60, 87, 95; Kiev center of, 92-93; manifestos of, 40; and national minorities, 107; of Nechaev group, 66; nihilist form of, 17-31; peaceful propaganda of, 64-65, 66, 67, 69, 78-83, 85-98, 110-18, 128, 135, 137, 177, 180; police harassment breeds, 62-63; populist direction of, 61, 63-64, 67, 68, 77, 78-83, 85-98, 107, 110, 177, 180; of provincial land-

DATE DUE

5 Jan 81			
OC 04			
NO 4			
GAYLORD			PRINTED IN U.S.A.